ALSO BY JULIE MORGENSTERN

Organizing from the Inside Out

Time Management from the Inside Out

Organizing from the Inside Out for Teens

SHED Your Stuff, Change Your Life

Never Check Email in the Morning

TIME TO PARENT

TIME TO PARENT

Organizing Your Life to Bring Out
the Best in Your Child and You

Julie Morgenstern

Henry Holt and Company   New York

Henry Holt and Company
Publishers since 1866
175 Fifth Avenue
New York, New York 10010
www.henryholt.com

Henry Holt ® and 🅗🅟® are registered trademarks of
Macmillan Publishing Group, LLC.

Library of Congress Cataloging-in-Publication Data

ISBN: 9781627797436

Names: Morgenstern, Julie, author.
Title: Time to parent : organizing your life to bring out the best in your
   child and you / by Julie Morgenstern
Description: First Edition. | New York : Henry Holt and Company, [2018]
Identifiers: LCCN 2018001408 | ISBN 9781627797436 (paperback)
Subjects: LCSH: Parenting. | Time management.
Classification: LCC HQ755.8 .M647 2018 | DDC 649/.1—dc23
LC record available at https://lccn.loc.gov/2018001408

Our books may be purchased in bulk for promotional, educational,
or business use. Please contact your local bookseller or the Macmillan
Corporate and Premium Sales Department at (800) 221-7945, extension
5442, or by e-mail at MacmillanSpecialMarkets@macmillan.com.

First Edition 2018

Designed by Meryl Sussman Levavi

Printed in the United States of America

1   3   5   7   9   10   8   6   4   2

CONTENTS

INTRODUCTION
KIDS: AN INSTRUCTION MANUAL

When I learned I was pregnant with my daughter, I experienced an extraordinary feeling of having been given the privilege of raising a human being. But the minute Jessi arrived and I held her in my arms, I felt overwhelmed and full of doubt. This precious, tiny, helpless human being, full of promise and potential, was completely dependent on me— and I had no idea what I was doing. I was a pretty disorganized person, barely managing my own life. How on earth would I handle the huge range of responsibilities that came with being a parent? How would I give my child everything she needed in order to grow up happy, healthy, successful, and confident? How would I help her reach her full potential?

In short, like many parents, I wondered, how the heck do I do this job? In fact, what even is this job?

Wherever I sought answers to this dilemma (books, doctors, other parents), the advice I got felt like vague platitudes that were too general to be useful, reassuring, or practical: "just do your best," "don't try to be Supermom," or, my least favorite, "you are the expert on your own child." I was incredulous: how could I possibly be an expert on child rearing when I had never done it before, and each day brought a different challenge for which I had no skills or training?

For the first three years of Jessi's life, I was a (mostly) stay-at-home mom who did a little bit of work for a few theater companies, usually with Jessi in tow. I directed plays with her on my hip and read and evaluated new script submissions from home, going in for occasional meetings. When Jessi was three, I got divorced and a lot changed. Overnight, I became the sole breadwinner. I began my own business so I could work from home and save on child-care costs. Jessi started school—first half days, then full days. I worked hard to put food on the table and pay the rent, run a household, stay on top of laundry and bills, and be present for my daughter.

I was motivated to give Jessi the attention I'd craved as a child, but without role models (my parents were well intentioned but otherwise distracted), I didn't know how to do it. I felt lost. I wanted to be present, but I found it difficult to slow down to Jessi's pace when she was small. She wanted to pick up pebbles and ask about the color of the sky on the way to school each morning, while I felt pressured to keep things moving efficiently and fast, my to-do list screaming in my head. I also struggled to take care of my own needs because I was anxious about diverting any energy away from her. Case in point: I actually felt guilty leaving Jessi safely in her playpen for ten minutes while I went to take a shower, for fear she'd feel abandoned or neglected. Instead, I'd plunk the infant seat on the floor of the bathroom near the tub and take the world's fastest shower, talking to her the whole time.

I longed for instructive and concrete advice. Would someone please just hand me a job description? A manual? I didn't understand why time-management brochures weren't provided in the waiting rooms of my ob-gyn's and pediatrician's offices, or as part of the packet the hospital sent home to accompany my snugly swaddled newborn. Why weren't they available in generous supply in the office of every school, from nursery through high school?

I wanted a practical guide that would tell me how to prioritize and divvy up my limited hours and help me navigate the time and energy traps that come with the territory of being a parent. I needed a way of understanding, and framing, the job—a way of visualizing what I needed to do and how I might course correct when I got off track or overwhelmed. I wanted a deep and caring connection with my kid that didn't necessitate abandoning my own well-being. If I failed to be perfect, would Jessi be damaged for life? What did "good enough" look like? What kind of self-assessment would tell me if I was doing a good job or where I might improve?

This book is my best shot at the guide I so craved all those years ago. It aims to help parents find the quality time they crave with their kids, with their partners, with their friends, and on their own, by offering a simple way of organizing the job. This book is not an amorphous laundry list of tips and tricks or an insurmountable mountain for parents to climb. What I am offering is a concrete way to conceptualize and put boundaries around what the parenting job is and how it can be done well.

As a professional organizer and time-management coach, I've worked with parents around the globe for more than twenty-six years. It's been moving to see that wherever my work takes me, the goal of all parents is to "be there" for their kids. No matter the family structure, age, income, or background, parents come to me craving one thing above all: time to relax and be present with their children, without neglecting the other essential parts of their lives.

Parents want to do right by their kids but universally suffer from the feeling of time scarcity. Many worry they spend too much time working and not enough time at home. Some feel like they are devoting all of their time to the parenting role, leaving no energy for their marriage. Still others suffer from investing all they've got on taking care of others and not enough on their own health and self-care.

I've always seen my role as taming the chaos in my clients' lives so they are free to make their unique contribution. And I believe there is no more powerful place to make one's unique contribution than in raising another human being.

The responsibilities of parenthood can feel simultaneously ambiguous and infinite, where it is hard to see the edges in order to manage the job with confidence. Lack of clarity often leads to "time clutter," with too many precious hours focused on low-value activities, like worrying about whether you are spending your time well. Organizing the job and approaching it systematically will allow you to take control and make confident time choices, while being fully present in each thing you do.

Designed for parents with children of all ages and at all stages, from birth through high school and beyond, this book will provide you with a logical way to think about your job as a parent—and the time balance you have to achieve. It will guide you when you get off track, give you tips to shore up your weaknesses, and provide concrete, practical strategies (backed up by scientific evidence) to develop new skills.

It is designed to help you relax, feel confident, and make the job of parenting your own, while harnessing your strengths and fortifying your weaknesses.

As a parent, you will be able to create the space for quality time with your kids and yourself, and to see the edges of the deeply complex and complicated job you have taken on.

It's the manual I wish I'd had.

HOW TO USE THIS BOOK

This book is written to be by your side from the birth of your first child until the launch of your last, throughout the entire bumpy ride of the parenting years. That's because the challenges of and questions about how to divide your time never go away—they just change.

Sound audacious? Maybe. But who ever masters this job? None of us.

Readers will start by identifying their own strengths and weaknesses at whatever juncture they currently find themselves. What hijacks our time, captivates our focus, scares us, or gets neglected will change as fast (and as frequently) as your kids do. You can return to this manual time and time again. It is written to be revisited.

I'd recommend reading it, as you would any manual, beginning with the overview (chapters 1–4). Once you've digested those four chapters, dip in and out of the remainder of the book according to your needs.

HERE'S HOW THE BOOK IS STRUCTURED:

Part 1: Time and Attention

This section introduces a new framework for the job of being a parent. By organizing the job, you are better able to control where you spend your time and attention. You'll get a basic introduction to the goals and framework that can guide your allocation of time across the full parenting years.

Chapter 1: Undivided Focus: What Parents Crave
Chapter 2: Loved and Listened To: What Kids Need
Chapter 3: Organizing the Job: A Simple Blueprint
Chapter 4: A Guide to the Quadrants

Part 2: Self-Assessing

Part 2 starts with a self-assessment that helps you zero in on which areas need work and directs you to the appropriate chapters. (You can come back and take this assessment any time you feel off track.) Then, when it comes down to it, there are only four parent-specific time-management skills required to master the juggling act. We'll do a deep dive into those four skills, which in turn enable you to assess and fortify your agility at moving between roles. Everyone should read these chapters.

Chapter 5: Where Do You Gravitate?: Your Quadrant Scorecard
Chapter 6: Four Time-Management Skills You Must Master

Part 3: Raising a Human Being: Doing Your P.A.R.T.

In this section you'll learn practical techniques to make and contain time for the four core responsibilities of parenting. Read these chapters as your needs dictate: whenever you feel you are either spending too much or not enough time in any one area of responsibility.

Chapter 7: Provide
Chapter 8: Arrange
Chapter 9: Relate
Chapter 10: Teach

Part 4: Being a Human Being: Fueling Your S.E.L.F.

In this section you'll learn how to make time to nurture and take care of yourself, so you don't put off self-care until your kids leave home for college. Revisit these chapters whenever you need to step up any form of "me time" that is getting short shrift.

Chapter 11: Sleep
Chapter 12: Exercise
Chapter 13: Love
Chapter 14: Fun

Part 5: Life Happens

This section includes strategies to steadily handle the overall job of parenting, no matter what life throws at you in special circumstances.

Imagine you're a pilot. I want you to use this book like a pilot uses the control panel of an airplane, adjusting different knobs as you sail through clear skies and hit patches of turbulence. Use it at any age and at any stage to get reassurance about what you're doing well; fortify your weaknesses; find concrete, practical ideas; redirect your efforts; and—most important—relax and know that you are doing just fine.

This book is a synthesis of my expertise as an organizer and time-management coach, my extensive review of the research in the field of human development, and my own experience as a parent. The lessons you learn here can be directed to caring for any child in your life, not just your own. With every kid you encounter—nieces, nephews, grandkids, friends' kids, classmates, neighbors—you have the opportunity to connect and make them feel recognized and valued for the fascinating, creative, and evolving little humans they are. What this book will provide, regardless of your family structure, career track, or economic status, is a manual that helps systematically tackle the job of parenting—by simplifying it, organizing it, and giving you concrete tips and strategies to keep all the balls in the air.

The payoff is the time to revel in the fun and joy of parenthood and the knowledge that you're giving your kids what they need, whether they're newborns, twentysomethings, or any age in between. You will spend less time on worrying and feeling guilty, and more time on what matters most—time, attention, and presence.

PART I

TIME AND ATTENTION

1

UNDIVIDED FOCUS:
WHAT PARENTS CRAVE

My client Bianca was a busy working mother who needed my help to make the space in her life for quality time with her family. In order to "be there" for her kids, Bianca arranged to work from home two days a week. That reduced her commute and ensured that she was physically on the premises, but she found it hard to relax and be present for anything—kids or job—because she was constantly distracted by her monstrous to-do lists. In her work as a sales executive, there was always another prospect to cultivate, market to crack, or pitch to prepare. On the home front, with three kids between the ages of eight and eleven, keeping up with the constant demands of scheduling, chauffeuring, homework help, shopping, meal planning, and "scraped knee" moments was exhausting. Her mind was always lost in the black hole of recalling everything she hadn't done.

"Every single moment of my life feels divided," Bianca confided. "I never feel settled. I don't have any pure moments." Bianca wished she could go to a Zumba class or have lunch with a friend without feeling guilty about it. She craved peace of mind. Above all, she wanted to be *present* for her life.

Working parents aren't the only ones who struggle with feeling stretched in a million directions—stay-at-home mothers and fathers experience the same pain. Running a household is hardly for the faint of heart: it's a tremendously difficult logistical task that is underestimated in terms of its complexity. It requires an unusual combination of skills rarely found in one person—the ability to hold to a strategic vision of the big picture, pay fine attention to detail, and be simultaneously organized and flexible.

Overcomplicating each thing we do is a trap into which all parents can fall. During my tour of Bianca's home, I discovered dozens of ways in which she was unconsciously making things harder than they needed to be. Evidence of her "never done" feeling was everywhere—mountains of forms to fill out, bottomless piles of laundry and unfinished projects in almost every room. She cringed with guilt when she revealed unsorted stacks of memorabilia stashed in drawers and closets all over her house, just waiting for the day she could sit down and organize them. The most emblematic example? An ironing board permanently open in the doorway of her bedroom closet, with a dozen button-down shirts waiting to be pressed. When I asked, she explained that crisp button-down shirts were her style. I pointed out that cotton shirts were a high-maintenance way of dressing for a busy mom. With everything she had going on, couldn't she switch to permanent press or cardigans? Bianca was so overwhelmed that she hadn't even paused to consider it.

With so much on parents' plates, we need instruction on how to scale down smartly so that we can be present for ourselves, our work, and our families. Your shirts don't need to be ironed. But your kids require your presence to thrive and grow, and you require it to stay whole.

A CHALLENGE FOR EVERY GENERATION

Parents have grappled with the time scarcity and attention dilemma for ages, each one trying to get it right. Although we like to say that we live in the age of overload, and in many ways that's true, it wasn't really easier to be a good parent in the 1960s or earlier.

The Greatest Generation and the lesser known "Silent" Generation raised their kids during the '30s, '40s, and '50s and focused on creating opportunities for children by building a new world, but there was less emphasis on cultivating the emotional lives of their kids. Baby boomers, whose children were born in the late '60s to the mid-'80s, modeled self-actualization, teaching their children they could be anything they wanted, but they were also stereotyped as workaholics whose children—so-called latchkey kids—often felt sidelined by their parents' ambitions. Gen Xers, who mostly became parents in the late '80s to early '00s (a.k.a. "aughts"), have been labeled as helicopter parents, hovering to keep a watchful eye on their kids and clearing their paths of obstacles to protect them, perhaps reacting to being latchkey kids. But hovering does not necessarily mean connecting and often leaves those overly protected children ill-equipped with life skills for the *Adult World*.

In the spirit of our collective effort to "get this parenting thing right," millennials, parents currently in their early twenties to mid-thirties, raising kids born after 2000, are spending more time with their children than any previous generation, in part because they understand the need for quality time with their kids. But because of careers and other demands, they often sacrifice sleep and other crucial components of self-care to do it. There are also enormous cultural, social, and personal pressures to be the perfect parent and best partner. Instagram, Facebook, and other social media platforms intensify this pressure, as everyone is putting forward their best parenting selves—selecting images and posts that present their lives and relationships in the best light. Today's parents and caregivers across all generations overschedule their lives in an effort to be responsive to their kids but end up exhausted and struggling to "be present" as a result. These are broad generalizations, but it's fair to say that parenting has always been tough.

The pressure for modern parents to be perfect is fierce, and the question of how to manage your time so you can give your kids undivided attention and take care of yourself looms larger than ever. Parents of all ages now face the modern-day problem caused by the prevalence of technology in our lives, of being together but apart, with everyone connected to a distracting device.

While researching this book, I was astounded to learn that there is still no single, clear description of the parenting role. One not-so-obvious reason is that the field of child development is relatively new, as Jennifer Senior so beautifully illustrates in her excellent book *All Joy and No Fun*. For much of history, she explains, parents provided food and protection to children, and in return, children provided labor in the fields or the family business or took care of their siblings while parents worked. But around the 1920s, a shift took place with the advent of child labor laws, psychologists studying human development, and parents aspiring for a better life for their children than they themselves experienced. In other words, we shifted to a culture focused on supporting a child's growth and development. Instead of preparing kids to replicate our lives, we prepared them to forge better lives than our own. That meant that in addition to teaching our kids how to drive a tractor, make a dollar, cook a meal, and steer clear of wolves, we became responsible for developing their emotional lives. And yet, no one has quite figured out the right way to balance this new, expanded workload.

Once I started reading the research, I was amazed to learn that social scientists have discovered direct links between the time and attention children receive from their parents and children's level of what is called executive function, which includes the abilities to organize, control impulses, make decisions, sift through complex information, and focus.

As Senior notes in her book, the impulse of each new generation to tend more closely to the social-emotional development of our children is bearing out in the research. Science today is exploding with knowledge that nurturance and attention impact even more parts of our lives than imagined: happiness, health, income, academics, and relationships.

Time and attention from our primary caretakers enable humans to make their unique contribution; they yield enormous benefits for the happiness and continuation of our species.

SLOWING DOWN TIME

Once, at a conference for professional organizers, I had a funny exchange that I think could only happen between two productivity consultants. My colleague posed a question to me as a riddle: "How do you get time to slow down?" I answered without missing a beat, "You become fully present." She broke into a smile and said, "Bingo!"

There are only twenty-four hours in a day, but it's remarkable how long a day is, how rich an hour is, if you are paying attention. It's equally remarkable how quickly time can slip through our fingers—whizzing past in a blur, unaccounted for—when we are distracted.

When you devote your undivided attention to something simple, like a workout, you're focusing on the way your muscles are engaging and you are making tiny adjustments. You're lifting or swimming or doing your crunches with better form, and that half hour is going to count for a lot more in terms of the results you see. The same principle applies to doing your job or paying your bills or spending time on a hobby that energizes you.

When you give your undivided attention to a person, the effect is seismic. By fully focusing on your friend or your spouse or your sibling or your child, you communicate an empowering message: You matter. You are seen. You are important. That recognition fills a fundamental human need in all of us, no matter how old we are. When people give us their full, undivided attention, we feel it in our souls.

Undivided time and attention is the single greatest gift you can give to any person, including yourself. If you can only manage ten minutes for yourself to grab a cup of coffee and a snack, it's better to slow down and be present for it rather than scarfing down a cold slice of pizza and whizzing through your to-do list.

Time and attention are essential nutrients for every one of us. They are also the most valuable resources you can use in the service of any task, as they allow you to make your unique contribution in each thing you do.

But it's hard to pull off giving or receiving undivided attention, as vital as it is. It's easier to be distracted than to be fully present. There's pressure to do everything all at once. Hours, days, weeks, and months can go by before we know it. And parents feel this time compression more acutely than anyone. We wake up and suddenly the kids have reached another milestone, and we missed it because we were so busy. How often do we think, *If only I had another day in the week?* What parent doesn't wish they could slow down time?

WHAT IS UNDIVIDED ATTENTION?

We know we want it. We feel it in our bones. And we are painfully aware of its absence from our harried lives. We use a lot of different terms to try to describe that thing we're yearning for: quality time, mindfulness, focus. At heart, it comes down to being able to connect, enjoy, and fully engage with people and activities in the moment you are experiencing them. It means not feeling the uncomfortable pressure of being rushed, and accepting the time it takes to complete the task at hand— whether it's getting your child to bed or waiting in line at the deli counter. Later I am going to describe this as "being present"—though it's often also referred to as a flow state or practicing mindfulness.

Dutifully logging in the hours or just being physically in the room doesn't cut it. If you finally get out for a date night and you spend the entire time texting with the babysitter "just in case," that's not presence. If you are sitting through the sixth game of Tetris with your daughter while obsessing over all the work you need to get done tomorrow, that's not quality time—not for you and not for your child. If you are putting in ten-hour days and going through the motions at work but getting nothing done because you are exhausted and worried about the latest family drama, that's not being here now.

Whether you are reading to your child, asking your spouse how their day was, or working out, you don't want to be distracted—doing one thing and thinking about something else. When you are fully present with each thing you do, life is generally better. Even filling out a school form or taking a trip to the mall is more satisfying when we're not feeling rushed and we're able to give it our undivided focus. You feel gratified and positive. Your kids feel important, your partner feels loved, your job feels secure, and you feel healthier and whole.

THE LESS TIME WE HAVE, THE MORE PRESENCE MATTERS

You might be thinking that giving your undivided attention to each and every thing you do as a parent is a stretch. I agree. It's unrealistic to expect yourself to be fully present in every moment of your day.

While it would be nice if we could all develop the mental muscles to be 100 percent present, in the real world that's a level of saintliness we can't expect to achieve. And yet, being present can't just be a once-a-month thing, nor can you put it on hold until the kids grow up (after all, depending on the number of kids you have and when they leave the nest, you could spend eighteen to thirty-five years of your life in full-on parenting mode). You deserve better than to always feel rushed, stressed, or worried that you're failing or missing something. Presence is a basic daily need.

Developing the muscle and skill to be present will make a huge difference in your ability to handle the vast job you have as a parent. The truth is, the more limited our time to spend on each task, the more we benefit from giving that task our full attention. That's right: *the less time we have, the more presence matters.* Understanding the power of time and attention and learning how to turn it on is critical for our own happiness and our children's well-being.

WHY IS IT SO HARD TO BE PRESENT?

Even Buddhist monks who spend the majority of their waking lives meditating can't count on reaching that perfect state of mindfulness all the time. And if being present is hard for all thinking, feeling humans, it's a thousand times more difficult for parents. Why? I can think of at least five reasons:

The sheer workload of parenting is daunting. We feel like we're trying to keep a million balls in the air at once without being taught to juggle. We're constantly afraid of dropping a ball on the periphery of our vision. When you have a zillion things to do, focusing on one at a time is the last thing we're thinking about. Being present requires us to slow down.

Being present isn't always comfortable. When we give our undivided attention to a task or a person, we may be forced to face our own shortcomings or sense that we don't know what we are doing. Children can be surprisingly hard to relate to. Do you remember what it was like to be four? Or two? Or nine? Or sixteen? We may worry that we'll do things wrong or that we can't do everything that's required of us. When that attention is directed toward someone, we become vulnerable—what if the other person isn't ready to be present with us? When we aren't confident, we gravitate toward what we know we are good at. For many of us *doing*—rushing around, crossing things off a list—is easier than *being* with another person, especially a child.

Being present takes energy—and parents are tired! Partly, that's because we put our own self-care last. We figure that the kids have to come first (and work is a close second—especially if that is how we provide for our kids). But self-sacrifice ultimately backfires if you leave *nothing* for yourself. You'll drag through the parenting years feeling exhausted, stressed, and a little resentful. That in turn will silently undermine your ability to be present for your job, your kids, and your spouse or partner. Recharging, even when it feels counterintuitive, has got to be part of this marathon job.

Parents hold themselves to impossibly high standards, wanting to do everything perfectly, or why bother? Perfectionism works against presence and pleasure. Kerry J. Daly, associate dean of research from the University of Guelph in Ontario and founding director of the Centre for Families, Work and Well-Being, published a fascinating study called "Deconstructing Family Time." In exploring subjects' ideological visions for quality time, there was often a disconnect between parents' aspirations and their reality, due to time constraints. As a result, parents often beat themselves up, feeling that whatever amount of time they give to each thing is not enough—which means they barely enjoy the family time they do have. That same problem holds true for our work time and our "me" time. One working mom told me that she can't enjoy or focus when she exercises because she feels defeated and discouraged before she even begins. She never knows when she'll get back to the gym, she thinks, so why bother? It's time to shift that all-or-nothing mind-set.

We are missing skills, knowledge, and training. While there are courses and tests for how to drive a car, write an essay, do calculus, and even cook a healthy meal, there has never been a universal manual on how to manage the parenting job. In fact, our educational system has historically been remiss in addressing the basic life skills that create a smooth and functional existence—raising kids, managing time, organizing space, running a household, balancing work and personal life. The result is that millions of parents feel confused, unsure, and overwhelmed. They're going through life distracted, unknowingly cheating their kids and themselves out of the essential time, attention, nurturing, and security they need. Remedying that state is what this book is all about.

In my work as a professional organizer, I always suspected a connection between the time and attention we receive as children and our ability to be organized as adults. My approach to organizing, called Organizing from the Inside Out, is based on the belief that each system, in order to last, must be custom designed around a person's unique way of thinking, natural habits, and goals. It's a method that requires me to ask the right questions and listen carefully so I can understand how my clients think, what is important to them, and how they operate naturally. When it works, the outcome is a customized schedule, space, team, or project that supports who they are, what they want, and where they are going.

To do my work, I have to listen. I have to pay attention. Throughout the years, clients have often remarked how nurturing and rare the kind of listening I provide feels, and how effective it is in designing systems that bring out their best selves. Over time, after hearing things like *I don't recall ever being listened to like this as a child* and *I've never stopped to think what I really need or how I like things* from my most organizationally challenged clients, I often wondered if there was a connection between the time and attention we received as children and our ability to be organized as adults. Creating order involves designing systems that support who we are, what we want, and where we are going. It requires thinking that we (and our systems) are important enough to pay attention to—a message given to us by our caregivers, or other adults in our lives, who take the time to show us that we matter.

We are all in need of nurturance and attention—whether it's the attention of others or attention we pay to ourselves. We know instinctively, and the research reinforces, that life is more fulfilling when we are able to be present—truly undistracted and attentive—in our closest relationships, in the work we do, and in the time we spend on ourselves.

In this chapter, we've focused on how much *you* crave being present. In the next chapter, we'll focus on the value of undivided attention for your kids.

2

LOVED AND LISTENED TO: WHAT KIDS NEED

In chapter 1 we explored the value of being present in each thing we do. In this chapter we'll explore why that's beneficial for a child—because nowhere is giving our undivided attention more important than when we're interacting with a young person.

A few years ago, I attended the fortieth reunion of Greenfield Elementary School in my hometown, Philadelphia. I was one among a sea of hundreds of alumni from across the decades, all there to see one man: Mr. Martin K. Brown, our beloved principal, now in his eighties. Earlier that summer, another alum discovered Mr. Brown's Facebook profile. Hundreds of his former students flocked to "friend" him, and within months we all descended upon Philadelphia for an elementary school reunion.

It was extraordinary to experience, as I moved through the crowd, reuniting with friends who looked exactly the same as when they were ten (I swear!) along with many people who attended long after we'd graduated. The stories and accolades emerged one by one of the extraordinary love and lifelong impact Mr. Brown had on each of us. It turns out, our years at Greenfield were among the most formative of our lives when it came to shaping our identities and building self-confidence. We could truly be ourselves at that school, and that sense of efficacy carried each of us through the rest of our growing-up years and into adulthood. Mr. Brown had a way of bringing out the best in every student lucky enough to have passed through Greenfield's doors. Here's what my former classmates had to say:

> *"He was the only authority figure I've ever loved."*
>
> *"When Mr. Brown was around, you just knew everything was going to be all right."*
>
> *"Mr. Brown gave me confidence—I was an awkward kid and he made me feel normal."*
>
> *"He created an environment that allowed us to soar."*

Mr. Brown was the kind of authority who left a lifelong impression—not just because he was such a wonderful person but because of how he made you feel. Every student felt important, taken care of, and that they belonged. The confidence we gained allowed each of us to go forth in the world, determined to be our very best and make a positive contribution. To this day, I think about my time at Greenfield whenever I need to connect to my most authentic, capable self.

As parents, caregivers, and family members, we'd all love to have even a fraction of Mr. Brown's impact on the children in our lives. How on earth did he do it? I sat down with Mr. Brown to explore what lessons we might learn from him about nurturing the children in our lives. His primary goal, he said, was to create a positive environment—a place where kids felt comfortable, encouraged, and free to be themselves.

To achieve that, he told me he invested his time and attention in specific ways:

- **He spent time getting to know us.** Mr. Brown considered the students the clients of the school, so he spent time learning our interests, our personalities, our families. He paid attention. Even forty years later, at the reunion, we marveled that he not only knew each of us by name, he remembered the names of our siblings and parents. And because our leader recognized us, we felt we mattered.

- **He organized his day around "being there."** Mr. Brown believes that kids feel "safe" when they know someone is in charge and present, so he made it a point to be visible. He did not want students to see him only when they got into trouble, and only associate his presence with punishment. So, he structured his day to include stopping by classrooms, by the lunchroom, in halls, and at recess, even to read poetry on occasion.

- **He was always happy to see us.** Whenever we got into trouble—schoolyard fights, talking back to teachers, lateness, missing homework—Mr. Brown had a knack for resolving conflicts quickly, with everyone's dignity intact. Because he had taken the time to get to know us, when kids acted out, he didn't need to yell or threaten. Instead, he'd say (with a glint in his eye), "I know you can do better." He meant it, and we listened.

Perhaps you had a Mr. Brown in your life growing up—an adult who listened, understood, and really appreciated you for who you were. Even now, as an adult, think about who in your life makes you feel that way. My guess is that's a person who really listens, cares, and truly "gets you."

THE LINK BETWEEN UNDIVIDED
ATTENTION AND HAPPY, HEALTHY KIDS

Beyond food, shelter, education, discipline, and values, kids need to feel loved and listened to in order to thrive.

Kids want to know they matter, and you communicate that very directly through the gift of time and attention. When kids believe they are worthy, they have the confidence to go out and make the most of themselves. They do better academically, emotionally, and socially and are less prone to risky or self-destructive behaviors. They are more resilient in facing life's challenges. Even the worst life situations are better when supported by a warm, nurturing parent.

A parent's undivided attention has a *profound* effect on not just the social and emotional development but also a child's cognitive development and physical health, all the way through adulthood. Psychologists, neuroscientists, sociologists, economists, public health professionals, and educators have all found that relationship-based caretaking, delivered through love, time, and attention, affects almost every marker of success in adulthood, to a greater degree than perhaps anyone imagined.

Researchers at the Harvard Center on the Developing Child explain that young children experience their world as an environment of relationships: the treatment we receive from our parents and other caregivers influences how we interact with the world and in all of our relationships. Sensitive, responsive caretaking leads to the development of:

Self-esteem and social competence. Responsive relationships engage children in the human community in ways that help them define who they are, what they can become, and how and why they are important to other people. It gives them a sense of we-ness, of the world as a safe place, which in turn leads to more confident exploration, responsible citizenship, and economic productivity.

Executive function and resilience. The architecture of a child's growing brain is literally shaped by "serve and return" communication. What does that mean exactly? When a baby or young child babbles, gestures, or cries, and an adult responds appropriately with eye contact, words, or a hug, this exchange builds and strengthens the neural pathways in the brain required to support the development of communication and social skills. When a child "serves" and we consistently "return," it influences the development of executive function— including the ability to reason, think, focus, control impulsiveness, and navigate difficult situations. It supports cognitive ability to retain and use information, filter distractions, organize, set goals, and adjust to changing demands.

Buffers against adult-onset chronic illness. Children raised in poverty are more prone to developing chronic illness later in life (e.g., autoimmune disorders, high blood pressure, pro-inflammatory conditions), due to the wear and tear on the body caused by physiological stress. However, in a series of landmark studies, British Columbia psychologists Gregory Miller and Edith Chen found that about 45 percent of those with low socioeconomic-status childhoods were symptom-free throughout adulthood. The one thing these folks had in common: nurturing mothers. Sensitive, responsive parents make children feel safe. "Those greater risks later in life seem to be offset if the [parent] paid careful attention to the children's emotional well-being, had time for them, and showed affection and caring," says Miller.

Academic and career success. A twenty-year retrospective study sponsored by the Robert Wood Johnson Foundation tracked kids from the age of five to twenty-five. The findings suggest that kindergarten students who are more inclined to exhibit "social competence" traits—such as sharing, cooperating, or helping other kids—may be more likely to attain higher education and well-paying jobs.

Reduction of risky behavior in adolescence. Multiple studies have found that close relationships with parents and caregivers significantly reduce the likelihood of delinquency, drug and alcohol abuse, and getting mixed up with other common dangers in the adolescent years.

The power of undivided attention comes down to this fundamental truth: human beings need to know that they are important in order to feel secure and confident and to develop the physical, cognitive, and emotional health necessary to successfully navigate the world. Undivided attention makes humans feel safe, important, and loved.

QUALITY TIME IS A WAY OF BEING

Every expert I interviewed emphasized the same mind-set shift about the concept of "quality time." Quality time is not something you carve out as a discrete amount of time with accompanying visions of warm, perfect moments—the stuff kids will remember forever. It's a way of being with your child that can make all of your interactions together good-quality interactions.

The scientific community defines quality time as sensitive and responsive caretaking. Sociologist Jane Waldfogel describes it best in her book *What Children Need*. Waldfogel defines responsive parenting as providing love and attention customized to a child's unique emotional and physical needs, which is achieved by paying attention and being attuned.

Sensitive and responsive care allows a child to feel known and understood, valued and valuable to someone else. It also provides a sense of connectedness and security, which influences self-efficacy and confidence—and teaches your children that they are important enough to influence the world around them. Think of Mr. Brown.

We happen to live in a time when good parenting is often equated with more time. Today's parents—men and women, of all socioeconomic levels—are spending far more hours with their children than parents did in the 1970s. Consider this: between 1975 and today, moms have almost tripled the amount of quality hours they spend with their children from 7 to 20 hours per week. Dads are putting in more time, too. Between 1965 and 2011, fathers more than doubled their time spent on child care from 2.5 to 7 hours per week. As University of Toronto sociologist Melissa Milkie told me, what makes today's parents distinct from parents of the 1960s is that for the most part, today's parents have consciously opted to have children (rather than automatically following a societal expectation that everyone follows: graduate high school, go to college, get married, have babies). As such, they recognize that being a parent is an investment of time they choose to make.

While that is the good news, the bad news is that for many parents, putting in that extra time comes at a cost—sacrificing sleep and self-care, failing to tend to their relationships, struggling through extremely hectic days that feel anything but relaxed and connected. Overdoing it has given rise to the term *intense parenting*, which can create more tension than nurturing.

QUALITY OR QUANTITY?: FOCUS ON CONSISTENCY

For decades, parents have debated the question of quality vs. quantity when it comes to time with their children. But the research points to a whole new way of thinking about it. From a developmental standpoint, the quantity of time isn't the primary issue. According to the experts, *reliability* is the most important factor.

In the best of situations, parents and caretakers provide sensitive and responsive care all or most of the time, which leads to what mental health professionals call a secure attachment.

Secure attachment is a basic need from the beginning of life, says marriage and family therapist and cofounder of CORE (Center of Relational Empowerment), Dr. Amanda Rios. "Without a certain level of attention and love," Rios explains, "children do not thrive and can develop significant interpersonal challenges."

The nature of a child's attachment to their caregivers is formed by the reliability of the love and attention they receive. The more consistent the time and attention we receive from our caretakers, the more secure our attachment.

When a parent is sensitive and responsive all or most of the time, children get the consistent message that they are valued, important, and secure, and that their needs will be met. As Dr. Rios explains, this gives them the confidence to go out in the world and explore. If you are sensitive and responsive some of the time, but not predictably, it sends a confusing message that interferes with a child's self-confidence and sense of security. You, the adult, may understand that your lack of responsiveness is due to external issues (adult worries, stress, exhaustion), but when children's needs aren't met, they can draw the conclusion that they are not worthy of love and care.

EXPERT ADVICE   THE POWER OF CONSISTENT CARE

The more reliable the time and attention we receive from our caretakers, the more secure our attachment is to our caregivers, and the more fortified we are for thriving in the world.
   Here is how it works:

- **Secure Attachment** comes from consistent care.
- **Ambivalent Attachment** comes from uneven care.
- **Avoidant Attachment** comes from harsh or withdrawn care.

For more on Attachment Theory, originally developed by Bowlby and Ainsworth, read Jane Waldfogels' *What Children Need*.

The ability to develop a secure attachment has nothing to do with whether a parent works or not—it's all the style of interaction. As Waldfogel notes, children with working parents can develop secure attachments, just as children with nonworking parents (who are stressed and distracted) can develop ambivalent or avoidant attachments. The key lies in how sensitive and consistent the parent is—not how much time they have.

And just because you're not actively harsh to your kid doesn't necessarily mean you are being responsive. How familiar is this scene? Your child is doing his homework, while you're on your iPhone or cranking through emails on your laptop . . . even though you are supposed to be cooking dinner and having family time. Or, you cram in a bunch of quick calls to get a few more things done while chauffeuring your kids from one activity to another, totally missing the opportunity to connect. You may not even realize you're being unresponsive or insensitive, especially if you made the effort to pick them up or get home in time for dinner at all.

Providing the type of consistent, reliable time and attention that humans need to create secure attachments isn't easy. According to noted child psychiatrist and UCLA medical school professor Daniel Siegel, one-third to one-half of people grew up without the nurturing attention humans need to form secure attachments—that's nearly 150 million people just in the United States.

IT'S NEVER TOO LATE

You may have heard that 90 percent of who we become as adults is the result of what happens in the first seven years of life. Talk about pressure. It would be a pretty cruel joke if the greatest impact you have as a parent is when you are least experienced. Luckily, recent science has found that while the early years do matter very much, the later years do, too. Brain plasticity continues throughout life—our neural circuitry and brain architecture are able to grow and develop well into adulthood. We all make mistakes as parents, but kids are forgiving and resilient. The heart wants to connect. Think about it—even as adults we still feel the positive effects of time and attention from people who matter to us. We all just want to be seen and listened to.

This is all to say, no matter the age of your children, it's never too late to develop the capacity to be present, never too late for them—and you—to benefit. So if you are getting a late start and your kids are already tweens or even young adults, don't worry. Carving out the time to be reliably present with your kids at any age will provide physical, emotional, intellectual, and social benefits.

In the next chapter, "Organizing the Job: A Simple Blueprint," I'll introduce you to a revolutionary way of structuring the parenting years, which will form the foundation of taking control of your time and focus.

3

ORGANIZING THE JOB: A SIMPLE BLUEPRINT

Imagine starting a new job with a big title and huge expectations, but no experience, no job description, and people telling you to just "follow your instincts." Sounds impossible, right?

Yet this is how most of us come to the job of raising children.

When you first become a mom or dad, you instantly go from being responsible for your own life—already a tricky balance between self, work, and relationships—to an exponential explosion of competing demands. Like every well-intended parent, your goal is to manage it all: the endless stream of child-related needs and the responsibility to create a vibrant family life, run an ordered household, develop and maintain a satisfying work life, and take care of yourself, too.

At first you might think everything will be simpler when your infant finally sleeps through the night or when you can cross diapers off your shopping list. But every parent knows that no sooner does one challenge evaporate than another materializes to take its place. The truth is, feeling divided between conflicting priorities is the reality for the full span of the child-rearing years. It's a juggling act that evolves constantly as kids grow, careers change, relationships take twists and turns, and parents continue to mature as human beings.

The parenting years are, inarguably, the most time-intensive in a human's life and a period during which we suffer most from time scarcity. The parenting journey is delightful, rewarding, and challenging in ways you never could have imagined. You can't possibly foresee the overwhelming love—or the staggering workload.

PARENTS ARE HUMAN BEINGS, TOO

What really complicates matters is that during the prime child-rearing years, parents are also usually in the prime of their own career, relationship, and self-development years. It's one basic truth that is almost always absent from conversations about time. That means that even while we are responsible for raising the next generation, we are smack dab in the middle of our formative adult years—establishing credibility and building new skills in the workplace, learning how to love and partner with another adult, and discovering what is important to us and how to take care of ourselves as grown-ups.

Yes, we need to be there for our children—and sacrifice a great deal for them. But we need to be there for other things we are nurturing, too, not only because we are mentoring the next generation on what it means to be an adult, but because if we don't, those aspects of ourselves can deteriorate, atrophy, or even go into crisis, and the fallout from that is bound to impact our kids—in the form of strained marriages, professional challenges, and our own unhappiness or restlessness.

This is a tough balancing act, to be sure. It's impossible to find the edges of the parenting job without some sort of blueprint.

PARENTS NEED A JOB DESCRIPTION

In my work as a time-management coach with companies of all sizes, one thing I've observed is how challenging it is for anyone to be truly productive and good at their jobs when they are unsure of their roles and responsibilities. Job ambiguity, with unclear goals and roles, is a surefire recipe for inefficiency, insecurity, and overwork.

By contrast, a clear job description that itemizes specific roles and responsibilities positions each worker to master the challenge, develop the necessary skills, and allocate their time among various responsibilities. Clear roles also make teamwork easier—knowing where one job leaves off and another begins eliminates redundancy, makes sure every task is covered, and leaves everyone free to own and master their own role.

So why would that be any different for parents? Experts are hard-pressed to pin down a clear job description for parents. One psychiatrist I spoke to insisted that the job of parenting is ambiguous intentionally because it is different for every parent, family, and kid. He complained that anxious parents want a menu. My response? Well, yes, why not? All we are asking for is enough clarity to organize our time with some confidence and, from there, make the job our own.

Parents need a simple job description that sets clear edges and flags potential blind spots. We need a basic structure we can embrace and modify to fit our values, our kids' unique and changing needs, and our evolving circumstances. We need a way to keep track of how we are doing, a GPS to know if we are veering too far afield in any one direction. We need a menu, of sorts, to evaluate strengths and shore up weaknesses, to allocate, organize, and monitor time spent across roles and responsibilities.

Organizing the job gives parents the chance to create the time, confidence, and clarity required to give our kids the all-important gift of undivided attention. Organizing is powerful because it creates the "life infrastructure" that frees us to focus on what truly matters. A blueprint can take us from ambiguity to clarity, the first step in wrapping our arms around the job of being a parent. It positions us to immediately start considering where our strengths lie and what our blind spots may be. It can be used to reflect (*Where do I gravitate as a parent and where do I struggle?*), to monitor (*Now that I am aware of my tendencies, am I following through on more balanced choices?*), and to develop (*What is my plan to shore up my weak spots?*).

A NEW FRAMEWORK

I'm going to challenge you to stop thinking about parenting as one giant, amorphous, infinite bundle of responsibilities requiring limitless hours, and instead ask you to think of being a parent as you might think of any other job: a series of defined responsibilities with clear edges.

The way I see it, the way to organize the time-stretched parenting years is to picture your life in two equally important parts: *Raising* a Human Being, and *Being* a Human Being.

Then, imagine that each part is organized into *four components*, for a *total of eight responsibilities* you need to balance your time across during the child-rearing years.

It's that simple. Let's break it down.

Raising a Human Being and *Being* a Human Being

RAISING A HUMAN BEING: FOUR TYPES OF PARENT TIME

The first step to organizing the job of parenting is to separate the different types of parent time we need to raise little humans. These are the four core responsibilities you need to allocate your time across to be an effective parent.

Together, they spell out the acronym P.A.R.T.—as in *doing your part*:

- **Provide** (basic needs of food, clothing, shelter, safety, education, money)
- **Arrange** (schedules, transportation, paperwork, activities, social life)
- **Relate** (listening, soothing, reflecting, talking, enjoying, playing)
- **Teach** (values, life skills, self-control, social skills)

Take a minute to digest this breakdown. The P.A.R.T. model takes some effort to absorb, because we're not used to itemizing parenthood in this way. But consider this—everything you do as a parent, from paying for food (**Providing**) to filling out school forms (**Arranging**), from playing a board game (**Relating**) to showing your kids how to make a sandwich (**Teaching**) falls into one of these buckets of responsibility—each of which is vitally important. And while sometimes they overlap, each type of parent time requires a very different set of skills, energy, and brainpower.

Kids Perceive Parent Time Differently

Now, here's where it gets especially interesting. While parents are well aware of the long hours we're putting in, each type of parenting time creates a dramatically different experience for our children. In other words, although you may feel that the total hours you put into parenting count all together as "time in," your child sees and perceives the various activities you spend time on differently than you do.

Why is that? Well, some of the activities you do for your children are *Visible* to them, and others are *Invisible*. Some of the activities you do as a parent occur in the *Adult World*, and some take place in your *Child's World*. A visual might help.

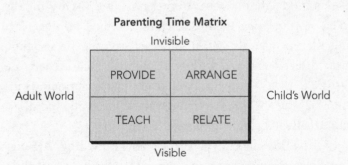

Parenting Time Matrix

	Invisible	
Adult World	PROVIDE	ARRANGE	Child's World
	TEACH	RELATE	
	Visible	

Let's ponder this for a moment. **Provide**, which is time spent working and managing money, takes place in the *Adult World* and takes a huge amount of time, yet the hours we spend providing are largely *Invisible* to our children. In other words, we can break our backs providing—sacrificing our lives for our kids, working long hours—yet children don't register the hours of toil it takes to provide them with the resources they need.

The same can be said of **Arrange**—time spent organizing schedules, carpools, appointments, filling out paperwork, and registering for school programs. These activities take place in the *Child's World*—and so your children will certainly notice if you drop the ball—but the amount of heavy lifting it takes to make their lives run smoothly is largely *Invisible* to them. In fact, you are often doing this arranging at night after they go to sleep, or squeezing it into small breaks during your workday, or while they are at school, specifically to keep it from interfering from your face time with them.

Relate and **Teach** are each highly *Visible* to your children as they represent time spent directly interacting with them. But they differ in a subtle and powerful way. When you **Relate**, you are in the *Child's World*, talking about and doing activities that are of interest to them. This is the crux of the quality time parents and children crave and scientists are discovering the value of—time spent talking, listening, soothing, reading, playing, sharing interests. When you **Teach**, you are also spending time directly engaged with your child—which is therefore *Visible* to them—but when you **Teach**, you are bringing kids into the *Adult World*, imparting values, life skills, and discipline that will help them succeed as adults.

Using this matrix, you can see how **Providing**, **Arranging**, **Relating**, and **Teaching** differ in terms of how your child experiences and benefits from them, and what they feel like to us. It also explains the frequent disconnect between how *parents* perceive the time they spend on their kids and how *kids* perceive that same time. How often do we hear of parents working grueling hours who feel they've sacrificed their whole lives to provide a good life for their child, yet the child grows up feeling like their parents were never "there" for them? Or the parents who spend all their time organizing their kids' schedules and the house to make their lives run smoothly, yet are never able to be present because they are always distracted by a to-do list?

When you look at the matrix this way, you can also see how easy it is for even the most well-intended parents to have difficulty creating space for quality time with their kids. Because goodness gracious, there's a lot to do.

But before jumping to considering how you personally are doing in each of these four parenting domains, take a moment to step back and consider whether this model feels complete to you. My interviews and surveys with parents across the spectrum confirm that the P.A.R.T. model does indeed capture the boundaries of the parenting job. What a relief!

So that covers *Raising* a Human Being, but let's not forget *Being* a Human Being. It's not difficult to see how easy it is for parents to neglect their own self-care.

BEING A HUMAN BEING: FOUR TYPES OF SELF TIME

As parents, we're also responsible for our own well-being. We cannot neglect ourselves and hope to keep things running smoothly for our kids.

Yet the truth is that we often overestimate our ability to function effectively on a depleted gas tank. Parenting is a marathon. It's a huge commitment of time and energy—a hike that twists and turns through hidden hills and valleys. To stay the course, you need to be strategic about sustaining your focus and energy.

There are four essentials of self-care required to keep from running out of steam and interfering with your ability to do your P.A.R.T. as a parent. Together, they, too, spell out a memorable acronym, S.E.L.F., as in fueling yourself. I think you'll find these require little additional description:

- Sleep (enough rest to rejuvenate your body, mind, and energy)
- Exercise (physical activity essential for body and brain)
- Love (romance, friends, and extended family)
- Fun (hobbies, passions, and relaxation)

SLEEP	EXERCISE
FUN	LOVE

Take a minute to think about this: sleep, exercise, love, and fun are four separate sources for recharging and renewing the spirit. Each has its own function. Not only do parents very often sacrifice most of their S.E.L.F. time in order to focus on their kids, but when they *do* take time for themselves, they often only do one small activity. But the truth is, no individual S.E.L.F. activity is enough to keep you going. As an adult in the prime of your own development, you need to consciously allocate your S.E.L.F. time among these four different sources of energy and identity. You may not be able to spend as much time on each of these as you did before kids, but you must work out some combination of activities to go the distance. **Sleep**—enough rest to rejuvenate your body and mind. **Exercise**—physical movement that boosts your energy and confidence. **Love**—connections to other adults for nurturance and support. **Fun**—the hobbies and relaxation that make you, you.

So, there you have it, a clear and concrete job description and framework for looking at the time demands and responsibilities of the parenting years: four types of parent time and four types of self time that, together, describe the juggling act involved in both *Raising* and *Being* a Human Being.

While doing your P.A.R.T. and taking care of your S.E.L.F. add up to eight areas of responsibility, it's pretty manageable. It's not twenty-five responsibilities, and not a million. By seeing the edges of parenthood and breaking it down into a limited number of responsibilities, you will find it easier to create the space for quality time with your kids and for yourself.

HOW THE FRAMEWORK HELPS YOU DO YOUR JOB

By organizing and containing the job, you can take more conscious command of your time, free from the ambiguous state of worry that you might be forgetting or neglecting something. Here's how the eight-part parenting matrix framework can help:

It helps you be present. You'll be aware of exactly where you are spending your time at any given moment, and thereby determine where you might need to go next. When you are not anxious about something lurking outside your peripheral vision, you are free to be fully present exactly where you are, feeling confident you are investing time in something vital.

You can organize your time in a way that frees you to be present and know when you will get to another responsibility.

It helps you course correct. Mihaly Csikszentmihalyi, the founder of the positive psychology movement, defines flow as "the optimal state." People in "flow" experience effortless concentration, enjoyment, and satisfaction; they feel in control, happy, strong, involved, creative, free, excited, open, and clear. "Flow" is achieved when we know what we need to do, know how we're going to do it, and have a way to measure our progress. Defining the job clearly gives you a way to track and monitor how you are doing. By having a more objective, complete set of responsibilities to keep an eye on, you can create your own program of development—embracing the things you do well, building the skills you need to improve, and staying in balance among all your responsibilities. It will also help you break unconscious patterns. Without a job description, people tend to parent by instinct—either doing exactly what our parents did for us (because it felt right and good) or trying to do the opposite (because we felt shortchanged somehow). But as we've seen, each generation seems to swing the pendulum back and forth—overcompensating in one area. This structure helps ensure you don't spend all your time in one or two buckets, unwittingly neglecting the others.

It helps you to go a little easier on yourself and give yourself credit for what you do well. Parenting is a helluva time challenge. And each of the eight responsibilities requires vastly different skills, competencies, and abilities. Nobody is equally adept at all eight—and that's okay. You can be kind and nurturing to yourself as you rise to the challenge, learn, and develop.

Awareness can help you quickly right the ship whenever you get off track.

Clara and her husband, Sean, came to me because of a huge time shift that took place when their daughter entered adolescence. When their kids were younger, the family had developed a great rhythm with plenty of quality time. Both parents always got home in time for dinner, cooking time doubled up as being nearby for homework help, and weekends were spent doing fun activities as a family.

Now, time spent together as a family wasn't quite so enjoyable, especially when it came to their teenaged daughter, Nina, who seemed to always be grumpy and intent on rejecting offers for help or guidance. Clara thought she needed to perhaps cut her work hours so that she could be there more for her daughter, who was struggling with many of the issues that often befall adolescent girls. Competitiveness about where she fit in with her friends, who had better grades, who had a boyfriend, and so on, was wreaking havoc on her daughter's moods. To begin the process of exploring where we might be able to trim and adjust things to make space, I drew out the four-quadrant parenting matrix for Clara. Clara's eyes went wide with a huge realization that solved the problem in an instant.

By simply looking at the matrix, Clara realized that she and her husband were unconsciously spending all their time with Nina in "teaching" mode. They could see her day-to-day life becoming more fraught with teenage angst, and as her parents, they instinctively wanted to protect and support her. Out of love, they always assumed the roles of mentor and guide. But Nina didn't always want to be in learning mode. It was too hard, too stressful. Nina never felt like she was able to relax or just *be*.

Clara didn't need to cut back on her **Provide** time. She and Sean needed to devote more of the time they were already devoting to Nina to just relaxing, connecting, and having fun without an agenda or pressure to learn. What Nina needed from her parents in order to fortify herself was less **Teach** and more **Relate**.

Clara and Sean immediately made the shift, and everyone in the family felt the tension drain and the connections during family time become stronger.

Understanding the distinctions among the four types of parent time gave Clara and Sean a different and useful perspective. It also helped them see that although the types of parent time can seem similar, and even overlap (as in the case of **Teach** and **Relate**), each has its own unique and distinct purpose and value, and understanding and applying that knowledge can help you stay balanced and fueled.

In order to manage the eight quadrants, you need to learn how to do two things:

- Dedicate enough time for each responsibility.
- Contain the time in each responsibility so you don't get stuck there or bring unfinished "business" from one quadrant into another.

This book will help you do that. But first, let's fortify your motivation and commitment to the task at hand by exploring the unique value and purpose of each of the eight areas of responsibility in P.A.R.T. and S.E.L.F. and why each is essential to your children and yourself.

4

A GUIDE TO THE QUADRANTS

PROVIDE	ARRANGE
TEACH	RELATE

SLEEP	EXERCISE
FUN	LOVE

Each of the four types of parent time and self time have their own unique purpose, and none can be neglected completely without some significant cost to you and your child. But it's a new way of thinking about the roles and responsibilities during the child-rearing years—and parenting remains a vast and complex job (even with the job description)—so it's worth doing a deeper dive.

This chapter will strengthen your understanding of the value and time demands of each of your roles and help you do your job with more awareness. The eight-quadrant structure provides you with a simple, concrete view of what (little and grown-up) human beings need, to keep you from unwittingly overdoing or underdoing any essential responsibility and help you be able to quickly compensate when life, circumstances, or the gravitational pull of your own preferences throws you out of whack. As parents we certainly can feel when we are out of balance, but we often don't know why.

As you read through the descriptions of the four P.A.R.T.

and four S.E.L.F. quadrants, you'll be able to wrap your head around the eight responsibilities and why each is vitally important to your children, and to you.

It may occur to you that each responsibility is so important and so different from the others that any one alone could practically be a full-time job. (That's why Parts 3 and 4 are filled with tips and tricks on how to shrink each responsibility to its smallest footprint.) Fear not: with awareness, intention, and organization, you *can* manage all eight responsibilities, in the right amounts, at the right moment, adapting and adjusting as you go—like a pilot adjusting the knobs during a flight.

So let's explore the eight unique quadrants in greater detail and consider how each is distinct. For each quadrant, we will identify:

- Activities Involved
- The Unique Value
- The Time Footprint

P.A.R.T.—FOUR TYPES OF PARENT TIME

Ray, forty-three, hired me to help him find time to take care of his own health. Having battled his weight his whole life, the scale had been creeping back up, thanks to life's circumstances: he was in the midst of a divorce and feeling the stress of trying to divide his time among work, shared custody of his three kids, and his new social life, which included dating for the first time in a long time.

Ray told me how close he was to his grandfather, an Italian immigrant who lived with Ray and his family when he was growing up. Each afternoon when Ray came home from school, his grandfather was there with a big hug, an apron on, and a spatula in hand. "What do you want to eat?" his grandfather would ask. Then, whatever Ray wanted, Grandpa would whip up from scratch: lasagna, grilled cheese, spaghetti and meatballs. And it wasn't even dinner! Pure love. Pure comfort. (And growing waistline).

This story beautifully illustrates what so many well-meaning parents (and parental figures) often do, which is to try to give our kids what was missing from our own childhood experience. Ray's grandfather had grown up very poor and often hungry. His gift of love to Ray was food. In untethered abundance. His intentions were pure—to protect his beloved grandson from experiencing the pain he felt as a child. He wasn't thinking about potential health consequences. He only wanted to be sure that Ray never felt deprived as he had.

Parents are often driven to protect their children from experiencing the pain they felt when growing up. Whether that was lack of food (so you overfeed), lack of money (so you overprovide), or a chaotic household that lacked order (so you overarrange). The tendency to overcompensate can backfire.

Kids enter the world ready to receive the full balanced set of needs (food, shelter, clothing, safety, love, time, and attention); they don't enter the world with the deprivation you experienced. If we overcompensate unconsciously, we run the risk of overdoing and overloading our kids with way more than they need in one department, while being completely blind to other roles we have to play.

The quadrants can keep those unconscious forces in check. You will inevitably be drawn to one or two of these roles more than the others, based on your personality, natural talents, upbringing, or values, so just being aware of the four distinct responsibilities will help you stay balanced.

PROVIDE

Activities: Working, managing finances; creating a safe and secure environment.

Position in Matrix: Invisible/Adult World

Value: At its core, providing is about furnishing children with the most fundamental resources for survival: food, shelter, clothing, education, medical care, and physical and emotional safety. These are the essential rights of every child and the legal obligation of every parent. These basics create the conditions for children to go about the business of learning, growing, and developing. In short, it creates the freedom for kids to be kids.

For most parents, whether you work outside the home or not, providing is pretty instinctive. We are genetically wired to protect our kids and give them food for their bellies, a roof over their heads, clothes on their backs, and a safe home and community around them. But to do so is very time-consuming and can be a source of stress and worry if not adequately tended to.

Without the basics covered, children are at a huge disadvantage. If kids feel physically and emotionally unprotected, they will become distracted with basic survival concerns. And when parents feel they are unable to provide adequately for their children, it is often hard for them to be fully present and provide the time for relating or teaching, because they are distracted with self-criticism, guilt, and worry. Providing a safe home and caring community protects your children both within and outside the walls of your home.

Time Footprint: Providing can take a huge chunk of time as a parent and be hard to contain. There are both onetime setups (like finding a job, selecting a neighborhood, choosing a doctor, childproofing your home) and ongoing time commitments—such as working, managing finances, and cultivating a safe and caring community. But there are many practical strategies involved in creating and containing the time around work, finances, and the cultivation of a community, as we'll see in chapter 7.

ARRANGE

Activities: Organizing schedules, spaces, paperwork, housework, transportation, traditions.

Position in Matrix: Invisible/Child's World

Value: Arranging entails time invested in designing, managing, and orchestrating the logistics in running a home and family. It is what we do to make our lives run smoothly. The tasks in **Arrange** enable you to create an infrastructure for living—an architecture that allows the days to run smoothly and predictably.

Time invested in organizing your family life yields huge dividends for both parents and children. It saves significant amounts of time and money otherwise lost to doing things inefficiently, scrambling at the last minute, searching for misplaced items, making duplicate and triplicate purchases of items you already own, and/or buying things at premium prices. It enables kids to partake in activities and programs available to them, because the school trip form is filled out and submitted on time, the transportation arranged, the lunch packed.

Arranging provides the invisible architecture of support that enables kids to partake in the world, prepared and proud. Done well, the arranging disappears into the background, and kids barely notice it at all. But when we fail in our responsibilities to adequately arrange, kids and their caregivers feel it. Kids feel the sting of being humiliated (when they arrive late, miss the school trip, have the wrong clothes for gym class). And any mom or dad who got so absorbed with work or other pressures that they forgot to pick their kid up from a party, or register their child for camp, knows the painful surge of guilt that is hard to ever forget as a parent.

Research shows that a calm, predictable schedule frees kids (and you) from worries or anxiety about what to expect from day to day. Predictability helps foster healthy development in children and reduces stress for parents. As a result, it creates opportunities for quiet and peaceful connections with the family.

Time Footprint: Arranging can consume huge amounts of time and energy, at the expense of time and brainpower available for other activities. Running a multi-person household is a difficult, complex job that is often underrated or underappreciated. In chapter 8, we will learn how investing time to automate and streamline can shrink the tasks here to the smallest footprint, so that the household can run quietly in the background, with minimal upkeep.

RELATE

Activities: Talking, listening, reading, playing, and participating in children's hobbies and interests; going on outings and adventures.

Position in Matrix: Visible/Child's World

Value: Spending time with your children in their world—discussing topics and doing activities of interest to them—is the most direct way of demonstrating to children that they are important, that they matter. Nurturance and connection help to shape our brains. Developmental psychologists and neuroscientists agree that children need to feel loved and have the attention of their caregivers in order to securely attach and properly develop. Relating provides the foundation on which a child learns to explore and interact with the world.

Time spent relating gives your child a sense of self, worth, and value in the world, which equips them to thrive on every level of development—cognitively, physically, emotionally, and socially. It's sacred time that is fundamental to their happiness, and yours. When you spend time with your child, your presence imparts the message that *you matter enough for me to spend time with you, to understand you, to pay attention to you.*

Relating gives you the opportunity to get to know your child as a person—understanding their unique point of view, interests, feelings, ideas, sense of humor. It positions you to truly become that person who knows your child best.

Relating also gives you, the parent, the opportunity to reexperience the world through another person's eyes. Slowing down to the pace of a child can be a built-in stress reducer if you allow it to be. We all need to take breaks from the intense pressures of work, running a household, and being an adult. Hanging with your kids can be a soothing break and a chance to relax and connect with your own inner child.

Time Footprint: Relating doesn't have to take a ton of time; sometimes even fifteen to twenty minutes of undivided attention will deeply satisfy a child. But of all the four core parenting responsibilities, this is the one that can be hardest to deliver—even if it is the most rewarding—as it requires you to slow down to the speed of your children and shut off all other concerns, worries, and to-do lists. As parents, we are years away from having been kids ourselves, so the challenge here is to shift our mind-set and allow this time to be truly connected, parent to child. We will learn strategies for effective relating in chapter 9.

TEACH

Activities: Imparting values, life skills, and discipline that enable kids to succeed in school and in life.

Position in Matrix: Visible/Adult World

Value: Teaching is a fundamental role that society counts on parents to do. The time you invest guiding and mentoring your children in values, knowledge, and skills positions kids to be independent and safe when out in the world on their own. It also creates a moral and practical rudder for them to become productive, contributing members of society.

Directly teaching and mentoring kids through conversation, discipline, setting limits, and encouraging self-regulation makes kids feel supported, guided, looked out for, and not alone.

Effective discipline and life skills also create more space in your schedule for quality time spent relating. First, when kids develop life skills, they can share in the workload of arranging (e.g., getting themselves dressed, helping with chores), freeing up time you would otherwise devote to household tasks. Second, and perhaps just as important, striking the right balance between discipline and instruction makes the time you spend with your child more pleasant. Time spent in the **Teach** quadrant can help to minimize tensions, battles, and power struggles that could otherwise make the quality time you want to spend with your kids unpleasant.

As we know, kids learn as much through role modeling as they do through direct "teaching." It's easy to forget that kids watch and listen to every word you say, whether you are talking directly to them or not (and perhaps especially when you are not). Being a role model requires you to be conscious of your actions, and to invest time in practicing and internalizing the behaviors you want your kids to emulate. It's an opportunity to learn the skills you didn't see modeled growing up so that you can model those skills for your children (a hidden bonus to parents on the time invested in teaching).

Time Footprint: You teach in three ways by 1) role modeling—kids absorb and mimic the behaviors you demonstrate, so to some degree, you are always teaching, whether you are aware of it or not; 2) spending time with your child and observing them to gauge where and how they need guidance; and 3) direct interactions, in which you are offering instruction. Learning to both make and contain the time for all three is the subject of chapter 10.

S.E.L.F.—FOUR TYPES OF SELF TIME

The four distinct components of S.E.L.F. care are just as important as doing your P.A.R.T.; in fact, the two are intimately connected. As parents, we're responsible for our children's well-being *and* our own. We cannot neglect ourselves and expect things to keep running smoothly for our kids. If we don't practice self-care, we become emotionally and physically discombobulated, and our kids' lives become chaotic and unsettled. If we don't find ways to fuel ourselves, we certainly cannot be fully present.

My client Milos was in his mid-thirties when his twins were born. He and his wife were college sweethearts, happily married for many years, with a rock-solid partnership they knew would be a great foundation for co-parenting. He was an economist whose career was skyrocketing, and with the birth of his daughters, he was determined not to take his foot off the pedal—of anything. He was fully committed to fueling his career and his marriage while being the most amazing dad in the world.

Then, when his twins were eighteen months old, it all caught up with him. His wife expressed her worries: "The guy's walking around brain dead." Milos had completely sacrificed self-care in order to be the best worker, best husband, and best dad. Now he was so exhausted that he was ineffective at everything he was trying to do. This wasn't a crisis that emerged out of nowhere. It took months of him walking around in a stupor before he and his wife fully realized what was happening. He was in serious need of an energy repair.

For most parents, committing to self-care involves a shift in mind-set. You probably already feel like you're spread too thin among all your competing responsibilities, and you may feel guilty taking time for yourself. You might think, if I haven't given my ALL to my job, my kids, or my spouse, then how do I justify taking time for myself?

The answer is that you must. Even if you haven't done enough for your job, or your kids, or the house, refueling—even in small portions—must be a part of the daily equation. Investing in yourself as a human being is making a parallel investment in your ability to focus and be present for everything else you do, which includes taking care of your family. In short, in answer to the question you might be asking—"Is self-care selfish?"—the answer is unequivocally "no." Most of us know this already, but chapters 11–14 will help make it a reality.

SLEEP

Activities: Nighttime sleeping (and who couldn't use more of that?) and naps.

Value: Every parent knows what it's like to be sleep-deprived; it simply goes with the territory of parenting. Maybe you have a child who wakes up four times a night, or you're waiting up for a teenager, or you feel like the time you spend scrolling through Facebook after midnight is the only "downtime" you have. No wonder so many of us walk around feeling exhausted and sleepy.

The problem is this: sleep is not optional. It restores our bodies and gives us the ability to stay emotionally regulated. When we're rested, we can maintain perspective. We process a lot of our problems in our sleep (hence the phrase, "sleep on it"), and we wake up with solutions that may have eluded us the day before. When you sleep, the brain does its magic and restores you, mind and body. Given that much of parenting is problem-solving, we truly need our rest to do that part of our job well.

Conversely, lack of sleep adversely affects our health, our ability to think clearly, our mood, and even our ability to maintain a healthy weight. Sleeplessness makes it more difficult to do our jobs, and it's much more challenging to be patient with our children. Being sleep-deprived creates a feeling of "running on empty," and it hinders our ability to be present for anything we do, from planning a birthday party to dealing with our boss.

We end up having to redo tasks in order to correct mistakes we made because we were exhausted and bleary-eyed. No wonder "nap rooms" have become increasingly popular in corporate and other work environments. Research shows that a ten-to-twenty-minute nap boosts productivity and awareness.

Time Footprint: Everyone needs a different amount of sleep, though most experts and studies say adults need seven to eight hours per night to function well, with naps of ten to twenty minutes as needed to fortify you. In chapter 11 we will figure out how much you need to function and how to make sure you get it.

EXERCISE

Activities: Any form of physical movement—cardio, stretching, weight-bearing exercise—whether at the gym, walking, biking, dancing, or doubling up exercise with everyday housework. Also included here are other forms of physical health including going to the doctor, physical therapy, and eating healthily.

Value: We all know that exercise is good for us. It seems like every day there's a news story about how cardiovascular exercise can add years to your life and how a sedentary lifestyle gives rise to a host of chronic health issues. We know physical activity relieves stress, increases focus and performance, and literally makes us feel better.

When it comes to exercise, it's especially important to remember that children mirror what their parents do. Modeling this part of S.E.L.F. care for your kids helps to create healthy habits into adulthood. If a parent is sedentary, there is a good chance their children will be, too. However, parents who eat healthily and exercise with their children on a regular basis are teaching them many valuable lessons.

Sometimes we make the mistake in believing that exercise is about vanity. However, it's not just about looking and feeling our best, but about *being* our best as people and as parents. Many parents get hung up on spending more time away from their children. If we spent all week away from the kids at work, do we deserve to play tennis on Saturday? If we're so zapped from being with the kids all week, shouldn't we just sleep through that spin class and conserve our energy?

On a biological level, movement recharges you, and it brings a host of physical and mental benefits. It can improve your cardiovascular health and muscle tone, reduce bad fat, amp up your stamina, and strengthen your bones and your joints. A good workout releases dopamine, giving you a natural high that improves your interactions with others. It sends oxygen to your brain and gives you a break from worrying that is almost meditative, enhancing your ability to solve problems.

Those are all excellent benefits, but exercise also vitally affects cognitive ability in the long term. A 2014 study by the University of Minnesota featured in *Psychology Today* found that young adults who run or participate in aerobic activities preserve their thinking and memory skills for middle age. Another study, from Finland, found that middle-aged people who are physically active are more likely to be protected from dementia in older age. What's more, a clear mind promotes presence.

Exercise gives you confidence that carries into other aspects of your life as well. You'll be less likely to lose your temper when your three-year-old spills grape juice on the rug or your preteen says you're stupid and she hates you.

When you're physically fit, it's easier to harness the time

and energy to keep up with your kids, whatever their age or yours, and it's easier to meet your personal goals. At the end of the day, exercise makes it easier to get the quality sleep you need.

Time Footprint: The good news is that there are many ways to integrate exercise into your life. The key is to unlock old notions of exercise being defined as ninety-minute workouts three times per week. Science has discovered that even five-to-ten-minute workouts can make a difference. In chapter 12 we will discuss how carving out the time for this essential part of self-care is more manageable than you might think.

LOVE

Activities: Conversations, activities, and connecting time with your partner, your friends, and your extended family.

Value: People rarely talk about the isolation that sometimes accompanies parenthood. It's a serious issue during those first few sleep-deprived months, for sure, when new moms (who may be on maternity leave from work) are suddenly home alone with a newborn. The challenge (and expense) of child care can make it hard to get out and see friends, even when and if it feels comfortable for you to leave your tiny human in the care of a babysitter. Too often friendships fall away when children enter the picture, because it's simply harder to find the time to maintain those relationships.

But close adult relationships sustain us. Yes, the romantic kind, but also our core connections with friends and extended family. Studies of people who live the longest, happiest lives consistently reveal that community and connection are key components. A main conclusion of the Grant Study at Harvard, which followed its subjects for seventy-five years, was that strong relationships are the most important ingredient to well-being over a long life.

Your connections to your kids are fulfilling, yes, but spending time with them still puts you in a giving role. Adult relationships and community allow us to restore our energy through getting support, understanding, companionship, perspective, validation, and a break from child-centered topics. They boost our confidence and help us maintain our sense of humor and calm. Some of our most cringe-worthy parenting moments are funny in hindsight when shared with a friend. There's nothing like a good laugh to help get you back on track.

Time Footprint: Finding the time to sustain relationships—through a quick cup of coffee, a weekend walk, or a dinner out without your kids—can help you connect to your "pre-kids" self. It's important that these adult connections take place with enough frequency to feel as if they're fueling you—as a person, and therefore as a parent. If nothing else, remember this: it's scientifically proven to be good for your health to maintain friendships, even when we begin our roles as parents. Chapter 13 will address this in greater detail.

FUN

Activities: Hobbies, passions, personal projects that fuel your curiosity and creativity, and time spent simply relaxing and unwinding.

Value: Think about what you used to do that brought you joy before your kids were born. Maybe it was playing an instrument, or painting, or writing. Maybe it was craft work, or a game you loved and excelled at. That avocation was a genuine form of self-expression and pleasure. You shouldn't force it to lie dormant until your kids are grown. You may have added "parent" to your identity, but you are still a writer, a singer, a knitter, a painter.

Our passions and pastimes center us by connecting us to ourselves. When we're able to see ourselves for who we truly are, we can see other people more for who they truly are.

Just as exercising releases endorphins, so does pursuing a passion or doing something fun. Cultivating a hobby or passion is one of the most efficient ways to recharge and boost your mood and energy level for everything else in your life. Our passions rev up our creative juices and enhance our problem-solving abilities. When we're engaged in doing something we love, we tend to know what to do, how to do it, and how to measure our results—the three conditions that lead to that desirable state of flow. This increases our overall confidence and happiness.

Time Footprint: As with exercise, parents often struggle here, because they fear they're being selfish for pursuing their passions, or they are made to feel this way by society or even by well-meaning friends and family. Making time for your personal pleasures is the opposite of selfish. The hour or even half hour you spend away from your kids will make it possible for you to be more fully present for all the hours you do spend with them. Understanding the importance of fun in your life as a parent is the subject of chapter 14.

Now that we've explored P.A.R.T. and S.E.L.F. in greater detail, let's find out where you excel and struggle in managing this job.

PART II

SELF-ASSESSING

5

~~~

WHERE DO YOU GRAVITATE?: YOUR QUADRANT SCORECARD

It's human nature to gravitate toward one kind of time over another when it comes to P.A.R.T. and S.E.L.F. We're naturally attracted to the things we're good at, while we avoid what we don't know how to do.

Do you have an inkling of which roles you pay attention to more than the others? Any ideas on which roles you habitually sacrifice or put off? I bet you do.

The P.A.R.T. and S.E.L.F. framework helps parents to know where their time is going and to be purposeful about how they use it. It serves as a practical rudder to keep you on track and in balance, and less overwhelmed by what otherwise feels like an infinite job with no edges.

The assessment in this chapter will help you recognize your current strengths and determine where you need to build skills or pay more attention. The results will allow you to target which chapters in parts 2 and 3 to read for tips and tricks to get in balance.

So, let's figure out where you stand right now. You can

retake the self-assessment every time you feel off balance—
your answers may change based on the age of your kids, or
what's happening with work, your relationships, your health,
and the rest of your life.

Remember the end goal here: gaining opportunities to be
fully present with your kids, your work, your hobbies, your
partner, and your friends and family.

THE QUADRANT SCORECARD

Instructions: Step 1: For each of the eight responsibilities,
indicate whether you feel you are spending too much, not
enough, or just the right amount of time.

Step 2: Rank each of the statements that follow on a scale
of 1 to 5. At the bottom of each section, total the numbers for
your total score for that section.

TIME TO PARENT REPORT CARD

Provide			
The amount of time I spend **Providing** is: (circle one)	Too Much	Not Enough	Just Right

When it comes to **Providing**, I feel: (circle number that is true for you)

1=Never, 2=Rarely, 3=Sometimes, 4=Often, 5=Always

Confident in my skills	1	2	3	4	5
Organized, with systems to make this easy and efficient	1	2	3	4	5
Able to relax and be fully present	1	2	3	4	5
Able to contain time to prevent it from spilling over into other responsibilities	1	2	3	4	5
Comfortable engaging support from family and friends to enable this	1	2	3	4	5

TOTAL "PROVIDE" SCORE

Arrange

The amount of time I spend **Arranging** is: (circle one)	Too Much	Not Enough	Just Right

When it comes to **Arranging**, I feel: (circle number that is true for you)

1=Never, 2=Rarely, 3=Sometimes, 4=Often, 5=Always

Confident in my skills	1	2	3	4	5
Organized, with systems to make this easy and efficient	1	2	3	4	5
Able to relax and be fully present	1	2	3	4	5
Able to contain time to prevent it from spilling over into other responsibilities	1	2	3	4	5
Comfortable engaging support from family and friends to enable this	1	2	3	4	5

TOTAL "ARRANGE" SCORE

Relate

The amount of time I spend **Relating** is: (circle one)	Too Much	Not Enough	Just Right

When it comes to **Relating**, I feel: (circle number that is true for you)

1=Never, 2=Rarely, 3=Sometimes, 4=Often, 5=Always

Confident in my skills	1	2	3	4	5
Organized, with systems to make this easy and efficient	1	2	3	4	5
Able to relax and be fully present	1	2	3	4	5
Able to contain time to prevent it from spilling over into other responsibilities	1	2	3	4	5
Comfortable engaging support from family and friends to enable this	1	2	3	4	5

TOTAL "RELATE" SCORE

Teach

The amount of time I spend **Teaching** is: (circle one)	Too Much	Not Enough	Just Right

When it comes to **Teaching**, I feel: (circle number that is true for you)

1=Never, 2=Rarely, 3=Sometimes, 4=Often, 5=Always

Confident in my skills	1	2	3	4	5
Organized, with systems to make this easy and efficient	1	2	3	4	5
Able to relax and be fully present	1	2	3	4	5
Able to contain time to prevent it from spilling over into other responsibilities	1	2	3	4	5
Comfortable engaging support from family and friends to enable this	1	2	3	4	5

TOTAL "TEACH" SCORE

Sleep

The amount of time I spend **Sleeping** is: (circle one)	Too Much	Not Enough	Just Right

When it comes to **Sleeping**, I feel: (circle number that is true for you)

1=Never, 2=Rarely, 3=Sometimes, 4=Often, 5=Always

Confident in my skills	1	2	3	4	5
Organized, with systems to make this easy and efficient	1	2	3	4	5
Able to relax and be fully present	1	2	3	4	5
Able to contain time to prevent it from spilling over into other responsibilities	1	2	3	4	5
Comfortable engaging support from family and friends to enable this	1	2	3	4	5

TOTAL "SLEEP" SCORE

Exercise

The amount of time I spend **Exercising** is: (circle one)	Too Much	Not Enough	Just Right

When it comes to **Exercising**, I feel: (circle number that is true for you)

1=Never, 2=Rarely, 3=Sometimes, 4=Often, 5=Always

Confident in my skills	1	2	3	4	5
Organized, with systems to make this easy and efficient	1	2	3	4	5
Able to relax and be fully present	1	2	3	4	5
Able to contain time to prevent it from spilling over into other responsibilities	1	2	3	4	5
Comfortable engaging support from family and friends to enable this	1	2	3	4	5

TOTAL "EXERCISE" SCORE

Love

The amount of time I spend with other adult relationships is: (circle one)	Too Much	Not Enough	Just Right

When it comes to **Love**, I feel: (circle number that is true for you)

1=Never, 2=Rarely, 3=Sometimes, 4=Often, 5=Always

Confident in my skills	1	2	3	4	5
Organized, with systems to make this easy and efficient	1	2	3	4	5
Able to relax and be fully present	1	2	3	4	5
Able to contain time to prevent it from spilling over into other responsibilities	1	2	3	4	5
Comfortable engaging support from family and friends to enable this	1	2	3	4	5

TOTAL "LOVE" SCORE

Fun			
The amount of time I spend on **Fun** and hobbies is: (circle one)	Too Much	Not Enough	Just Right

When it comes to having **Fun**, I feel: (circle the number that is true for you)
    1=Never, 2=Rarely, 3=Sometimes, 4=Often, 5=Always

Confident in my skills	1	2	3	4	5
Organized, with systems to make this easy and efficient	1	2	3	4	5
Able to relax and be fully present	1	2	3	4	5
Able to contain time to prevent it from spilling over into other responsibilities	1	2	3	4	5
Comfortable engaging support from family and friends to enable this	1	2	3	4	5

TOTAL "FUN" SCORE

Tabulate Your Scores: (low=5; high=25)

PROVIDE	ARRANGE
TEACH	RELATE

SLEEP	EXERCISE
FUN	LOVE

Total P.A.R.T.: _____ (between 20 and 100)

Total S.E.L.F.: _____ (between 20 and 100)

ANALYZING YOUR SCORES

First, take a look at the relationship between your P.A.R.T. score and your S.E.L.F. score. Are they about even? If so, you are giving equal amounts of attention and ability to both parts of your life—whether that is a lot or a little.

If you notice that one score is significantly higher than the other, it indicates you have organizing skills and the capacity to create systems but are directing them to one half of your life more than the other. Consider why that may be. Is it a value system that you grew up with? Is it based on the model of how your parents parented you, or is it an intentional contrast to the way you were raised?

It also makes sense that parents devote varying levels of attention to each responsibility at a specific moment in time based on each child's personality, their ages and stages, and what's happening in your own adult life. You are growing as a human being all the time, too, nurturing and conquering your own challenges in your work, self-care, love relationships, and personal interests. The needs of every individual and family are fluid and constantly changing.

And sometimes we have little choice. Circumstances with finances, jobs, relationships, and our own health force us off balance, overtaking our time and attention in ways we aren't even aware of, causing us to spend more time in an area than we want or preventing us from giving other things the time they need.

No matter the cause—mind-set, skill, or external circumstances—all we often need to get things back in balance are awareness, a practical approach, and a little self-kindness.

Once you have assessed your P.A.R.T. and S.E.L.F. scores, read the quadrant-specific chapter (e.g. **Provide**, **Arrange**, **Exercise**, **Sleep**) for tools that will allow you to: 1) make time for things you've been giving short shrift, and 2) to contain the time spent in roles that have monopolized your schedule. By the same token, don't be afraid to go into chapters where you had pretty good scores. You may get much-appreciated confirmation that what you are doing is right, and may pick up a tip or two.

FIVE COMMON PARENTING PROFILES

Lest you feel alone in your score, let me assure you we all fall into common patterns as caretakers. Following are five common P.A.R.T. profiles that are easy to fall into—often based on external circumstances, personality style, natural strengths and challenges, and the influence of our own upbringing.

Using your scores from before, read on to see which profile you most strongly identify with. At the end of each profile, I've included a reference to the chapters that will help you address any imbalances and challenges you are likely to face.

High Provide, High Teach / Low Arrange, Low Relate

STRENGTHS: WHERE YOU SHINE

Whether you are well-off financially or working multiple jobs to make ends meet, if you fit this profile, you are likely to be an excellent provider, and you very likely enjoy working. You are committed to taking care of your family financially. You want to provide the best of everything: not just a comfortable home and material goods, but also a quality education and unique learning opportunities for your child. You are committed to providing not just the material means for success but the emotional guidance as well. You enjoy teaching and educating your children in order to prepare them to be successful and fulfilled in the *Adult World*.

You could also fit this profile if you are struggling financially and need to work two to three jobs just to survive, even if you don't love your work. In the limited amount of face time you do have with your kids, you feel compelled to use it to give them guidance and discipline so they can create a better life for themselves.

CHALLENGES: WHERE YOU STRUGGLE

You may not spend a lot of time—or may feel like you don't spend a lot of time—with your children because you are so intensely focused on providing. And when you do carve out time with your kids, you feel obliged to teach them. (**Arrange** and **Relate** can feel like luxuries in this scenario, so they get deprioritized.) Providing and teaching are incredibly important parenting tasks, and they are easier to measure than the more intangible emotional connections we make with our kids. The problem with most of the time spent in these quadrants is that all of the activities take place in the *Adult World*. To feel fully loved, seen, and nurtured, your kids also need you to spend time in their world, just listening, relaxing, and exploring their interests without an agenda.

POTENTIAL CONSEQUENCES OF IMBALANCE

Throughout history, this role has been captured by the traditional patriarchal archetype where the father works to provide material goods and opportunities, but when he is at home, he is teaching his kids how to succeed. Now that many families are two-income families, women, of course, are stepping into this role as well. All parents who fit this profile need to learn how to contain the amount of time they spend providing. They need to make sure that during their family time they are not always teaching but *connecting* with their kids.

Recommended chapters: chapter 8, "**Arrange**," and chapter 9, "**Relate**"

High Provide, High Arrange / Low Teach, Low Relate

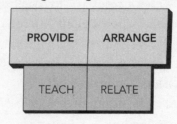

STRENGTHS: WHERE YOU SHINE

You are someone who gets things done and gets them done well and in a timely manner. Highly productive and very organized, you love the feeling of checking items off a to-do list. You work hard for your family when you're at work, and you stay on top of what needs to happen at home, meaning the home environment is peaceful and organized. You run a tight ship.

CHALLENGES: WHERE YOU STRUGGLE

If you find yourself identifying with this profile, you like work that can be easily quantified and marked "done," which can be hard to measure when you're relating with or teaching your kids, as these activities are intangible and difficult to frame in any one particular way. There are no checklists for emotional connection, and it can be hard to gauge how kids are absorbing what you teach or explain to them. When you get home, you might find yourself swapping one to-do list for another (i.e., work to-dos for household to-dos) because checking things off a list feels familiar and comforting. One client of mine put the phrase PEOPLE FIRST, TASKS SECOND on his cell phone screensaver to remind himself that every day when he got home he needed to combat his tendency to get lost in his at-home to-do list.

POTENTIAL CONSEQUENCES OF IMBALANCE

It's great to be and feel productive, but you must make time to relax and remain connected with your kids, without any lists or agendas. One client of mine struggled with the one-on-one relating; the activities were hard to measure, and the benefits felt largely intangible. She found it hard to slow to the pace of her child and to relax into the mystery of the connection between parent and child. Although this client was a high earner who could afford to offer every possible activity and material item, her child was unhappy and never seemed satisfied. When she looked at the matrix, she realized that what her child was lacking was not food, or the best schools that money could buy, but undivided, genuine time and attention from her mother. Many parents in this profile might do a great deal *for* their kids but not a lot *with* their kids. If you find yourself here, you need to focus on relating and teaching—in other words, less *doing* and more *being*.

Recommended chapters: chapter 9, "**Relate**," and chapter 10, "**Teach**"

High Arrange, High Teach / Low Provide, Low Relate

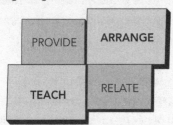

STRENGTHS: WHERE YOU SHINE

You are firmly committed to guiding your children to give them the best shot at organized, trouble-free, capable, and self-sufficient lives. You've got the household management down to a science! You understand that making sure their lives run as smoothly as possible creates a foundation that is vitally important to their development and opportunity to learn. Something about your own childhood caused you to place very high value on order, self-sufficiency, and being responsible. You are so committed to teaching your kids all they need to succeed, you might even homeschool as a way of preparing them for success.

CHALLENGES: WHERE YOU STRUGGLE

Parents who fit this profile may have given up careers to focus on raising a family, but spend all their time at home emphasizing logistics and preparing their kids for success in the world. Sometimes these parents find themselves pouring all of their energies and time into arranging and teaching—so much so that they might as well be gone and at work, because these tasks keep them from relating to their kids or practicing necessary self-care. Sometimes people in this profile feel guilty for not contributing to the family's financial resources, and they feel they must excel at teaching and arranging, even if neither of these responsibilities comes naturally or fuels them. There's a bit of "all work, no play" mentality that can be exhausting for parents and kids.

POTENTIAL CONSEQUENCES OF IMBALANCE

One of my clients, Jenna, was a married, stay-at-home mom with two kids. All of her time was dedicated to doing the homegrown option of everything, and she made every moment a teaching moment. In short, although she wasn't providing for the family financially, she was literally working all the time—and so were her kids. She poured all of her time into arranging and teaching, with the result that she had no energy left to connect with her kids or her spouse. This is the danger of imbalance: lots of work, all with good intention, but not necessarily delivering the intended outcome of focused, uninterrupted quality time.

Recommended chapters: chapter 7, "**Provide**," and chapter 9, "**Relate**"

High Arrange, High Relate / Low Provide, Low Teach

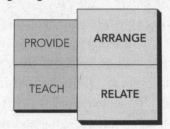

STRENGTHS: WHERE YOU SHINE

You are skilled at running a household where all the trains run on time. You also carve out time to spend focused attention with your kids. In other words, you spend a lot of time organizing your *Child's World*, and a lot of time *in* your *Child's World*. Your kids feel safe and secure in this predictable environment. They feel connected to you, as well as fully loved and valued. In short, they know they matter, and they will blossom as a result.

CHALLENGES: WHERE YOU STRUGGLE

If you are a stay-at-home parent, out of either choice or circumstances, you may periodically struggle with feeling guilty or resentful that you're not contributing to the financial resources of the family or not having the opportunity to express a vital part of yourself through work. That can lead to a lack of confidence about what you have to teach your child, which may make you shy away from your role as guide and mentor. You may also be confused about what you should be teaching versus what schools, educators, or your spouse are responsible for imparting. These lines are not necessarily explicit or carefully defined.

POTENTIAL CONSEQUENCES OF IMBALANCE

Many nonworking parents feel obliged to run an impeccable house if the other parent is the provider, as it may feel like their way of making a contribution. But if this is not work you enjoy, all of your relationships will suffer—with your spouse, with your kids, and with yourself. My client Kirstin gave up her career, her professional identity, and her ambitions to be a stay-at-home mom. She wanted to do her part, so she poured all of her creative energy into arranging and relating. But the arranging tasks that occupied all of her time did not fulfill her as her work had, and she was unhappy.

Recommended chapters: chapter 7, "**Provide**," and chapter 10, "**Teach**"

High Provide, High Relate / Low Arrange, Low Teach

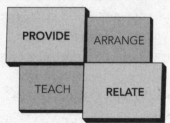

STRENGTHS: WHERE YOU SHINE

You are good at nurturing and investing in your work life to make sure your job is secure and are proud of the opportunities and life you are able to provide for your children. You work hard, get things done, and do what it takes to get ahead. Any time off is spent fully devoted to connecting with your children. You walk through the door and the focus is entirely on them: checking on how they are doing, having fun, connecting, relaxing—and understanding what's going on in their world. Your kids have a good life and feel loved and important—they know they are the apple of your eye. You are very close to your kids and a good role model for success in the world.

CHALLENGES: WHERE YOU STRUGGLE

You may be the primary provider for your family, who finds household logistics and mechanics either terribly boring or distracting. So you avoid it. You also don't want any of the limited time you have with your kids to be "diluted" with tension or conflict—so you shy away from disciplining or taking on the role of teacher, preferring to be the *fun* parent. You may be either letting these things go completely by the wayside or trying to fully delegate these to someone else—your spouse, an extended family member, or a hired helper—to free up your nonworking time from these burdens. There's also the chance you might be letting these things slip because you feel like you just don't have the skills to do them on your own.

POTENTIAL CONSEQUENCES OF IMBALANCE

If you have delegated the arranging to someone else, and it's all being handled expertly, and you appreciate the work they are doing, it can work beautifully. If you are completely hands off on arranging and the person tasked with it does not find it fulfilling or doesn't have the skill set, you could end up with unnecessary tension that is a distraction for a smooth-running household.

A common mistake I see in people who avoid logistics is that they minimize how time-consuming and hard planning can be, thereby not giving enough time or credit to the people in their household who pick up the slack. That disconnect between what is required and what it takes to complete creates tension and often keeps all of the work from being done. If arranging goes by the wayside, and the house, schedule, and paperwork are in disarray, you and your children may get distracted when things go into crisis mode.

Being all fun and no discipline will also likely backfire from time to time—when your kids do something extremely out of line or dangerous, and you suddenly need to step in as the disciplinarian, and your kids are taken by surprise. It's great to be a friend to your child, but children also need and desire guidance and discipline.

Recommended chapters: chapter 8, "**Arrange**," and chapter 10, "**Teach**"

Parenting is a lifelong journey, a continuous ebb and flow. It's not a race to win or a set of principles to master. Consider retaking the self-assessment every three months as you work on your skills and awareness, and as circumstances and demands of your family and life evolve. Check in on your progress and gain confidence as you master new skills and habits that boost your feelings of control and fulfillment.

We've already accomplished so much together: identifying undivided attention as a worthy and transformational goal, establishing a new and clear definition of the parenting job, and exploring a framework for being more mindful and strategic about how we use our time.

Still, no matter how skilled you become at each of the eight quadrants, there is one set of universal time-management skills that apply to all of the quadrants, enabling you to wrap your arms around the whole juggling act, and shift between roles with more agility. Let's look at those next.

6

FOUR TIME-MANAGEMENT SKILLS YOU MUST MASTER

No matter how practiced you are at the eight responsibilities in P.A.R.T. and S.E.L.F., what's actually required of parents is the ability to continuously and seamlessly transition among all eight roles, and that's tougher than it looks. Like a master juggler who effortlessly tosses bowling pins (or scarves or balls) to a specified height at a specific arc and rhythm, so, too, must parents hone the essential time-management muscles that allow you to switch among eight roles while keeping every single one in motion.

This, more than anything, is what makes it hard for caretakers to be present. Parents often complain about the mental stress of juggling so much—how hard it is, on your brain, to be changing gears all the time. It takes enormous skill to "be here now" while still making sure that everything elsewhere is taken care of.

Time management is a broad discipline I've taught for twenty-six years to people living in a wide array of circumstances. There are four time-management muscles I have found to be uniquely valuable to parents. Mastering just these four enables parents to switch among roles while avoiding any unnecessary distractions or time potholes that only exacerbate the feeling of being stretched too thin. When these muscles are underdeveloped, we can't manage a wide scope of activities (which is what parenting requires).

Consciously develop these skills, and this whole juggling act gets easier:

- Apply Selective Perfectionism
- Resist the Siren Call of Technology
- Master Mindful Transitions
- Build a Village and Delegate

APPLY SELECTIVE PERFECTIONISM
The Challenge

What is perfectionism? Perfectionism is the pressure we often put on ourselves to do things extremely well. True perfectionists tend to judge their performance in the starkest of terms: either they've done things brilliantly or they're a complete disaster. In some settings—a difficult class in school or a challenging work environment—this drive can serve us well and earn us praise. But when applied to parenting, perfectionism can sap the joy from everything you do, lead you to work yourself to the bone, and crush your ability to be present as you obsess about whether you did or will do a good enough job in each of your endeavors. Bottom line: unbridled perfectionism will disrupt your capacity to experience contentment and joy.

Why You Must Master It

Freeing yourself from the logistical burden and psychological paralysis of perfectionism liberates you to manage the wide scope and scale of everything you need to do and helps you stay grounded over the long haul. It prevents you from expanding an already difficult job into an impossibly ginormous one, so that you can handle the workload with more ease and agility.

Furthermore, one of the best things you can do—especially as a parent—for your kids and peers, is demonstrate in your own actions that you don't have to be perfect to be good or likeable or successful. In the age of illusory social media profiles, if we were all more open about sharing the things we struggle with, we might be able to disrupt the culture of the perfect parent. Who doesn't prefer someone who's accessible and real, anyway?

Here's the Big Idea: Think MAX-MIN-MOD

As a parent, with so many things to do every day, it's easy to lose perspective and always think you have to do things par excellence. Perfection is a drive for safety—no fear of criticism or wrongdoing. Yet, the phrase "it doesn't have to be perfect" is relatively meaningless . . . what the heck does that mean, anyway? MAX-MIN-MOD is a tactical handbrake that slows you down enough to ask yourself: "Before I do this, what am I trying to achieve?" Then you can consider, "What's a good enough job?"

Here's how it works. For any task or activity that threatens to swallow you whole—or that you're procrastinating about because it's so overwhelming to complete to perfection—define three levels of performance: Maximum (MAX), Moderate (MOD), and Minimum (MIN).

First, MAX. What is the maximum I can do? What does truly perfect look like? Write down, very specifically, all the actions you envision that would add up to the most stellar job. Next, ask what is the minimum I could do? (Yes, skip Moderate until the end.) Imagine you have run out of time, you can't skip out on the task, but you need to do the most basic version that will still get the job done. Then, define MOD. What is something above the bare minimum, if you have a little more time to make it special but not go crazy?

Here are a few examples. Let's say you are going to:

Send a cake to school for your kid's birthday
- MAX: Bake a cake, from scratch, in the shape of your child's favorite character, with individualized party favors for every child.
- MIN: Buy cupcakes at the supermarket.
- MOD: Bake cupcakes from a boxed mix with frosting from a can. Top your child's cupcake with a little figurine of his favorite character.

Have friends over for dinner
- MAX: Cook a huge pot of yummy stew, a gorgeous salad, and your famous cornbread that everyone loves.
- MIN: Order takeout, have everyone chip in, and serve it in pretty serving bowls.
- MOD: Assign each of your friends a dish to bring, potluck style, and make a batch of your famous cornbread.

Clean up your house before friends come over for dinner
- MAX: Completely declutter the front hall and closet (finally!); deep clean the kitchen and bathroom;

vacuum, sweep, dust, and put a pot of orange slices and cinnamon sticks on the stove to make the house smell festive.

- MIN: Toss all the clutter in some reusable shopping bags and cart them to the back bedroom, and spray the house with cinnamon-scented potpourri.
- MOD: Grab a few coats out of the front-hall closet to make room for guests' jackets, stash kids' toys in their assigned bins, wipe down the bathroom, and light a scented candle.

Once you've defined three levels of performance, you can choose the one that's most appropriate for the circumstances, the time you have available, and what else you have on your plate. Sometimes you'll choose MAX, sometimes MOD, sometimes MIN. The muscle is breaking the all-or-nothing thinking that leads to overwork or paralysis, and recognizing you have options.

More Tips to Apply Selective Perfectionism

Practice doing a task less than perfectly every day, just to acclimate yourself to the feeling of easing up on the blind, mindless drive for perfection. One of my clients did this at work, where his perfectionistic tendencies monopolized his time at the expense of his family. Every day for a month he did something less than perfectly, no matter how anxious or worried it made him. To his great surprise, no one cared. As it turns out, his version of perfect was other people's idea of obsessive and unnecessary. Start with a lower-stakes task and allow yourself to do a so-so job.

Trade perfection for presence. When you catch yourself revving the engines of perfectionism, stop to consider what's most important. Is it to get the thing you're working on to a flawless state, or is it showing up in the state of mind ready to connect with your kids, spouse, coworkers, friends? You can obsess over every word of a PowerPoint presentation for work *or* you can rehearse a few times and be ready to take questions. You can squeeze in one more errand while your kid finishes up with his math tutor *or* you can just relax and be ready to greet your kid when he's finished. The goal is to find the most efficient and effective way to get things done, not the most exhausting. Consciously preserve your energy for your attention, your brain, and your heart wherever you are going, and for whomever you are with.

Believe in resilience (yours and your kids'). Worrying and parenting go together like peanut butter and jelly. It's part of the job description. Yet, people from all walks of life who are able to take things in stride (and therefore don't lose hours fretting over every little decision) operate from an inherent belief in their own resilience and resourcefulness. Basically, they know if they make an imperfect decision, they'll be able to recover. And they are able to translate that sense of resilience to their children. It allows everyone to relax and move forward instead of being paralyzed by perfectionism.

RESIST THE SIREN CALL OF TECHNOLOGY
The Challenge

My assistant Tatiana grew up in Silicon Valley, and for her graduation project in college, she did a study on whether technology brings people closer together or drives them farther apart. Her conclusion? Technology brings you closer to people who are geographically far away but more disconnected from people who are physically close by. Take a moment to absorb that.

We are so mindlessly connected to our devices—constantly checking email, texts, social media—that it's hurting our ability to be present for anything: our children, our work, and even our gym time! From the parent's perspective, it's understandable. We have so much to do that we feel like we need to fill every micro-moment with another task, another phone call, another connection. But do we really? At what cost? And we don't even realize we are doing it. Go to the playground and you'll find all the moms and dads on benches looking at their devices. It's so second nature now that no one even thinks about it. Or, we choose to feel guilty and do it anyway.

Technology can deteriorate our ability to create the space for quality time on anything. It also shortens our attention span, drains our energy and patience, and contributes to sleep deprivation and irritability.

Why You Must Master It

We have all kinds of wonderful gadgets and devices at our fingertips. The challenge is using them to help us, not distract us. We've become a world of "phone zombies." Let's be honest. Being a parent has many joyful moments. But parts of it are also boring and the temptation to just take a quick look at Twitter or Instagram can be hard to resist. It also makes us feel less isolated. But think about it from the perspective of your child: when a parent is on a device, the child makes assumptions about where he falls in the pecking order. He may even feel unsafe and unseen.

It's as easy for children to get addicted to technology as it is for parents. If they see you cradling your phone 24-7, is it any wonder why? Perhaps you've spent time in the company of a Snapchat-addicted teenager or met kids with very limited social skills who spend the majority of their waking hours glued to a screen. Social-emotional skills have been studied to boost success in school, work, marriage, and life. Learning and retention have been studied to be more lasting when they take place away from screens. That can only happen by mixing "online" connections with connecting "IRL" (that is, "in real life"). It's possible both to use technology to your benefit—to be more efficient and to get things done—*and* to put technology in its place by being mindful and selective about its use.

Here's the Big Idea: Become a Media Mentor

Just like table manners and four-letter words, kids imitate what their parents do. If you want your kids to have a healthy relationship with technology, model it yourself! The best thing you can do is actively mentor your kids in their relationship to technology by developing and communicating your own personal rules and establishing household rules to use technology with intention. Make conscious choices about what you use technology for and when.

Show your kids, through your own deliberate choices, that just because you can use technology for everything doesn't mean you should. For example, maybe because you work on a screen all day, you read paper books at night. Maybe if you are playing a board game and someone can't remember a fact, the house rule is *don't* Google it. Stay connected to the people at the table, relying on (gasp!) memory alone. If no one comes up with the answer, look it up later, while you are alone. Apps like Google Maps and Waze are enormously helpful, especially when you're trying to get someplace fast. But if you're on vacation or exploring a new spot, technology keeps your head down, buried. Instead, consider pulling out an old-school map or asking for directions.

Be bold and stand tall in decisions about when and for what your kids can use devices such as iPads and cell phones. It's a slippery slope—today's devices can be used for homework, social media, and entertainment. But don't back off and throw your hands up in surrender. It's particularly important to limit social media time and entertainment time on devices—and show your kids that there are other places to connect and get validation. This is especially important once they get to middle school, when the need to belong and be liked leaves adolescents particularly vulnerable—a kind of 24-7 punch to the gut on whether they are being "included" or not.

Recognize how physiologically addictive technology is—so don't be surprised when they balk or throw tantrums when you say time's up. Think of it like cotton candy. No matter how much they scream for more, at a certain point you just say no because you, the adult, know it's not good for them.

Media mentorship begins at birth, and www.zerotothree .org offers a very practical and insightful suite of tools called Screen Sense, which recommends ways to manage screen time for young children. But we know that no matter how you manage screen time when your kids are small, the challenges and pulls of technology only get stronger as kids get older. The good news is, no matter how hard it is to break bad habits (yours or your kids'), it's never too late to hit reset, for the health and development of your growing child.

The American Academy of Pediatrics is an outstanding

resource that continuously monitors the research on the impact of screen time and puts out guidelines for appropriate media use at different ages. Their recommendations are based on brain development and social-emotional needs. You can also check out their wonderful online tool to help families create their own media use plans at www.healthychildren.org /mediauseplan.

More Tips to Resist Technology's Siren Call

Park it at the door. In the Japanese tradition, there is a station by the front door where everyone removes their shoes and puts on slippers. It's an act that not only keeps dirt out, it also sets the tone for the home as a sacred space. You can do the same for technology. Consider creating an attractive and prominent docking station—a beautiful storage box by the front door—where everyone parks their cell phones upon entry. A sign above the station, with an inspiring phrase like BE HERE NOW or LOVE THE ONE YOU'RE WITH, can communicate the spirit of your family values. During designated times, family members can retrieve their phones from the docking station, but otherwise the physical separation can make it easy for people to be present and more conscious about their use of technology.

Detox your family. Lots of families—I might even argue *most* families—have a less than healthy relationship to technology. But it's entirely possible to turn things around (just like it's possible to eat more healthily, or exercise more, or get more sleep at night). Plan a three-day detox, during which most activities should involve a full-body experience: play catch, go bowling, play a board game, make pasta from scratch, do arts and crafts. It will be difficult for you *and* the kids! You'll want to check your phone, just for a second. You may even feel anxious and antsy about it, but tolerate that discomfort and don't give in. Soon enough your brain will shift to a different gear and you won't need the technology hit.

Make technology the fifth choice, not the first. We all know how easy it is to use technology as a babysitter. It's an easy (and cheap!) choice to entertain the kids when you need a little time for yourself. There's nothing wrong with giving your kid—and likely yourself—a break, by allowing a little screen time, as long as that time is intentional and bounded by time parameters you feel comfortable with as a parent. The problem is how addictive technology can be—before long, the minute they get bored, kids beg for a show or a device. Instead of making technology your first choice for distraction, make it your fifth, or don't make it a choice at all. Come up with a menu of four other things you can turn to before you resort to technology. You can even have the kids make up their *own* list and coach them to use it to scratch the boredom itch.

I interviewed Simon Isaacs, cofounder of Fatherly.com, a very cool dad-centric website geared to fill the gap of parenting advice, news, and product recommendations for men. Simon is a total techie who built a business on the Internet—he knows the benefits of technology. But he also knows its dangers. He has a personal goal to never, ever make his kids feel as if what's on the screen is more important than they are. He developed a policy for himself that when he is home and one of his kids comes up to him to talk, he instantly shuts the laptop or flips over the phone. No delay, no finishing what he was doing, he just closes or turns over the device and gives his kid his undivided attention. This policy is nonnegotiable for him—and is a mechanism for determining what sort of work he does when at home: he never does anything he can't be interrupted doing.

There's a saying about parenting: "The days are long, but the years are short." In the blink of an eye, kids are out the door. Be here now.

MASTER MINDFUL TRANSITIONS
The Challenge

Switching gears—between work and home, between the fast-paced *Adult World* and a kid's dawdling pace—is one of the biggest challenges parents face. Some people have an ability to hyper-focus: wherever they are, the rest of the world disappears. They go so deep, and are so intent on what they're doing, that they lose track of time and their surroundings. These people have an especially difficult time switching gears and can get stuck in one role at the expense of the others.

Others switch gears so frequently—bouncing from one thing, to the next, to the next—that they fail to be fully present for any one single role. These parents constantly interrupt themselves (by changing tasks so frequently) and are easily derailed by competing priorities.

That's why you might find yourself losing your temper in the first few minutes after you walk in the door from work, despite your best intentions. Or why you feel frustrated after you've busted your tail to clear time to take your kid to the playground and it feels like it's taking hours for her to pull on her socks and shoes. And why you're aggravated by the constant interruptions that are part and parcel of parenting. It's hard to manage the complex juggling act of parenting if you struggle with transitioning among tasks and mind-sets.

Why You Must Master It

When it comes to making smooth transitions, the ultimate goal is to be truly in the present—with your kids, job, spouse, friends, and even with yourself when you're at the gym or having a quiet moment. When you make a full and complete transition, and are truly "here now," at work, home, with your kids, friends, or spouse, you can get significantly more quality out of significantly less time.

Without this agility, you could get stuck in a particular mode and "give me a minute" can turn into an hour . . . and in that time, the opportunity for connection vanishes. Being able to quickly move from one task, or one pace, to another is among the most important skills a parent can develop.

Here's the Big Idea: Set Your Intention Before You Cross Any Threshold

When you are crossing any threshold—and switching from any one quadrant to another (**Provide** to **Relate**, for example, after a long workday)—build in a minimum of ten minutes before you arrive home to shift gears. The most common challenge working parents share with me is, "I walk in the door after a long day and just need a little space before I can handle my kids and the house and all that stuff." But kids don't get that you need a little time to clear your head—they've been missing you all day!

When walking through your front door, instead of thinking about your workday, or tomorrow's to-dos, shift your focus. Ask yourself, "When I walk through the door, what is my intention?" Maybe it is to be present for your kids and partner, or to make your family laugh.

The same is true when you leave home and go to work. Getting out the door in the morning can be hectic and stressful. Don't carry that stress into the workday—it will dilute your ability to be present at work, which means you'll get less done and feel obligated to stay later at the office or get back on the computer after the kids go to bed to compensate.

Keep in mind that when you are transitioning from one mode or quadrant to the next, you need to prepare yourself not only to give something different but also to receive what the people on the other side of that door have to share: their love, their worries, their stories, their needs. Don't be surprised. Be ready.

Avoid the "just one more thing" syndrome. Who hasn't been tempted to do just one more thing before leaving the house or running out of the office? Departures can already be a stressful situation. Don't make them worse by shoving in another task and leaving no time for a gentle transition. Every time the impulse crosses your mind, trigger your "transition ritual." It could be as simple as counting to ten or taking four deep breaths. Help yourself transition mindfully instead of in a herky-jerky mad dash.

EXPERT ADVICE | **ROAD MAP THE EVENING**

Claire Lerner—mom, friend, and renowned parenting educator—shared that most parents feel extremely stressed from the time they get home from work until the time they put their children to bed. And when parents are stressed, children often exploit the situation to gain control. Her remedy for this situation? Parents should connect by phone for five minutes before they get home every day to create a game plan for the evening. This helps parents collaborate and work around each other's priorities. If Mom has a mandatory call at seven p.m., she can do dinner and the bath, but not bedtime books. Instead of watching the evening unravel, Mom and Dad will be (and feel like) a united team.

More Tips to Master Mindful Transitions

Create a kick-butt to-do list. Whether you prefer a digital or paper planner, keep a single, reliable list where you can capture all of your to-dos as they come to mind throughout the day. Whether it's for work, your kids, or household chores, this will put your mind at ease and give you confidence that no task (however big or small) will be forgotten. If you are interrupted in the middle of a task, write down your next action item, take the interruption, and resume exactly where you left off.

Help kids mentally prepare to make transitions. If transitions are hard for adults, they are doubly tough for kids who lack your perspective. Try this method to ease transitions for your children: 1) let them know how long you will be in a certain space and what your expectations are for when you'll be leaving; 2) give kids a ten-minute warning (cell phone alarms are great for this); 3) show empathy when they buck at the idea of wrapping up—"I know it's hard to leave when you're having so much fun"—and offer assurance that they'll have another chance; and 4) help them get excited about the next thing they're about to do. Seems pretty simple, right? Right. But skip even one of these steps and you could be in for a bumpy ride.

Give transitions the time and space they require. Most people underestimate how long transitions really take. The best thing you can do for yourself and your family is to get real about timing. Identify the transitions that give you the most trouble (getting up, dressed, and out the door in the morning is a common one) and deconstruct them. First, using a stopwatch, time how long it actually takes for each kid from wake-up to out the door—you may say forty minutes, when in fact it's forty-seven. Second, figure out what mechanics can be done in advance (e.g., making coffee, packing lunches). Third, be consistent: make it all second nature, like a reflex. Even for kids who really struggle with transitions, the process can be made much easier if all you have to focus on is the mental shift rather than the logistical part as well.

BUILD A VILLAGE AND DELEGATE
The Challenge

In chapter 2, I introduced Melissa Milkie, a University of Toronto sociologist who for decades has been studying how families spend their time. Her research shows that it's only in recent years that two people (or one!) have tried to raise a child without help from anyone else. But today's generation of parents have a few unique characteristics, including how seriously they take the decision to have kids, as opposed to, say, parents in the 1950s who were just as likely to have kids to fulfill society's expectation of what it meant to be an adult. Today's parents' sincere intention can lead to a sense of intense responsibility, and that can keep parents isolated as they try to do it all on their own.

Of course, delegating isn't always easy. First, you have to have someone to delegate to. And that can be a psychologically loaded task, especially for parents, who are eager to maintain a sense of control and want things to be "done right."

Some parents know what they'd like to delegate but have a hard time doing it—because either they can't find or pick the right person to delegate to or they've had poor experiences with delegation in the past. (In most cases, a "poor experience" translates to the task taking far longer than anticipated, or not resulting in the desired outcome, often because the delegator's expectations were unclear.) Lacking the know-how is one of the common obstacles to people delegating regularly.

Why You Must Master It

If you want quality time for your kids and yourself, you must learn to delegate. The job of parenting, with eight discrete roles to juggle, is bigger and more challenging than any one parent (or two or three) can handle. The best use of your time is getting to know your kids and prioritizing your own self-care so you have the energy to connect and nurture. It's worth the effort to identify ways you can share the burden with others, whether it's with babysitters, extended family, neighbors, or friends.

Here's the Big Idea: Build Your Village

As a parent, whether you are single or married, have one kid or ten, it's not uncommon to feel totally isolated. Your only hope for managing the job comes from building a village of people with whom you can share the journey of being a parent. That includes practical support (sharing carpool duties, recommending a new pediatrician) and emotional support (empathetic exchanges with others going through the same challenging experiences you are—potty training, middle school, the college application process). Cultivating the connections of the people who become your village will take some initial effort, but the return will be a thousandfold.

Milkie advises thinking of your family unit as beyond the people who live in your house. As the African proverb goes, "It takes a village to raise a child." No family should be an island. Your village becomes an invisible safety net of support that surrounds you and your family in good times and bad.

After my marriage ended, I found an apartment in a neighborhood that had great public schools and lots of families. I probably had the least money of anyone on my block (and often struggled to pay my rent for the first couple of years postdivorce), but being there connected me to a community of people that eased the loneliness and burden of being a single parent in so many ways. I'd sit on our front stoop and chat with the neighbors, while Jessi played with other kids on the block. I joined the local PTA out of a sense of duty—to show Jessi that even though I was a single parent, I wouldn't be so different from her friends' parents. But the PTA gave me much more, a circle of friends—five families (three married couples and two single moms) who became my village. We took turns walking the kids to and from school; the older kids babysat the younger ones; we celebrated New Year's, July Fourth, Memorial Day, and Labor Day together. I'm sure I'd have been a lesser parent without their friendship and support. Parents who are isolated, living in an area where it's harder to connect with neighbors, will need to work harder to find that village, but it may be the greatest investment of their time.

Invest the time in building your community. You may not think you have time to get involved in your local community (whether it's at a co-op play space, church, local parenting group, or school) until you realize that a couple of hours invested in building your network will buy you hundreds of hours back in time and peace of mind. Through these institutions in your community, you'll start to build a circle of people with whom you have common needs and on whom you can rely for things like carpooling, babysitting co-ops (where a group of families share babysitting with one another), and hand-me-downs.

More Tips for Delegation

Don't deny people the joy of feeling valued. My client Betsy felt guilty about asking anyone to care for her two-year-old son. She figured, he's my child, he's my responsibility. And, in some regard, she was right. But she took her sense of responsibility to the extreme, believing that asking for help was akin to "pawning him off." She felt as guilty asking anyone else to tolerate spending any potentially unpleasant time with her young son—who might be whining or crying, as two-year-olds do—as she did taking time away from her little guy. Not surprisingly, this left very little, if any, time for S.E.L.F. activities. I turned the tables and asked how it made her feel when someone asked her to watch their child. She said it made her feel good, trusted, and useful—and that it gave her a chance to be an important person in another kid's life. That change in perspective helped her become more comfortable with build-ing and relying on her own village.

Be clear about what really matters. One of the hardest things about delegating—especially when your children are involved—is that everyone has their own way of doing things. The key is to boil your basic requirements for what "good" looks like to three (or fewer) criteria. For a babysitter, that might mean: 1) keep the kids safe; 2) don't give them sweets (because it makes putting them to bed even harder); and 3) make sure they fin-ish their homework. Delegation will go much more smoothly if you, as the delegator, decide what success looks like and tell your babysitter before they start the task.

Make delegation conversations into their own kind of quality time. If you avoid the "dump and run" approach—assuming someone knows what you want and how to do it—delegating can offer the chance to get to know someone else, share skills and experiences, and enable both parties to feel as if they are making a contribution. Delegating, done in a respectful, reciprocal way, is a way to grow close to someone else.

Assess someone's level of expertise before you assign the task. As a parent, you'll delegate to people who have a wide range of expertise: everyone from a mother's twelve-year-old helper (who doesn't know how to hard-boil an egg) to your child's grandmother, who may have a ton of experience with children but is less familiar with how you want your family to operate. Is the person you are delegating to a rookie or an expert? Are you treating that person with the appropriate level of respect (or direct instruction) based on what you know of their background? Your approach can change depending on the person to whom you are delegating. The person you are delegating to can be at one of three levels—beginners, equals, or experts. You should adjust the time you invest and what you discuss accordingly.

Beginners: These can be friends, family, kids, or a spouse who may not be as knowledgeable about the task at hand. Explain the project, and then walk them through the steps to getting there. Review their efforts along the way and provide feedback, but let them finish it—no matter what. Always reward their effort.

Equals: This is when people you delegate to do a task they've done plenty of times before, even if they do it differently. In these cases, explain the task and be clear about your overall goal. If the way it is done really matters (i.e., money or safety are at risk), explain the specifics of how it should be done. Otherwise, name the job and the goal, and let them do it their way.

Experts: Working with professional child-care providers, teachers, and doctors can be tricky—you don't want to micromanage them, but it's also hard to tell where you leave off and they begin. When choosing any expert for a task, be clear about what you are looking for: solid credentials, a good reputation among people you trust to do the job right, and people with whom you have a good rapport. Then for the ultimate partnership, recognize that you are the expert on your child, and that the professionals you tap for help are experts in their discipline (teaching, medicine, child development, reading, etc.). A teacher, for example, should be an expert on how a child learns, the method of instruction, and specific subject areas. You, as the parent, are the expert on your kid. Once you get that right, it's so much easier to collaborate.

To create the space for quality time for our children and ourselves, we need to balance our time across eight domains of parenting: four in Raising a Human Being (that's P.A.R.T.) and four in Being a Human Being (that's S.E.L.F.).

These four time-management skills—1) Apply Selective Perfectionism; 2) Resist the Siren Call of Technology; 3) Master Mindful Transitions; and 4) Build a Village and Delegate— enable you to make and contain time for each without getting trapped in one quadrant at the expense of another.

Take a moment to reflect here: Where do you need to build up your skills? Which one trips you up the most? Which one will make it easiest to switch back and forth among the eight roles? Which skill would give you back the most time and energy if you focused on honing that muscle?

Everyone can benefit from refining and continuing to develop these advanced time-management muscles. Each could be the topic of an entire book, let alone a chapter. I've tried to focus here on the things that get parents in the most trouble and too often derail the pursuit of quality time. If you are interested in focusing more on your time-management skills, there are many more comprehensive resources out there—including my own book, *Time Management from the Inside Out.*

Let's go now to P.A.R.T., to dive into tips for making and containing time for each role you play in Raising and Being a Human Being.

PART III

RAISING A HUMAN BEING:
DOING YOUR P.A.R.T.

7

PROVIDE

	Invisible	
Adult World	PROVIDE	ARRANGE
	TEACH	RELATE

Ginny loved her work. A vice president of marketing for an ad agency, in many ways her work defined her. She found the chance to innovate and to solve problems for clients incredibly stimulating, energizing, and satisfying. Creative work ignited her soul. Her ambition was to develop an impeccable reputation in her field, and perhaps, one day, to start her own firm. Her work ethic, of which she was very proud, led her to say yes to many projects and do whatever it took to deliver excellence.

Yet, Ginny's passion for her work made her feel guilty. It took time away from her kids (ages seven, eleven, and thirteen) and her mind out of the moment when they were together. Her brain was constantly churning with work challenges, and if she had an idea, she was driven to execute it. It was hard to turn work off at night and on weekends. She wondered constantly if she should put her goals and passion on hold, to be a better parent for her kids.

Of the four parenting responsibilities, providing for our children is easily the most time-consuming and emotionally charged. This one, of all the P.A.R.T. categories, can easily co-opt every well-meaning parent's time and focus away from the other core responsibilities.

IN OUR PARENT TIME SURVEY
WORK IS HARD TO CONTAIN

52.24% of parent respondents reported that quality time with their kids is an important priority, but said that it often gets preempted by work or other demands.

We want to create the best life for our kids, and we know that requires making and managing money to provide the essentials: food, clothing, shelter, and a safe, secure environment. Work can also be a source of personal fulfillment or extreme discontent for parents. So whether you are working in a job you are passionate about or one that just puts food on the table, the challenges presented in this chapter present the primary dilemma of parents everywhere: how do I balance earning and managing money with making time for my family? This chapter offers practical, doable tips that will help you strike this balance more easily.

THE IDEAL STATE:
CONTENT AND CONTAINED

The interesting thing about work is how it crosses boundaries in all areas of our lives. Obviously it's a source of money—and that, in and of itself, provides freedom and opportunities. But for many people, work is also a source of fulfillment, self-development, and self-expression. In fact, according to a recent study published by the Kellogg School of Management at Northwestern University, 89 percent of people say work is "meaningful" to them, whether they work full-time, work part-time, or even volunteer.

The vast majority of the moms and dads I work with struggle to find the right balance between work and family. Some, like my client Ginny, are so passionate about their careers that they struggle to be present at home; others find that their dissatisfaction at work spills over into their ability to enjoy the quality of their family time. Those who *aren't* working—either because they've lost a job or made a decision to be a full-time caregiver—can be distracted because they miss the sense of purpose that work provides.

The ideal state when it comes to **Provide** is to be content and contained. When we are content and contained, we find meaning and value in our relationship to work and are able to give it our undivided attention and get things done. We are able to be fully present when we are at work, and then we can turn work off at the end of the day and go home to be fully present with our families.

But being present and developing a content and contained relationship with work is difficult, due to a 24-7 work world, inefficiencies at the office, and any number of other practical and emotional complications that trip us up.

More than any other obstacle to containing the time and mental space **Provide** consumes is the two-ton gorilla of emotions: guilt. Guilt that we are not doing enough for our families because we work, and guilt that we are falling short at work because of the demands of our family lives. And if we aren't working, guilt that we are not contributing to the family income, or providing a good role model, or being true to our whole selves.

Guilt is a menacing voice in our heads that distracts us from doing the job—in any of our roles, P.A.R.T. or S.E.L.F.—because it divides our attention. And we know that undivided attention is the Holy Grail—for us *and* for our families.

In the process of working on this book, I've gotten to know the work of Ellen Galinsky, president and cofounder of the Families and Work Institute. (Although I don't know Ellen personally, I sort of feel like I do! She's become a personal hero.) After decades of debate about whether or not mothers should work, Galinsky had an innovative idea that might settle matters: why don't we "Ask the Children"? She and her team conducted a landmark study by that name to explore kids' perspectives on working parents.

Her findings were fascinating. And totally surprising.

First, according to Galinsky's research, there is no correlation between whether a mother works and kids' developmental outcomes. None. We can put that worry to rest, once and for all. Stop and absorb that.

The big insight is that it's not *whether* we work, but *how we feel about work* that impacts kids. When we are conflicted about working, we communicate that guilt to our kids—directly and indirectly—and that's what affects them. Guilt, for example, might make us reluctant to talk about work we love. Instead, we say things such as *"I wish I didn't have to work." "I hate to leave but Mommy/Daddy has to work." "You want me to buy things for you, right?"* which creates haphazard messages about the meaning and value of work.

Second, Galinsky found that what children wish they could change about their parents' work lives was not necessarily to have their parents work less (only 10 percent of kids chose this). What kids said they *do* want is for their parents to be less stressed and less tired by work when they are together (34 percent)—which gets back to the importance of managing our attention and presence when we are with our children.

And finally, Galinsky discovered that kids want parents to love their work, *just not more than they love them*. That seems essential information for the parent who is passionate about her work, as well as the parent who is working just to pay rent and put food on the table.

So, take heart, parents. Breathe. Whether you work out of necessity, passion, or a combo of the two, extract guilt from the equation. Guilt about work is total mental clutter that only serves to steal additional time and energy from being present for quality time with your kids and for yourself. It turns out our kids are resilient and pretty smart. Guilt doesn't deserve so much of your attention after all—and that makes getting to a state of "content and contained" a little bit easier.

FINDING WORK'S SWEET SPOT

I've always loved this quote from Annie Dillard's book, *The Writing Life*: "How we spend our days is, of course, how we spend our lives." Time has a slippery, ephemeral quality, and the key is to be conscious and thoughtful about both work and family time, to prevent precious moments from sliding by in either department. Here are a few key ideas to think about and execute when finding the balance:

Create edges. Ellen Galinsky's research discovered that parents enjoy their work when they can contain it, when they can be efficient and focused, and then, at the end of the day, they can leave work at work. Based on my work with thousands of parents, I agree. Because we live in a time of swelling work-loads, it's up to you to create the edges on your workday and on your workweek. Don't expect your boss to do it for you. Do some of your coworkers take pride in being available by email 24-7? That doesn't mean you need to be. To avoid being trapped by unspoken assumptions on either your part or your company's, discuss expectations for after-hours con-nectedness with your boss. Are you expected to answer emails at night and on the weekend? If it's a true emergency, can you agree that the company will reach out by phone? By defining clear edges, you can more easily give work your all during work hours and, when you are done, leave that piece of it behind and be fully present for your family.

Talk about work in a healthy way. We know from Ellen Galinsky's research that the better you feel about your work, the better it is for your kids. If you love your work, be inten-tional about how you talk about it as a source of fulfillment, meaning, and self-development. This can be a model for how you want your kids to think about school. If you don't like your work, try your best to embrace what you do like about it: the paycheck, the flexibility, your coworkers, or perhaps the opportunity to work outside of the home. What's important is the feeling of choice: you are choosing this job, right now, for whatever it might offer you. Kids can receive—and remember—that message.

Think about work in stages and phases. Two years is a huge amount of time in the life of a child but a blip on the radar for an adult. As you debate your relationship to work, it helps to think in terms of ages and stages. The trick, here, is to dance to two beats—to the time of your child's development as well as to the time of your career's development. Imagine you are crossing a stream by hopping from rock to rock rather than trying to jump from one side to the other in one huge leap. If you base your career decisions on your child's growth and stages, then you don't feel trapped or locked into a job that, in the short term, isn't fulfilling but is a means to a financial end. By the same token, you might take a job that's a bit soul crushing, knowing that in a year or so you can make the transition to a job that fulfills you. Knowing that what you're doing now *is not forever* can help you make decisions that are in your own interest—and in the interest of spending quality time with your kids.

FOCUS ON RESULTS

On the flip side of feeling guilty that work is taking away from family life, many of my clients who are working parents feel guilty about having family life take away from their work duties and end up putting in extra time, or mental space, worrying that they are not keeping up with their childless peers. In my experience, working parents are among the most productive in the workplace, because they are so worried about being perceived as falling short. The goal is to be super focused and productive while at work, so it's easier to tie your day in a neat bow and be present for your kids and family when you're at home. Here's how:

Treat each day like a résumé. You were hired to do a job based on your unique talents, skills, and experience. Get clear on what's being asked of you, and get your job done. Résumés speak in terms of accomplishments, not activities. If you organize your time wisely and keep a laser-beam focus on achieving results, you should be able to record and report what you've done at the end of each day. Make it a habit to document what you've done for colleagues and supervisors. This creates a trail of accomplishment, and it also helps you *feel* accomplished.

Cut workday clutter. Sometimes people get stuck bringing work home at night or on the weekends, not because the company expects them to but because they piddled away their productive hours at work with bad habits like procrastination or perfectionism. Avoid the massive time suck of Facebook, other forms of social media, and personal emails. Just like our goal is undivided attention with our kids, when you're at work, really be there—focused, fresh, and ready to put in the time.

Anticipate derailments. I also call this tip "stage-manage your life." Stage managers prepare for any disaster by playing the "what if?" game before each show. *What if*, during a live performance, the curtain doesn't open or the phone doesn't ring on cue? When you're a working parent, learn to think like a stage manager. Spend a few minutes at the end of every day looking ahead down two highways, Work Life and Family Life, both of which can be highly unpredictable. Think about what might derail you in the next few days and how you might manage any potential surprises. By anticipating what might be headed your way, you can take preventive measures, and, even if a crisis occurs—at work or at home—you will spend less time digging out of the mess because you've thought about how to solve it in advance. Be prepared.

Learn the art of the "gracious no." Guilt about your limited hours as a parent can trap you into saying yes to every request from colleagues (or your boss), even though you know it's way above your capacity. But, if constantly agreeing to extra requests is stopping you from getting your core responsibilities done or forcing you to bring work home at night and interfere with family time, you need to talk about it directly and objectively. Instead of being defensive when you are being asked to do too much, develop the art of the gracious no. Don't speak of it as a choice between "your work" or "this person's work"—you are all doing the company's work. Frame the conversation in an objective and positive way. For example: *"I'd love to help out, but I need to deliver on this deadline/project before I add anything else to my plate. Can we speak when this is done?"*

Be a good citizen (in a fraction of the time). Greet people with genuine kindness and interest. Ask how they are doing and wait for the answer. Know your colleagues' birthdays and remember to send them a note. These small gestures don't take a lot of time, but they go a long way in building rapport with your coworkers, which makes the workplace more enjoyable for everyone. If you can, ask if and in what ways you might help alleviate another's workload. By proactively offering assistance, you can plan for the extra work rather than being at the mercy of last-minute requests. You will also make it clear that you're a team player.

SEEK FLEXIBILITY, BUT BE WARY OF TIME TRAPS

Most working parents want and need jobs that offer some degree of flexibility. It allows them to be there for their kids on a regular, predictable basis and in moments of need or emergency. According to *Forbes*, there are four secrets to finding a flexible job:

1. Target small to midsize companies, as large companies tend to be less flexible.
2. Don't assume a full-time job can't be done on a flexible basis.
3. Hold off on requesting flexibility until the end of the job interview.
4. Suggest a two-to-three-month trial period and frame flexibility as a win-win scenario for both parties.

But not all flexibility is equal. Some of the *most* flexible situations are actually the most demanding in terms of time. Here are a couple of guidelines to keep in mind:

Flextime. If you are able to negotiate a more flexible schedule (e.g., working from home one or more days a week), make sure you ask your supervisor to identify his or her biggest concerns so you can address each of them. In my experience, employers have four common worries about work-from-home employees: 1) low productivity (make sure you know and achieve your deliverables, and document your daily output); 2) missing out on casual conversations (it's easier than ever to manage this issue thanks to technologies like Skype, FaceTime, and Google Hangouts); 3) absence of team building (make sure you show up, in person, on key days such as for staff meetings); and 4) inaccessibility at a busy time (if a company is offering you flexibility, you should be flexible for busy times in return).

Entrepreneurship. Take it from a fellow parent who started a business with a young child: the hours may be flexible, but a new enterprise often requires more hours (and brain space) than you ever imagined. Even part-time "side businesses" such as renting out extra space (Airbnb, rehearsal space to a local band, etc.), reselling items on eBay, or making money with a well-established skill (like teaching piano lessons or part-time copy writing) can come with a crushing time burden that is hard to predict in advance. What's more, income can be unpredictable, which might force you to put in even more hours out of fear of not earning enough. That said, there is something empowering about calling the shots and (hopefully) feeling passionate about your own company. Whether full-time or part-time, being an entrepreneur is a series of trade-offs, just like everything else: Know what's most important to you. And filter every business idea you contemplate through this strict time lens: minimal activity for maximal reward.

MANAGING MONEY

Whether you work full-time, work part-time, or are a stay-at-home parent, earning money is only one aspect of providing. The other side is spending the time to manage it well, so you are able to make trade-offs between time spent working and time with your kids, stretching your money to provide the essentials: food, shelter, clothing, and education.

We all know money is not an endless resource—far from it. Yet shockingly few of us have been trained in the basic life skills associated with money management: writing and sticking to a budget, balancing a checkbook, thinking through a basic savings plan. I give dozens of talks each year, and when I deliver a presentation about time management, I often ask audience members to fill in the blank at the end of this sentence: "*I procrastinate whenever I have to . . .*" The most common answer is "manage finances." Why is that? Managing finances is emotionally charged—challenging basic fears and making us feel vulnerable. We're afraid we might discover that we don't have enough. There's shame and insecurity connected to money, especially in a culture that is driven by so much consumerism. Parents are vulnerable to it, and so are kids.

Yet, not looking at or not managing money well can lead us to work longer and harder than we really have to, to worry constantly about finances, and to buy things as a substitute for the time we crave to spend with our kids and for ourselves.

Raising kids is an expensive proposition, and investing the time to look at and manage money as a tool will help you feel in control and more confident about various work-time trade-offs, no matter how much or how little you have in your checking account.

Here are some practical ways to contain the time (and mind space) you spend managing finances:

Decide how much money is enough. It will surprise no parent to learn that raising a child costs a lot of money. Oddly, though, many of us live in a state of blind anxiety about how much we actually need in order to provide a good life for our kids. That lack of clarity can create time binds such as overworking to keep up with our neighbors (or what we think our neighbors are making), spending more than we save, or entirely avoiding taking any time to manage our finances. If you know—even roughly—how much you truly need, and for what, you can make more informed decisions about working for passion or utility, for a paycheck or greater flexibility. A great starting measure to put it all in perspective comes from the Economic Policy Institute's Family Budget Calculator, which can tell you what income a family needs in order to attain a modest yet adequate standard of living in your zip code (or any other neighborhood you may consider moving to). Where you live makes a huge difference, of course—the basic family budget for a two-parent, two-child family ranges from $49,114 (Morristown, Tennessee) to $106,493 (Washington, DC).

Create a regular time. Only one thing separates those who are good at managing their finances and those who aren't: time. Regardless of socioeconomic status, people who manage their money invest a consistent amount of time each day or week to tracking their finances. As a result, they feel in control and are able to make informed and responsible decisions about spending, saving, and investing. Yet, there's a fine line between staying on top of your finances and obsessively worrying and checking. One new mom on a tight budget said she spent too much time checking her bank account every spare moment, which also kept her from being present at work, at home, or in anything she was doing. We switched her to a regular time—once a week, on Saturday—to give her finances her undivided focus, then not obsess. I recommend dedicating at least sixty minutes each week, or ten minutes per day. Use the time to do a routine checkup: check your balances (the more intimately familiar you are, the more carefully you'll make decisions), monitor your bills (ensure you aren't surprised by bigger ticket items on the horizon), and eyeball your budget and spending (there's huge value in watching your expenses by category, so you can compensate if necessary).

Make a budget. My grandmother was a seamstress and a single mom who raised her kids on a factory income. She had a series of envelopes—rent, food, utilities, clothing, etc.—that she stored in the back of the grandfather clock in her living room. As she made money and cashed her checks, she dispersed it into these individual envelopes. She knew how much, if she had extra, that she could give to her kids or spend on herself—without feeling guilty. The best budgets— and those most likely to be used—are simple. Yours needs at least three categories: daily living (housing, food, bills), free spending (money outside of the money you owe others), and savings.

Don't trade time for things. Often, when we spend money on things we really don't need, we've fallen into a spending trap—filling a need that is only *represented* by the item but will not actually scratch the itch. If you or your family find yourselves spending too much money on things, study your patterns of overspending. What items do you collect in excess: cookbooks, picture frames, gadgets, jewelry, toys for your kids? Then identify the WHY behind the BUY. Ask yourself what you're *really* craving. Too much exercise garb? Maybe with each new pair of yoga pants, you hope to get motivated to work out. Too much on takeout? Perhaps you need to share the workload at home. Constantly dropping cash on toys and games for your kids when they already have more than they can use? What you might *really* need is more time with your kids. By identifying the real desires behind your spending habits, you can find a way to meet those needs with time and skill, preserving the cash for true necessities, savings, and pure fun.

Keep financial paperwork organized. Choose a single space in which you do your finances and set up your records there (even if you manage most of your finances online, there are always some papers associated with financial management: original contracts, bank account info, school registration forms). Knowing exactly where your documents are will make it easier to manage your finances in less time and produce information needed by schools, banks, doctors, and so on, so you can handle any emergency swiftly and with confidence. In many households, one person manages the finances. If that describes your family, create a one-page index of where everything is stored (paper, digitally, or both), along with a master list of accounts (every bank, credit card, investment, and insurance account you have).

PROVIDING AND THRIVING

Providing is about creating the conditions—practical, financial, and emotional—in which your kids can truly thrive. For many of us, **Provide** is the biggest and most difficult piece of P.A.R.T. to deliver on and contain. But if you master it, you get big rewards. If done right, you can provide for your family and ensure that you derive the most positive aspects of work, no matter what kind you choose to pursue.

With a commitment to keeping a watchful eye on what you have and what you can spend, you open up options on what type of work you need to generate the true essentials—food, shelter, clothing, and a safe environment—while preserving energy and focus for being there for your kids and yourself, which taken together gives your kids the best shot at life. With all this in place, you can relax into connected, undivided time with your kids. You can enjoy invaluable moments that can't be quantified and make memories that last a lifetime.

Next up is "**Arrange**," where we will cover how to keep your kids' lives and yours organized, ensuring that all the trains on the home front are running on time.

8

ARRANGE

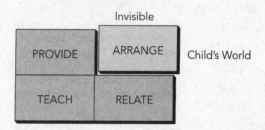

Becky, a divorced fifty-two-year-old mom with a ten-year-old and fifteen-year-old, wished she could spend less time thinking about, organizing, and nagging her kids about household logistics and maintenance and more quality time as a family. Her family didn't like the nagging, either. Unfortunately, as many women do, she'd become the person who decides what needs to be done, tells people what to do, and nags them to do their jobs. Tired of the amount of brain space and time it took to be her family's default arranger, she'd called me in for help. I asked her, "How much time would you gain back if you didn't have to be the resident supervisor?" "Two hours a day," she said without skipping a beat. "Along with a wagonful of stress I feel every day as I deliberate how to remind them nicely and minimize conflicts without deciding it's easier to just do it all myself."

Becky and her kids gathered with me at their kitchen table to explore everyone's point of view and to see how we could make things work better. We did an exercise I often do with families, divvying up a deck of cards with all the chores of **Arrange** printed on them, in terms of who does what. Her teenage son, Aaron, who'd felt very put upon about lawn and pet care, was humbled when he saw that his mom had twenty-four cards, while he had six, and his little sister had one. The discussion revealed that much of the nagging was the result of misunderstandings around timing. Angelica, the ten-year-old, expressed that she was very willing to do more but needed to be taught. The family reallocated the tasks, made a plan for teaching Angelica how to do them, and created a chore chart, including expectations on when things had to be completed; for example, the dishes have to be cleared as soon as dinner's done, but Saturday's vacuuming, dusting, and cleaning chores can happen anytime between waking up and five p.m.

THE OIL IN THE MACHINE OF LIFE

The work of arranging, like the architecture of a house, is an invisible infrastructure that creates the conditions for life to run smoothly. By creating systems that are simple, shared, and understood by everyone, your family can live on top of this structure.

Arranging helps kids feel secure and the house feel calm. It frees you and your family to live, work, and relax every day. When done efficiently and well, it creates the space for quality time with each other and gives you the ability to be prepared and present for your activities outside the house.

At its core, **Arrange** is the equivalent of the operations department of a household. And it is a massive logistical task. It involves orchestrating all of the organizing, cooking, cleaning, scheduling, transportation, paperwork, and activities of every family member. To manage it all, a person needs to be organized *and* flexible; creative *and* systematic; a big-picture thinker *and* a detail-oriented person. Very rarely are all of these qualities found in just one person, and even when they are, the job is still far too much for one person to manage solo.

MULTIUSER SYSTEMS REQUIRE COLLABORATION AND COOPERATION

Arranging for family life is different and more complex than organizing for a single person. Not only is the *volume* of stuff to organize greater, it requires you to *synchronize family members' plans*. That requires some advanced coordination skills.

Because arranging for a family takes so much time and brain space, it often prevents parents from ever being able to relax, connect, and be present. **Arrange** can easily take over your schedule (and your brain!) at the expense of other things you'd prefer to spend time on. Even families who successfully keep things in order often resent the amount of time it takes.

The two biggest pitfalls? Underdoing **Arrange**, because you find the tasks too tedious and prefer to focus on the big picture, or overdoing it, allowing the logistics of your family to become the dominant focus of your family life.

The goal is a happy medium, a predictable operating system that helps your family function at its best, achieve goals, and get the most out of each thing you do. In other words, be "organized enough."

> **IN OUR PARENT TIME SURVEY**
> ## HOUSEWORK IS UNEVENLY DIVIDED
>
> 63.77% of survey respondents reported doing more of the chores than their spouse/partner.
> 57.75% of parents surveyed reported that they only put a little to some effort into having their children contribute to household chores and maintenance.

DON'T DO IT ALL ALONE

Many people find that **Arrange** is more tolerable with a shift in mind-set. Instead of focusing on the thanklessness and tedium of all these annoying tasks, try to get excited and engage the whole family in the pursuit of figuring out which systems will work best for your household. When it comes to a multiperson household, choosing to be organized (or not) isn't a matter of personal preference, it's a matter of survival, with each participant seriously affected by the action or inaction of the other. Just imagine a naval ship, with all those different personalities on board, each deciding independently which cabinet the cereal bowls should go in. Getting breakfast on the table would take forever. Breakfast would never get served!

Sure, on the surface it can seem petty to debate about where the scissors live or when the vacuuming happens, but having systems in place that everyone honors is one of the most loving things you can do for your family. Why? A family's operational system is a living, breathing system that *supports* or *obstructs* the family when it comes to achieving its individual and collective goals.

Elevating the mundane to a family enterprise means

Arrange is no place for martyrdom. Stop thinking you have to do it all yourself (even if you do it best!). Engaging every member of the household in arranging tasks, including kids from an early age, is a good thing. It promotes a sense of responsibility and belonging; imparts the value of caring for others in relationships; and teaches critical life skills that translate easily outside the home to school, work, and any situation that requires cooperation. Plus, what kids want most is time with you, and one of the greatest motivations for sharing the work of **Arrange** is that it creates space for quality time for the family.

And, each time there is a significant shift in the ecosystem—another baby is born, a parent's work schedule changes, your fifth grader gets a teacher who piles on massive quantities of homework, or someone changes their diet—be prepared to retool your system. Consider yourselves the chief engineering team setting out to tinker with a broken machine. Talk to each other. Put on your forensic caps and sleuth out solutions to the problems!

HAVE A CONVERSATION

At its soul, organizing is an expression of who you are, how you think, and what's important to you. It's a structure that frees your time and mind for the things *you* want to spend time on. When people don't follow a system that's been created, it can feel like an act of disrespect, even a personal assault. But systems need to be designed for the whole family—not just according to how one person thinks, even if one person takes on the lion's share of the work.

That's why **Arrange** is such emotionally tricky territory.

Because it's easy to underestimate the amount of time it takes, families rarely talk openly about the responsibilities. Very often, as happened with Becky, one person becomes the "default" arranger and absorbs the entire job. Or individual family members silently gravitate toward certain tasks, based on what they notice or care about, but since no one talks about it, either they don't feel recognized for the work they put in or they feel criticized for what they don't do.

Lack of conversation about logistics is a breeding ground for resentment and conflict. When family members get into the habit of simply expecting things to get done, conflicts arise. The default arranger, especially, can feel trapped in a role he or she didn't sign up for.

A conversation can help overcome misunderstanding and resentment. Family life is dynamic, and discussing again what is required, and how it will get done, is fair game at every transition point. It's never too late to redivide the labor and hit reset.

Keep in mind where you and your family might be getting hung up. Does your family agree on what you want your home to feel like? Is it calm, cozy, formal, minimalist, a center for fun and socializing? Are your systems clear to all or are they only clear to you, the default arranger? Does everyone in the family understand what their responsibility is to maintain the systems you've put in place?

Expert Advice | **DISCUSSING ARRANGE WITH YOUR FAMILY**

1. Start with the shared goal, such as

   - *"We all want to create a warm and welcoming home that prioritizes time for relaxing and enrichment."*

2. Talk about the current situation without judgment or blame. If you've become the default arranger, be sure to take responsibility.

   - *"The logistics take far more time than any of us realize."*
   - *"Our family has fallen into a pattern that is causing stress and getting in the way of us spending time together."*
   - *"I know I took much of this on myself, but it's just not working."*

3. Shared space, shared resources, shared responsibilities.

   - *"We all live here. We all have a stake in the family's schedule and space. I think we should all have some role in creating our family organizing systems and maintaining them."*

4. Propose a solution.

   - *"Let's work together to figure out what we want, which systems will get us there, and a new division of labor. Then we'll create some systems that minimize the burden on all of us."*

There are certainly legitimate reasons when the work of **Arrange** falls more heavily on one family member than another. Adults with babies must take on more responsibility than parents of older kids. A stay-at-home parent is likely to pick up more of the work than a parent who works outside the home, for example. One parent may actually enjoy the work of **Arrange** and so gravitates to it naturally.

Even if you do most of the arranging, it's important that you don't do it in silence, without the appreciation and understanding from the whole family about how they are benefiting from your effort.

When family members are aware of all the details, however mundane, that go into running a home, it makes them more appreciative. Vice versa, the only way to truly divvy up the labor is to be realistic about all the things that have to happen—visibility enables delegation.

AUTOMATE THE PREDICTABLE

One of the best time-management lessons I ever learned was from Kate White, the editor in chief of *Cosmo* for many years, who also managed to simultaneously juggle marriage, parenting, and writing novels on the side. Putting out a monthly magazine, as you can imagine, is a chaotic business, as deadlines are missed and stories go wrong as the issue is going to press. I often observed Kate during that period and she was always cool as a cucumber—a calm in the midst of every monthly storm. How did she do it? Kate's secret was this: always get the predictable tasks done first (even if they aren't due right away), to leave room for the unexpected. It's a perfect lesson to apply to parenting.

Raising kids is all about the unpredictable: constant shifts in abilities, interests, questions, and needs. If you leave the predictable activities of cooking, shopping, waking up, laundry, and bedtime to the burden of daily decision-making, you won't have the energy and time to deal with the true surprises. So follow Kate's wisdom. Automate the predictable.

Creating and sticking to systems is not necessarily natural for every personality style. If you're someone who thrives on spontaneity and creativity—like my client Lisa, who bristles at the idea of routine (how boring!)—you might struggle in the "automate" department.

Lisa was an interior designer with her own business, who loved that every day was different. And since her husband, a teacher, was reliably home by four p.m. every day, she figured when a client session ran over, or she was behind on finishing a project, there was no harm in getting home later than expected. He could cover dinnertime and help with homework, and she'd be sure to give everyone her undivided attention when she got home. Besides, sometimes she surprised her family and had breakfast with them on days her appointments started later. So it all worked out in the wash, right?

Not really. It took a heart-to-heart with her hubby and kids to help her see how her unpredictability wreaked havoc on their evenings and days and explained why they weren't always so "ready" for quality time when she showed up. Consistency and predictability are key to a connected family life and, brain science tells us, essential to children's development. Knowing what happens, when, and how helps kids feel safe and secure because they know what to expect. Once Lisa saw her spontaneity through her family's point of view, she used the freedom of being her own boss to set predictable work hours her family could count on.

She booked mid-morning meetings on Tuesdays and Thursdays, so she could have breakfast with the kids, and stuck to Tuesday and Wednesday as late nights at the office— so everyone could plan accordingly. It took some retraining on Lisa's part (to change a lifetime pattern of freestyling her days), but she discovered that everything in life doesn't have to be spontaneous. In fact, the right amount of structure made more room for spontaneity and being present when together.

Keep in mind, we're not aiming for military precision in the schedule or a house that resembles the staged rooms in a magazine. There is no such thing as perfectly structured or perfectly organized! We're after efficient, predictable, tidy, and calm.

THE HOW-TO GUIDE

As we dive into ways to automate the four primary areas of **Arrange**, keep these two final points in mind to strike the right balance between making and containing time for **Arrange**, so it doesn't swallow you and your family whole:

Focus on hotspots. It takes time and skill to build organizing systems. For that reason, don't attempt to organize everything at once. First focus only on the hotspots—things that will deliver the most relief, calm, and time won back. Make a list of all the functions involved in running your household, pick two or three causing you the most stress or time lost, then invest energy and brainpower in fixing those. Remember, the goal is "organized enough."

Shrink each system to its smallest footprint. Don't make any system more complicated than it needs to be. The goal of organizing during the child-rearing years is to free up your time, energy, and focus for connection, not consume you. In other words, your kids and family would much rather spend quality time with you relaxing than on perfection-level house-keeping that gets destroyed in three seconds of play. Remember, if a system meets these two criteria—easy for everyone to follow, runs with minimal effort—it's good enough.

AUTOMATE FAMILY
ROUTINES AND TRADITIONS

Consistency in how the days flow creates the metronome of a family's life, synchronizing all family members, in spite of different schedules, personalities, and activities. Routines and traditions allow families to organize themselves to get things done, form an identity (as a unit), express their values, and spend time together.

Design the weekday around five anchors

There are five common touch points that offer every family the guidelines for structuring a predictable schedule. These five moments anchor a child's day, marking key transition points that free them to go off for adventures and come back to rest and share with you. They also happen to be ideal moments for connecting and letting your kids know that they are loved and valued.

Anchor 1: Wake up—The first few minutes of the day are one of the most important opportunities you have to make your kid feel loved and valued by giving them your undivided, positive attention. No matter how hectic the day ahead is, or how little sleep you had, try to be sure you wake up in time to be ready to wake them sweetly and calmly. If you are able to be fully present with your child for the first five minutes they are awake, it can carry them through the day.

Anchor 2: Get out the door—Morning madness beleaguers even the most organized families; coordinating bathroom, eating, and exit schedules is no small feat. Yet having a stressful morning leaves everyone feeling out of sorts and affects the workday and school day. The morning routine can be streamlined by doing as much as you can the night before (picking outfits, signing permission slips, presetting breakfast), and then getting real about how long what's left takes. This is one routine that needs to be mathematically timed out, accounting for staggered wake-up times, how long each person *truly* needs to get ready (e.g., if your six-year-old daughter likes to change outfits several times before deciding what to wear, build that in), and hidden tasks (wiping down the counter, feeding the dog, etc.).

Anchor 3: Afternoon/After school—If you can pick your kids up from school, you get to witness and participate in this key transition. Working parents may not be able to be there in person, but you can still handcraft and support this pivot point from school to after school in your child's day. Experts advise you make it a shift in rhythm from the school day: Who is picking them up? Where are they going: Home? A friend's? An after-school program? They will likely have stories from their day that they want to share. Can you take a ten-minute afternoon break to call or FaceTime them at that moment?

Anchor 4: Dinner—Study after study shows that families who have dinner together five times a week position their children for the greatest success. Kids from these families do better academically, socially, and emotionally, regardless of socioeconomic background and other life circumstances. Build a routine around dinnertime that reduces stress, gets meals on the table, and ensures everyone talks and eats together. This is your chance to develop the art of conversation. Check out the website The Family Dinner Project (thefamilydinnerproject.org) and the book *The Family Dinner* by Laurie David for tons of interesting conversation starters to keep everyone engaged, at every age. For example, *"If you joined the circus, what would your circus act be?"* (ages two to seven), *"What's the funniest or strangest thing that happened to you today?"* (ages eight to thirteen), *"Endings aren't all bad. Can you think of a time when an ending was positive?"* (ages fourteen to one hundred).

Anchor 5: Bedtime—Bedtime can be a soothing and predictable time that builds strong bonds between parents and children. When it comes to automating sleep, experts say going to bed and getting up around the same time every day is essential—and that wake-up time on weekdays and weekends should be within two hours of the same time. Create a consistent routine that factors in about forty-five minutes of wind-down time before bed and communicate it so your kid can master it. Pivot as much of your family's routine as you can around getting adequate sleep for everyone to be their best at home, at work, and at school.

Plan the weekends around seven units of time. Think of the weekend as seven units of time: Friday night, Saturday morning, Saturday afternoon, Saturday night, Sunday morning, Sunday afternoon, and Sunday night. Slot in the different things you'd like to do: housecleaning and chores, individual activities, physical activities, family hangout time, etc. Friday's popcorn and movie night, the payoff for the intense structured week; Saturday morning is lazy breakfast time; and so on. Be sure to include one longer block of time to hang with your kids talking, sharing an interest, or just playing, to give the opportunity for longer and deeper conversations to emerge.

Family traditions: Family traditions are based on your family's values and help your kids form a sense of identity and belonging: *this is how our family does things.* Traditions can be built around any of the touch points discussed. Maybe everyone shares one thing they are grateful for before going to sleep; or one Saturday afternoon a month, the entire family volunteers together. Birthdays, holidays, and special occasions can have their family handprint as well: birthdays might be celebrated with a custom limerick in tribute to the year, holidays feature a special recipe handed down from the generations. These mini-traditions are what makes your family *your* family.

When it comes to daily and weekly routines, try to be as consistent as possible and get everyone to honor them. Routines work best when everyone in a child's life follows them. That might not be possible 100 percent of the time, but you can at least share with grandparents, babysitters, and spouses (including stepmoms and stepdads), and ask that they do something similar. It's an easy way to create consistency for kids and demonstrate alignment among the adults in their lives. If this isn't possible, don't stress. Just provide your kids a "transition period" for the first few hours between switching homes.

AUTOMATE INDIVIDUAL
SCHEDULES AND TRANSPORTATION

In tandem with the family's shared routines are each family member's individual schedules and to-dos. They vary by person, season, and circumstance. This ever-changing flow of appointments, transportation needs, playdates, events, school trips, and sports practices is the air-traffic-control function that necessitates expert coordination and tracking to avoid a crash.

Centralize your calendar and information center. In the good old days, there was a single family calendar on the wall and that's all anyone ever used or needed. But life has gotten busier and our options to track it all have grown exponentially. Parents often have work calendars, kids have school planners, and different family members may prefer digital or paper, one app or another. Yet, the only way to sanely coordinate shared lives is by choosing one centralized family calendar to consolidate all schedules and be accessible to everyone. Tech-leaning people may prefer the sharing capabilities of an online calendar (such as Google or iCal); analog folks may prefer paper or a giant write-on/wipe-off magnetic whiteboard on the kitchen wall. (Chalkboard paint on one wall can do the job, too.) A calendar system is only useful if it is kept up to date and referred to daily. Designate one adult as the "keeper" of the master family calendar, whose primary job is to keep the kids and their own schedule up to date. Teens and other adults in the house must be responsible for transferring their schedule into the master family calendar for easy group coordination. A master shopping and errand list in the same location will round out the system, with everything in one place for scheduling.

Have a daily calendar huddle. With such busy and complex lives, we can't expect everyone to remember the schedule or to look at a calendar on their own. Reviewing the calendar together at the same time every day, even if everyone knows where to look, allows you all to sort new requests as they come in (transportation conflicts, forms to be signed) and ensure nothing falls through the cracks. It's also a chance to connect as a family—hearing not only what everyone is doing but how it's all going. Spending ten to fifteen minutes a day, even over dinner, will keep you attuned to each other and save hours of chaos and damage control.

Use transportation as a time to connect. Walking or driving kids to school or activities can be a great time for connection if you use the opportunity consciously. To maximize your drive time, ensure that the moments before you leave the house are as stress-free as possible to make the walk or drive more relaxed. Carpooling, or sharing the walks to and from activities with other parents and families, gives you and other parents a chance to get to know your kids' friends, learn about what's on their minds by listening in on their conversations, and build an extended community. Make a rule that no one is allowed to use a device during the walk or drive.

Build in unstructured time at home. Amid the hubbub of every day, child development experts emphasize avoiding overstuffing the schedule with extracurricular activities. There are many benefits to extracurricular activities—they allow kids to explore interests, they develop circles of friends outside school, and they also look good on college applications. But it's easy to go too far. Before you sign up your children, find out how much time it will take, factoring in travel time, the activity itself, and any extra time required outside of the class or scheduled activity (homework, practice, etc.). Remember that there is huge value in unstructured time hanging at home: you cooking, kids playing nearby, being relaxed and able to spontaneously engage in conversation, or play, on your kid's terms. The safety of knowing you are around and available for questions or casual conversation is invaluable.

AUTOMATE PHYSICAL SPACES

Organizing spaces is about creating environments that are comfortable and functional, putting the objects, information, and supplies that family members need at their fingertips. A functional and calm home increases the opportunities and energy for quality time together. If you need help organizing, there is no better resource than *Organizing from the Inside Out*. That book is dedicated to teaching you how to organize every room, closet, drawer, and shelf in a way that is natural and easy to maintain. To get you started, here are a handful of broad principles on which the book is based.

Think kindergarten. When it comes to organizing, every room, closet, and space should be designed around the concept of a kindergarten classroom: the space is divided into activity zones that reflect what takes place in each area. Group similar items together, get fun containers, label them, and teach kids to use them. With some tweaks, this system works for any space (closets, kitchen, fridge, garage). The zones in a family room, for example, might be: reading, entertainment, hobbies. For a kid's room, they might be: sleeping, dressing, playing, homework. A well-organized system, where every item has a convenient, well-labeled home, should enable you to do a very quick, ten-to-fifteen-minute tidying at the end of every day.

Create rotation systems. At any given time there are the things your kids are using, things waiting to be used, and things they have outgrown. The demarcation between those stages is often gradual, which leads to a ton of stuff to manage. Keep clutter at bay by building a system that allows for this natural flow. It's best to store the items waiting to be grown into, and things kids have grown out of, in their bedroom closet or near wherever you store their books and toys. That makes it easier to remember they exist and to move things in and out of commission as needed.

Declutter twice a year. To keep the volume at bay, tie decluttering to predictable annual moments: end of school year, birthday, holidays. Get rid of anything that is obsolete, extraneous, broken, torn, stained, or just plain annoying. Each space should be filled only with what you (and your family) use and love—so you can quickly find what you need when you need it and put it away with speed.

Create a launch-and-land center. Create a compact and efficient "launch and land" pad in the main entryway of your home to make departures and arrivals less hectic (no more frantic searches for car keys!). You don't need much space—think about building vertically: hang a row of hooks on the wall for coats, backpacks, and totes. Pack everything you need for the day the night before and leave it by the door. You can also create and laminate a checklist of everything you need to remember before you leave (permission slips, cell chargers, keys, soccer stuff, dance gear, or any other essentials) and hang it on the wall.

Conquer paper. No organizing challenge causes families more stress and anxiety than the avalanche of paperwork and memorabilia in their lives. You can tame the chaos with a few key strategies. First, get all the paperwork into one central location (not spread in various places throughout the house). Then, break it down into categories (e.g., finances, education, vital records) and assign each category to a specific adult owner, who is responsible for creating and maintaining the system for it. In addition, each owner should teach their spouse or other adults how the system works in case someone else needs to step in.

Wherever you can rely on digital, go digital. Get down to the smallest amount of paper as possible. Here are some starter hacks for different categories of paper:

- **Financial papers.** This includes bills, bank statements, investment and insurance papers, contracts, receipts for small and big purchases. When it comes to financial paperwork, no doubt digital is best, as the volume is high and online banking and record searching is easy. Still, if you like to have paper backup on things like annual statements, original contracts, and receipts, create a paper filing system. Consider one drawer or file box dedicated to financial papers, with folders for each account and category of receipts (handyman, after-school programs, etc.). Create a one-page file index at the front, listing what is filed on paper plus online, for easy access.
- **School information and permission slips.** The number of repetitive forms parents have to fill out year after year is maddening. Try a simple paper system stored in an accordion file with sections labeled for school forms, medical forms, camp forms, etc. When you have to fill out the *next* year's school form, just pull out last year's and copy all the relevant information. It works!
- **Vital records.** Designating one specific file drawer, binder, or document box with the most vital information (medical forms, educational records, insurance, passports, driver's licenses, birth certificates, etc.) can guarantee instant and reliable access. Nothing will make you feel more at ease. It's also nice to have these records digitally and one copy off-site, to make sure you can get your hands on these records anywhere, anytime.

- **Kids' artwork and schoolwork.** It can be torture to decide what memorabilia to keep and what to toss. Try this: Designate a bin in the bottom of each kid's closet to collect artwork and school work for the school year. Every June, go through the box with your child, pick the best-of, and transfer to an archival box labeled for that year. You can also create a gallery wall in their rooms to hang items they are particularly proud of, or a place in the family room or kitchen for favorites.

- **Photos.** The principles to tame the thousands of images we now collect are: Collect (establish a single program on your computer to gather all of your images—no matter which phone or camera took them); Organize and Streamline (create folders by person, date, event, or place, and yes, delete the blurry, bad, and six excess shots you took of the same image); and Display—choose your favorites to print for display on your desk or on the fridge or to hang on a wall; create a digital photo album to share with long-distance relatives; and post on Facebook, Instagram, or your social media of choice. There are several websites that now make photo books a snap. Put one person in charge as the family archivist.

- **Lifestyle.** This is the category that refers to family activities and stuff you need to run your household: school, camp, extracurricular programs, subscriptions, museum memberships, contact information for your "village"—of doctors, neighbors, handymen, and babysitters. Put all of this into one central three-ring binder with info slipped into plastic sleeves—so it's easy to update expired info without a hole punch—with dividers for each family member, each schedule, and each activity.

BABYSITTER MEMO

After much trial and error in forgetting to communicate key information to babysitters, Ginny created a Babysitter Memo that puts her, her children, and the caregivers at ease and frees everyone to relax and focus on quality time together rather than worrying.

Here's what she's got on it:

Contact info for parents (cell), neighbor, pediatrician, pharmacist, dentist.

Emergency contact numbers: Police, Fire, Gas, Poison Control

Home address and home phone

Medication or special dietary needs for each kid (including dosage and timing, food allergies, etc.)

Essential caretaking routines (or rules) that ensure the most seamless and soothing experience for both the babysitter and the child (e.g., homework rules, bedtime routines, how to handle it if your kid gets upset)

Pet care (walking or feeding dogs, cats, hamsters)

AUTOMATE CHORES AND ERRANDS

Housework and chores enable us to maintain our organized spaces and keep our homes and daily family life humming. Every family gets messy and dirty and uses things up, and replenishing and maintaining is part and parcel of the job. It can feel like a never-ending list of to-dos, but many of these tasks are predictable and can be systematized.

Set aside specific times and days. If you do housework in any free moment, you'll never be able to rest because there is *always more to do*. Instead, set aside specific hours to do specific chores: fold kids' laundry Monday nights, grocery shop on Saturday afternoons, and so on. Setting aside specific hours will force you to prioritize and let some things go. It also gives children enough notice and time to do their chores. Try batching logistics: when you are making doctors' appointments for your children, make them for yourself, too.

Build self-instructing systems. Hate being the nag, always reminding people what to do and how to do it? If you've ever wondered how someone could walk right past the pile of clean clothes on the bed without putting them away, it's because not everybody is focused on the same things. The only way to build cohesion in any multiperson system is to use clear and attractive labels, instruction tags, and checklists that remove any guesswork and any room for misinterpretation. A cute laminated index card with the words PUT ME AWAY tied to the handle of a laundry basket filled with clean clothes can motivate action without you having to be the nag. Clear labels on a shelf edge will ensure coffee mugs go on the bottom shelf, drinking glasses on the middle shelf, and wineglasses on the top shelf. One clever family made it easy for even the youngest kids to whip up their favorite homemade salad dressing recipe: they wrote the recipe directly on the bottle, drawing a line on the bottle for each of the ingredients with a permanent marker.

IN OUR PARENT TIME SURVEY
CLEANING COULD BE MORE EFFICIENT

We asked moms in our survey about which household routines they most wanted to streamline. This was the result:
Cleaning—75%; Laundry—55%; Cooking—45%;
Meal Planning—40%

Attach chores to other routines. Another way to reduce the brain space and time that chores take up is to make the chores invisible by attaching them to other routines. Throw in a load of laundry right before taking the kids to the park. Have your kids prep their backpacks right before brushing their teeth. Keep a shower cleaning spray next to the tub, and spray down the wall every time you take a shower instead of waiting to do it once a week. One client, who struggled to find time for meal planning, made it a habit to do it while the kids were doing their homework.

Stage-manage your life. The more you do in advance, the easier it is to execute the repetitive household chores that can become mundane. Do as much as you can ahead of time to minimize the time you spend on the chore itself.

Prepare breakfast and coffee for the morning the night before and preassemble dinner kits. Put oatmeal in the slow cooker before bed. Get the coffee measured and on a timer, with the water set. Assemble smoothie ingredients the night before and store in the fridge overnight. When you wake up, you just have to hit a button. Pre-assemble ingredients for dinner in a clear bin, into which you also toss recipe instructions. No thinking required, just go.

Automate meal planning with ten go-to recipes and a standard shopping list. Come up with ten fast go-to dinner and breakfast recipes and put each on an index card, with ingredients and instructions on the back. Have a matching shopping list. Each week, have your family select the meals they want out of a hat or box. Check the needed items on your matching shopping list, which gets tacked to the fridge on Sunday evenings, so people can add things to it throughout the week. Change it up every other month so no one gets bored!

Cut down on laundry sorting. Give everyone their own laundry basket and start doing the wash by person. Buy all matching socks, so you spend less time pairing them.

EXPERT ADVICE   **PUT YOUR CARDS ON THE TABLE**

This was the exercise I did with Becky and her kids. It'll do wonders for your family.

- **Make an index card for each task and chore involved in running and maintaining your household** (laundry, kitchen cleanup, yard work, grocery shopping, pet management, money management, meal planning, cooking, setting the table, clearing the table, etc.), being sure to have a separate card for each chore.
- **Who Does What?** Start by categorizing the cards by who does what. This immediately creates a visual of how evenly (or unevenly) the labor is divided. You may discover that some things are unclear—done by multiple people—or that some things are not done at all. Once you see how tasks are divided, have a discussion.
- **Redivide and Conquer.** Once you see how the labor is currently divided, lay all the cards back out in the middle of the table. These are the *family's* tasks, not just one person's. As a family, discuss whether all of the chores are necessary. Then, brainstorm ideas for what among the remaining tasks can be streamlined. Allow everyone to choose the things they like to do, have time to do, or can commit to doing. Then, discuss what is left on the table and how those should be handled. Do we rotate? Do we hire someone? Do we let it go? Do we find a better system that takes less time? It's essential to be clear on who does what and when. Playing it by ear may feel relaxed, but it adds a time-consuming activity to each chore: deciding who is doing what in a particular moment. Avoid the tension and conflict that can arise from this mistake and decide in advance.

AGE-BY-AGE GUIDE TO ARRANGE: INVOLVING YOUR KIDS ACROSS AGES AND STAGES

Responsibilities help build skills and connections and can be thought of in two categories: those that help your children become *self-sufficient* and those that engage your child as an active member of maintaining the *family systems*. My colleague Marcia Ramsland wrote a great age-by-age guide on getting kids to help around the house. The website raisingchildren.net .au is another wonderful resource for what kids can handle at different stages. Here's a guide integrating some of their insights to help you figure out what is reasonable to ask kids to learn and do at each age:

Infant (0–1)

Self-sufficiency: Babies thrive on interaction with you, but they also enjoy quiet time with a mobile or soft toy. Find moments to "separate" from your child to clean up the kitchen and do household chores.

Family systems: The first family contribution a baby makes is fitting into the normal nighttime patterns of the family. Do your best to think of sleep training with a positive attitude—it is something they can be proud to do for the family. It's their first act of belonging, which is so essential to a human's identity.

Toddler (1–3)

Self-sufficiency: Play "pick up" together before leaving the room or eating meals. Store their things within their reach: put toys on the lower shelves, books on middle shelves, stuffed animals in a basket, and the clothes in a closet or hamper.

Family systems: Encourage help with simple responsibilities, such as making the bed, dusting, getting the mail, sorting items for recycling, clearing plates from the table.

Preschool (3–5)

Self-sufficiency: Kids can help with self-care basics of getting dressed, brushing their teeth and hair, making their bed. Have them carry their own things to and from the car.

Family systems: Be a "family helper" with simple chores like putting out placemats and napkins at mealtime, emptying small wastebaskets, getting the mail, sorting the recycling, and picking up sticks and leaves in the yard.

School-Age (5–10)

Self-sufficiency: Kids begin to master routines to organize themselves. For example, before breakfast, make their bed, get dressed and groomed. After school, put away their own backpack, lunch box, school papers, and coat in the proper places. Write their own thank-you notes after birthdays and holidays.

Family systems: Regular or rotating chores, such as setting and clearing the table, loading the dishwasher, wiping down cabinets, emptying the trash, feeding the pets, folding and hanging laundry, putting away groceries, and helping to cook and prep for meals—including washing vegetables, prepping salad, and making salad dressing.

Tween (10–13)

Self-sufficiency: Arranging their own schedule, balancing school social activities and family time. Change their own sheets, organize, vacuum and dust their own rooms. Learn a basic budget system.

Family systems: More advanced chores such as vacuuming, mopping, cleaning bathrooms, preparing meals, cleaning out the refrigerator, making a grocery list, mowing the lawn, babysitting, and walking pets.

Teen (13–18)

Self-sufficiency: Kids can do their own laundry, learn to iron clothes and sew on buttons. If they drive, teach them to regularly fill up the car with gas and about vehicle maintenance. Manage a systematic cash flow and put money into savings. Let them pay the family bills a few times to see real-life expenses.

Family systems: Grocery shop, learn to prepare three to five different meals, and clean up the kitchen. Running "adult" errands such as taking things to the dry cleaner's and driving younger siblings around to their events. Painting, yard work, rolling up rugs, cleaning the stovetop and oven, washing windows and cars.

PUT PEOPLE FIRST

Remember the goal of all this work: to create more quality time for family connection. It's so easy, especially when we're busy tracking calendars and cooking meals and organizing stuff, to slip into the habit of *doing* instead of *being*.

Develop a certain tolerance for chaos. If you are one of those people who can't relax until everything's in its place, you'll have a hard time being available for connection. Remember that all good systems have a built-in level of flexibility and that one person's system can look like a total mess to someone else.

One mom complained about her husband's little piles in the corners of rooms that drove her crazy, concluding that he was lazy about putting things away, which made it hard for her to relax. When I asked her husband about the piles, he said they were materials for projects he was planning to do in each room, such as repairs. That was no mess; it was his visual reminder system. In fact, he did get to the projects. We purchased a couple of big beautiful floor baskets to place in rooms where projects were going on, and he simply stashed his materials inside. A perfect compromise!

Treat shared spaces differently than individual spaces. There are shared spaces and schedules, and individual spaces and schedules. Give everyone a space and time in their schedule that they can control themselves. Whether they keep it extra neat, a total mess, or something in between, having a space of their own to control allows each person's individuality to be expressed, without interfering with family systems.

Always start with hello. How often do you walk through the door and immediately start making a to-do list to replace the one you just left behind at work? Or do you walk in the door and immediately start getting out pots and pans, only half-listening to what your spouse or child has to say? I have a client who constantly reminds himself, as soon as he walks through the door, to put people before tasks. If you have a good system in place, you should know what to do and when you need to do it, so that the first thing you can focus on is your family. Ask, "How are you?" and then listen.

Done well, the work of arranging, like the foundation of a house, is an unseen infrastructure that creates the conditions for life to run smoothly. By creating organizational systems that are simple, as well as shared and understood by everyone, your family can live life on top of this structure. One of the most important parts of your job as a parent is discussed in the next chapter, "**Relate**," which successful arranging makes possible.

9

RELATE

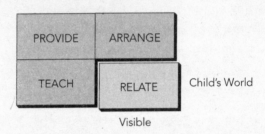

My client Jocelyn was married to her childhood sweetheart, Jack. They had one child, Nina, who was eleven years old. Jocelyn was a successful career woman, who scored herself high on **Provide** and **Arrange** but relatively weak on **Relate**. She was a real doer, with little aptitude for the slower pace of kid time. Yet, as Nina was getting older, Jocelyn felt a growing distance and wondered if she should arrange to leave work early a couple of afternoons a week to create more time to connect with her.

As we dissected her schedule, though, we discovered that Jocelyn was actually surprisingly good at relating in the mornings—she always woke Nina with a tender kiss and a smile, asked to hear about her dreams, and then they had an unrushed morning of getting dressed, eating breakfast together, and getting off to school.

The difficulty was evenings and weekends, where there *was* a breakdown in connection. When Jocelyn got home from work, she focused entirely on keeping the trains running on time: checking homework, getting through dinner, and making sure Nina went to bed early, for a full night's sleep, so Jocelyn could hop back on the computer to plow through more work. By the weekend, Jocelyn was so fatigued from the intensity of managing the week that she left Saturday and Sunday relatively unstructured—either tending to errands and chores as a family or piggybacking on her sister's family's plans—as she just couldn't bear to organize another minute. Jocelyn was basically on autopilot and couldn't think of activities for connecting that weren't connected to a to-do list.

Before Jocelyn asked to shorten her work hours, I suggested she change the nature of the time she spent with her family when she was with them. Being present doesn't necessarily take more time, but it does take more attention.

I suggested that Jocelyn make a few simple adjustments to be ready to relate when she was with Nina. First, I suggested she stop all work calls ten minutes before arriving home and use that time to consciously shift gears to focus her intention toward connecting with Nina (and Jack) the minute she walked through the door. Just like when she greeted her daughter with a kiss and asked how her dreams were in the morning, she would walk through the door and ask Nina how her day was. That ten-to-fifteen-minute conversation would set the tone for the evening and change the pace. After that, she could check homework and have dinner.

We added a little structure to the weekends to make sure they focused on quality time and being present, without putting too much of a burden on either parent. We designated Saturdays for quality family time, breaking the day into three discrete parts. In the morning, Jack and Nina spent time together, while Jocelyn went to the gym or off to get a manicure. In the afternoon, Jocelyn and Nina had one-on-one time, while Jack had time to do his own thing. In the evening, they had family time—going to a movie, a restaurant, or some other family-friendly activity. If you feel you are not spending enough time relating, start by changing the nature of the time you have, before you try to add more minutes and hours.

I've found that once you make the moments you do spend together of higher quality, it's easier to add more time, because the relating experience is (likely) more pleasant. It's a muscle or skill that you can actually build on—and see the results appear gradually before your eyes.

WHAT IS THIS THING CALLED LOVE?

At its core, relating is about building a relationship with your child, one in which you connect and understand your child as the unique individual she is, exploring her interests, thoughts, and feelings, and getting to know what is going on in her life. Relating requires entering your *Child's World*, on his level, at his pace, and being fully present.

While they often overlap, there is a clear distinction between **Relate** and **Teach**: when teaching, your primary intention is to have your child understand you, so they develop skills and values that will help them thrive in the grown-up world. In **Relate**, your goal is to better understand your child. *You* are the student.

Of all the quadrants in P.A.R.T., your job in **Relate** is probably the most irreplaceable job you have as a parent: you are, more than anyone else on earth, who your children look to for affirmation and recognition of their self-worth. It is through relating that you give your children their sense of self—that they are valued and valuable in the world. As discussed in chapter 2, kids want to know they matter, and you communicate that very directly through the gift of time and attention. And while most parents crave time to connect, finding the time and knowing how to **Relate** can prove the most elusive of all the quadrants.

IN OUR PARENT TIME SURVEY
PROTECTING TIME TO RELATE IS DIFFICULT

Parents struggle to stay present during quality time with their children, because their minds drift. The top four mental distractions are:
59.09% housework piling up
51.52% I am exhausted, and have very little energy
48.48% I get distracted by my cell phone (texts, emails, etc.)
42.42% work demands

BE HERE NOW:
WHAT RELATING LOOKS LIKE

Remember Mr. Brown from chapter 2? One of the many things that made him so remarkable was his ability to give his students his undivided attention, even while managing the adult responsibilities involved in running a school. As a parent, you have a similar challenge: connecting with your child, while fulfilling a multitude of responsibilities as an adult.

Relating requires being fully present, responding, and tuning in to your child in a way that communicates, "Right now, you're the most important thing to me." Here's how:

Stop what you're doing and give your child your full attention. Tune in to what is going on with your kid at this moment. No multitasking. Look at your child while she's talking to you.

Face-to-face, eye-level communication will help your child feel that you're talking with her, not at her. If you find yourself in a situation where what you are working on has to remain your primary focus, get down to your child's level, look them in the eyes, and say, "I know you really want to tell me that story, and I so want to hear it, but I have to finish x,y,z and then I can give you my full attention"

Slow down to the speed of your child. Shift gears when interacting with children to account for their different speed of processing. Karen Spencer, founder of Whole Child International, has used relationship-based caretaking to improve the quality of lives for vulnerable children worldwide. As Karen put it, children have magic in them—and understanding the different speed of response enables the deep connections we crave. The younger the child, the slower the turnaround. Wait until the baby's mouth is open to put the spoon in; don't ask your toddler or school-age child a question and then rush to answer for them. Even with teenagers, whose brains are still developing, recognize that it takes time for them to absorb and retain information.

Show interest and curiosity. Really listen, stay open, and encourage your child to expand on what he's saying. Explore his views, opinions, feelings, expectations, or plans. Watch your body language and facial expressions; your child can tell if you are annoyed, impatient, or disinterested.

Enter your *Child's World*. Focus on things that interest them. If it feels like torture to play the same boring game, listen to a repetitious story, or do something that doesn't interest you, focus on seeing what they see in the activity. Learn to notice—

without judgment—what excites or scares them, what challenges and engages them.

Limit the teaching. Avoid the impulse to turn every interaction into a life lesson. The goal is to enjoy and bond with your child, not to give advice or help, unless you are asked for it.

Relating is a way of being. It doesn't matter whether you are cooking, playing, relaxing, hiking, or even dealing with a tantrum—what really matters is that you are there, present, emotionally and comfortably connected. Nothing about "relating" time is transactional, something you put on your to-do list or squeeze into your day.

SMALL DOSES, FREQUENT FACE TIME

The million-dollar question is how much time do kids need to feel loved and secure? In my research, I've uncovered some hopeful news.

It turns out, children don't need large chunks of time delivered occasionally; they need short bursts of attention delivered consistently. A little focused time goes a long way with kids. Many experts say that the attention span of a child is about one minute for each year of their life. In other words, a one-year-old child can focus for about one minute, a five-year-old for five, and a fifteen-year-old for about fifteen minutes. In her TED Talk, "The Year of Yes," Shonda Rhimes learned that when her kids asked her to play a game, fifteen minutes was all they needed before they lost interest and walked away.

Interviews with children reveal that they are satisfied in less time than parents realize; they just want to be able to rely on that time, and for Mom and Dad to be truly focused—not multitasking or phoning it in. Five to fifteen minutes of undivided attention can transform your and your child's lives. Jeanette Betancourt, senior vice president of community and family engagement at Sesame Workshop, emphasized that relating time starts with the everyday caretaking moments that do not require any extra time. Brushing hair, getting dressed, eating meals, tucking kids into bed at night all provide a wonderful platform to relate to your child. If you view the cutting of your kid's nails as an opportunity to connect, instead of a chore, it becomes fun. If you view the drive to and from activities as a chance to communicate, rather than just transportation, it becomes relating time. Once parents realize they are doing these things already, Jeanette says, the next question is how to make the most of these moments, talk a little more, invite questions, give a hug for the sake of a hug.

But here's the thing: you need to be there as often as possible to take advantage of those little opportunities. Delivering responsive and reliable care requires structuring your life around being a frequent presence in your children's lives, so that you spend time interacting with them, getting to know them, and paying attention, in order to be good at interpreting and delivering on their needs. This is very liberating news for every time-starved parent.

The first five minutes pack a punch. Annie Pleshette Murphy, parenting expert, family therapist, and former editor in chief of *Parents* magazine, calls the first few minutes of every reconnection point with your child "the relationship savers." First thing in the morning, the first few minutes you reconnect with your children after school and before dinner, when you get home from work, the goal is to light up when you see your child. A warm and nurturing response will set the tone for the time together and actually stretch time—buying you loads of peaceful time where kids feel satisfied, so that the moments you do have together feel full. (According to Annie, that focus on the first five minutes works well for marriages, too.)

Kids need alone time, too. Moments when you are in the same space as your kids, but each involved in your own activities— you are getting a meal on the table, while your kid is nearby doing their homework—are healthy. Children of all ages— from babies to teenagers—benefit from doing their own independent activities, yet are secure and supported knowing you are nearby and available. Here's the condition: together but apart time only works if you are actually accessible to your children and available to engage in chat with them from time to time. You should avoid doing any "flow" tasks or work that requires your undivided attention.

Relate while you vacuum (not *in a* vacuum). Every expert I spoke to warned against a parent's tendency to think of household chores as something you need to rush through to make space for quality time with your kids. Let kids be involved with what you're doing. Relating over the little things—making dinner, washing the car, folding laundry, sweeping the kitchen floor—is one way to make sure you get in some good connecting time with your kids, even if you have a mile-long to-do list at home. Don't shun them, engage them. Those tiny moments of connection over seemingly mundane domestic tasks are often the most memorable for kids anyway.

Make the most of daily routines. Streamline routines such as waking up, getting dressed, eating meals, traveling to and from school or other activities. The more predictable and less rushed routines are, the easier it is to use them as moments for calm, focused quality time.

Schedule dedicated one-on-one time. A little bit of predictable special time every day to connect to your children can become the building blocks of connection over the years. Whether it's twenty minutes of reading every night or half an hour to shoot hoops, create a tradition of reliable daily moments your kids can count on to talk to you. Once a week or even once a month, dedicate a longer block of time to spend one-on-one, diving into a project together, going on an adventure, or pursuing one of your child's interests.

Relating time is a basic daily need that can be integrated into any encounter and interaction with your child. The goal is small doses, frequently and consistently delivered. That foundation will allow for the inevitable imperfect moments and overly busy times. Remember that, for the most part, your kids don't really pay attention to *what* the activity is—as long as it's with you.

FOUR RELATE ACTIVITIES

Like Mr. Brown, some parents and caregivers seem to know what to do, instantly, to be able to relate to children. We admire parents who are gifted at connecting with their kids and have created obviously close, respectful, supporting, and loving relationships. But it doesn't come so easily to everyone (which can be hard to admit). Many parents feel flat-footed, awkward, and uncomfortable. Some parents "get" the need to spend time with their kids, but relating to kids at every age and stage is tough, and learning how to do it (and enjoy it!) takes some knowledge and experience.

Let's break **Relate** down into four categories of activities: Talking, Reading, Playing, and Sharing Adventures. Each of these activities provides a good platform for connecting, bonding, and infusing your child with the unconditional message that they matter. If you think about it, these activities are the ways that all human beings communicate a sense of importance.

Here are some very practical techniques, culled from the experts, about how to successfully engage in all four categories with kids of all ages.

TALK

If the eyes are the gateway to the soul, conversation is the gateway to your child's inner thoughts, insights, and experiences. Every child is navigating the world for the first time; we can't assume we see what they see, notice what they notice, or conclude what they conclude. The aim of conversation at every age is to help you see the world through your child's eyes, find out what's on your child's mind, and demonstrate a genuine interest in who they are as individuals.

Create a safe space for your children to express whatever they are thinking and feeling. Your job is to be neutral, nonjudgmental, and curious.

Ask open-ended questions. Questions with yes or no answers (e.g., *"Did you have fun?"* and *"Do you like your teacher?"*) lead to dead-end conversations. Get your kids talking by using Who, What, Where, When, Why, and How questions:

- *Who was your favorite character in the movie?*
- *What was the best part of your day?*
- *Where do you want to go . . . ?*

- *When* did you discover that you liked poetry? When do you get upset?
- *Why* did you choose that topic for your story/drawing?
- *How* did you figure that out?

Listen more than you talk. Aim for a 70:30 ratio—you listening for about 70 percent of the time and talking for about 30 percent. Your job is to ask questions that will stimulate your child to talk. Nurture the discussion with phrases like "tell me more about that" and "that is so interesting."

Don't be afraid of feelings. When our children are upset, our instinct can be to take away the pain by minimizing the problem or jumping straight into fix-it mode. Yet, it has to be safe for kids to share all kinds of feelings with you, not just the happy ones. Empathize and name their feelings, without feeling like you need to fix them. Instead of dismissing or denying your child's emotions or worries, try teaching him or her that feelings come and go.

Talking Age-by-Age

Infant (0–1)

Follow your infant's attention and name the things that captivate them. "Do you see the lamp switch? That's how we turn on the lights." When you go outside, and she looks up at a tree, "Oh, that's a squirrel. Squirrels have fluffy tails and eat nuts. I wonder if it lives in that tree?" Leave a gap when it's your baby's turn to talk again. This teaches your baby about the pattern of conversation. Coos, babbles, and gurgles are an infant's version of language, so respond to their "words" with your words.

Toddler (1–3)

Play sports commentator on their discoveries. Toddlers are amazing learners. They are discovering that they can change the way the world works. Narrating their play is a great way to help young children understand how language can describe actions. You can even ask questions like, "What will you do next?" Or, "I see you put the ball inside the jar. Is there another way to do that?"

Preschool (3–5)

Reflect together on shared experiences. An example: "Remember when we went to the park and we had a picnic and then played on the swings? And then when it started to rain, we went to get ice cream and that was fun, too?" Let the child consider the order in which things happened, why things happened the way they did, and what the experience meant. Consider writing or drawing these stories as a way of creating permanent memories.

School-Age (5–10)

Have a daily debrief. At school, your child is busy learning, making friends, and tackling daily challenges. Talking about what's happening in their lives when you are apart is tremendously bonding and helps them feel cared for, understood, and secure. You can help your child develop empathy and understand different points of view by getting him to describe his own feelings and by talking about other people's feelings; for instance, "Why do you think that made Sally sad?" A daily dialogue puts you in the best position to guide and support them in all circumstances.

Tween (10–13)

Make it safe to talk about the tough stuff. Keep the lines of communication open as the tough topics come up: bullying, sexual orientation, drugs, alcohol, academic competition. Adopt a poker face. Avoid being critical or judgmental or even looking alarmed. Just listen. Mirror back what they are saying, and clarify your understanding: "Is that what you mean?" Then empathize: "That's a good point." "That sounds like it was very painful." Often empathy is all kids (and grown-ups!) need to feel whole.

Teen (13–18)

Engage in philosophical talk. This is a point at which kids are exploring different ways of looking at the world on the road to identity formation. If they are less willing to talk about details of their own lives, consider discussing the news or engaging in philosophical talk. Approach subjects with curiosity. Be willing to discuss a topic from all perspectives—the exploration may stretch your mind, too.

TUNING IN WHEN YOUR KIDS ARE READY TO TALK

Tamika has three kids—eight, ten, and twelve—and finds that getting them to open up and tell tales from their day has to be individualized. Each kid is different, of course. She figured out when they wanted to share and made herself available at those times of day.

She told me she gets the best information from Ashley, her twelve-year-old, when she's in the shower. "It's her time to spill the beans. If I want to know what happened at the lunchroom or at recess, that's the time I'll here it all," she said.

She noticed that her middle child, Sean, likes to talk before he goes to bed at night.

And Adam, her youngest, would relay every moment of his day the minute he got off the bus. "At least a few days a week, I make sure to do pickup—instead of our babysitter—so I catch all of his stories as they tumble out."

READ

While conversation connects you to your child's inner life, reading exposes children to other worlds. The bond that forms between parent and child while sharing stories is so powerful (and so vital for children's happiness and development) that the American Academy of Pediatrics recommends parents read aloud to their children from infancy through young adulthood. According to a survey by Scholastic, 83 percent of kids aged six to seventeen said they still love reading with their parents and cite it as one of the most bonding experiences of their childhood. Books can be powerful tools for relating to your child, as they are written and edited by professionals who understand the issues and interests children face at various ages and stages. Use reading to spur conversation. Involving your children in choosing what to read also boosts their love of reading.

Have fun with reading. Make sure reading is associated with pleasure, and quality time with you. Have fun with it. Build anticipation with a dramatic introduction of the book: read the title, author, and illustrator. Look at the cover and imagine together what the book might be about. As you read, vary your expressions and tone of voice to fit the plot. Use a different voice for each character. Pause when appropriate to create suspense. Engage your children in reading by encouraging them to finish sentences (when they are young), reading certain characters (as they start learning to read), reading aloud to you (you read one page, they read the next).

Talk about what you are reading. Talking about what you're reading gives it power, according to the National Association for the Education of Young Children (NAEYC), as well as the opportunity to promote closeness between parent and child. Talk about the book and how it relates to a child's real-life experiences. Do you know anyone like that? Did that ever happen to you? If you're reading a book about a family, for example, talk about how what happens in the story is the same or different from what happens in your family.

Contain bedtime reading. Bedtime reading is a great way to unwind, but it can also be hard to contain. What kid doesn't ask for "just one more book, please"? Decide ahead of time how many minutes or how many books is reasonable. For young kids, create a special bedtime basket into which they can deposit two or three books (or whatever the limit) so they can see when it's finished. *Plus*, there's no need to limit reading to just bedtime. Read aloud during chores (one person reads while the other does the dishes), in the car, at the doctor's office, on the bus, while waiting in line, on a field trip.

Reading Age-by-Age

Infant (0–1)

Encourage your baby to join in. Ask, "Where's the . . . ?" "What's that . . . ?" "Point to the car." "Meow like a cat." And wait for a response. Stay on a page as long as the baby is interested in it, and let the baby touch the book, look at the book, and turn the pages.

Toddler/Preschool (1–5)

Ask thinking questions. Toddlers and preschoolers are learning to cope with feelings and master self-help skills (dressing, brushing their teeth, etc.). They enjoy stories with characters who are having similar experiences to their own, according to Reading Is Fundamental (RIF). They also love stories with rhythm and rhyme. Foster participation while reading the book by asking thinking questions, such as: *Where did he go? Why did he do that? What might happen next?*

School-Age (5–10)

Read chapter books. At this age, children are learning to monitor their own behavior and enjoy books with more fully developed characters, plot twists, and descriptive language. Set the stage before you begin reading. Discuss what you read yesterday and what might happen next. Use Post-its or other page markers to divide the text into read-aloud segments. These segments should have natural breaking points and leave the child at a particularly good cliffhanger—so they look forward to the next night's reading.

Tween (10–13)

Read what your child reads. Get your own copy of novels your child is reading for school or for pleasure. You may get to reread books you enjoyed as a kid (Roald Dahl, anyone?). Reading together gives you more to talk about. Ask your child to imagine what he or she might do in a similar situation faced by a character. Help your child find the words to express their reaction and share your reactions as well. This helps kids develop their own emotional vocabulary.

Teen (13–18)

Share books of interest. According to Bank Street, kids aged fifteen to seventeen are more likely than younger kids to want books that let them forget about real life for a while (think fantasy series like *Harry Potter* or *The Hunger Games*), or to read books that feature issues kids this age are grappling with. Questions include, "How do I fit in?" "How do I stay true to myself when confronted with peer pressure?" "How will I find my life's work?" "How can I create a world free of violence or hunger?" Encourage your teen to choose a book related to an interest, a biography, a novel, a nonfiction topic, and so on. You can also read the newspaper together, whether it's for fifteen minutes over breakfast or just on weekend mornings. Establish a routine and talk about what you read.

Expert Advice

THE LEXILE FRAMEWORK

Here are wonderful questions you can ask to stay connected when kids are reading on their own:

Before your child reads a book, ask:

- Why did you select this book?
- What makes you think this book is going to be interesting?
- What do you think the book is going to be about?
- Does this book remind you of anything you've already read or seen?

While your child is reading a book on their own, try asking:

- Will you catch me up on the story? What's happened so far?
- What do you think will happen next?
- If you were that character, what would you have done differently in that situation?

After your child has finished a book, ask questions like:

- What was your favorite part of the book? Why?
- Who was your favorite character? Why?
- What was the most interesting thing you learned from the book?
- Why do you think the author wrote this book?

PLAY

Play is so important to child development that it has been recognized by the United Nations Commission on Human Rights as a right of every child. Children learn to interact with the world through play from a very young age. While, of course, kids need to play with other kids and on their own, playing with parents is a great way for your child to connect with you, in their world, on their terms. "You can discover more about a person in an hour of play, than in a year of conversation," said Aristotle.

Keep it varied and old-school. There are different forms of play—pretend, games with rules, physical, constructive, competitive—and each kind of play has its own benefits and characteristics. Simple wood blocks, dolls, a ball and bat, or a game of tag offer more opportunities for the child to direct the play than the fanciest games and digital toys.

Let your child lead. When kids play, they create a world that is perfectly suited to their current needs, interests, challenges, and goals. When you follow their lead, you have the opportunity to inhabit their world. If you are open-minded, it can be a fascinating place.

You have fun, too. The National Institute for Play recommends adults reconnect to their playful side, to build intimacy, release stress, and add joy. Get in on the fashion show, use duct tape on the floor to create a toy car highway, build a marshmallow city. Just have fun!

Playing Age-by-Age

Infant (0–1)

Play imitation games. Take turns making simple gestures (waving, for example). Infants can learn to copy the movements that go to song and, with practice, remember the sequence and cadence. Just think "The Itsy-Bitsy Spider," and "You Are My Sunshine." Demonstrate how to play with a toy—making a horse gallop or rocking a baby doll crib.

Toddler (1–3)

Let kids call the stage directions. Toddlers are beginning to develop an understanding of cause and effect. As you play, give your kids the opportunity to tell you what you should do.

Should you pour the tea? Should you feed the stuffed giraffe some rock soup? Allowing your toddler to regulate the behavior of others is a great way for them to develop their own self-regulation skills.

Preschool (3–5)

Engage in imaginary play. Preschoolers have great imaginations and like to practice new skills. Build a fort out of pillows; line up some chairs as a bus and let the kids do the "driving"; put on a play or a concert. Encourage their creative streak with crafts projects using items you find around the house: paper bags, toilet paper tubes, or old socks to make puppets.

School-Age (5–10)

Play games that require concentration and quick responses. Hand games, card tricks, jump rope, tetherball, and dodgeball are great physical activities that require quick decisions. Simon Says, musical chairs, and freeze dance are also great for building attention and cognitive flexibility because the child must track which rule to apply and switch actions as appropriate. Putting on a fashion show or a play also appeals to kids this age.

Tween (10–13)

Cultivate physical activities. Cultivating a love and passion for any physical activity—dance, soccer, basketball, running, etc.—can be one of the best combatants against peer pressure to smoke, drink, and do drugs throughout the teen years, because kids are motivated to stay healthy. Physical activities combine mindfulness, and movement can also help kids develop their ability to pay attention.

Teen (13–18)

Co-play video games. In an ideal world, you'd get your teen away from screens and their electronic devices, but if they are sincerely attached, here's a suggestion: rather than criticize, offer to co-play. Video games allow a kid to escape from the pressures of their own life and master something. By joining them, it allows you to have a better sense of how your child is spending his or her time and offers a point of connection on their terms. They may also learn more—or be able to better interpret what they are seeing on-screen—if they are playing video games with an adult.

SHARING ADVENTURES

Almost anything can be an adventure to a child: from going on a treasure hunt in the grocery store, to riding a bus for the first time, to learning how to build a robot. The key is to be fully present for the adventure by participating in discovery and exploration with your child.

Longer adventures (a family vacation, a trip to the beach, river, or amusement park) can take bigger blocks of time and don't have to be done every day, but they are an important marker of telling your child, "I will invest time in you." Adventures and outings also create the space for deeper dialogues (that might feel too rushed in everyday life) and create shared memories that become part of your history as a family.

Do things of interest to your child. The goal here is to focus on what engages your child, not to impose your own interests, says Laurence Steinberg, a noted author and professor of psychology at Temple University. If your kid is into science, make a battery out of a lemon together. If your kid loves to draw, sketch portraits of each other. Love basketball? Watch the NCAA finals together. Adore the ballet? Try to get tickets to a live performance. Understand the activities that are important to them and experience it through their eyes.

Discover something new together. Novelty helps make adventures fresher and more engaging for you and your children. Expose your kids to new experiences: cultural events, nature walks, practicing how to make homemade pasta, learning to build a model ship together, etc. By taking your children on adventures (big or small), you will discover what ignites their curiosity, what makes them laugh, where their passions lie, and how they interact with the world.

Be spontaneous. The "surprise" factor goes a long way in creating lasting memories. Child development experts Annie Pleshette Murphy and Laurence Steinberg say that the most memorable moments from childhood aren't the fanciest vacations, they're the little surprises—"Let's go on a walk around the block in our pajamas," "Let's go get an ice cream cone before dinner!"

Sharing Adventures Age-by-Age

Infant (0–1)

Go out, anywhere. Literally anything—anything—feels like an adventure to your infant, who is seeing the world for the first time. Let them touch the grass, stare at leaves in the wind, listen to waves at the beach, watch ducks in the pond.

Your job is to help your baby simply notice the wonder all around him.

Toddler (1–3)

Go on a scavenger hunt. Toddlers are still discovering the world and can actively participate in the observation. Turn any walk into a leaf-counting hunt or a scavenger hunt (find something that feels rough, silky, pointy, round).

Preschool (3–5)

Go on a picnic. Involve your kid from start to finish: pull out a cookbook, let your child pick a recipe, help prepare and pack it. A peanut butter and jelly sandwich can be thrilling! Or, have a picnic inside, using a theme like "pack the rainbow," so your kid learns to assemble a balanced meal.

School-Age (5–10)

Ask your child to teach you something they learned in school. It could be how to do a move she learned in gym class, how to write a haiku, or the importance of recycling to save the earth. Then come up with a fun project that builds on those skills. Cowrite a cookbook, start a family newsletter, do an art project that recycles magazines, use cardboard tubes or old gloves to make finger puppets.

Tween (10–13)

Get involved with the community. As peer pressure and self-doubt begin to take hold, it's a great time to get kids involved in the world at large—to gain some perspective and feel they are doing some good. Have them write letters to soldiers serving overseas, visit an old age home together, volunteer in the community, do a bake sale to raise money for a charity, do a local history walk.

Teen (13–18)

Hang out however they wish. Teenagers have packed schedules of their own, so it's harder to find time to spend together. Reserve one to two hours a week just for the two of you—and be open to doing whatever they are in the mood for—going on a bike ride, hitting up a local coffee shop for a treat, exploring a local bookstore, writing poetry, doing a crossword puzzle together, etc. Let them lead.

REAL PARENT VOICES

CASUAL CONNECTIONS DURING THE TEEN YEARS

Roy discovered the best-kept secret about raising kids is that you think it's when they're babies that they need you the most (and they do, at least when it comes to physically helping them put their pants on). But the teenage years are when your presence is even more important—not for constant communication but for drive-by, casual interactions. He was able to negotiate working from home three days a week to be around for his teens a little more often.

IT'S NEVER TOO LATE

Okay, so what if your kid is eight or fifteen and you feel like you've never done this relating thing quite right? Maybe you've pressed your own interests too hard. Or made too many relating moments into teachable moments. Or been overly judgmental in the past and worry that it's too late to connect with your kid in a real way. Perhaps you have new kids in your life through divorce, remarriage, or friends and are trying to build a relationship.

I have good news: according to the experts, it's never, ever too late to create and benefit from connecting with your children. The human brain isn't fully formed until the age of twenty-six. So, while those early years (ages zero to five) are a peak brain development period—as are the years in early adolescence—brain development in humans continues for at least five to ten years after the completion of physical and hormonal maturation.

RELATING IS AS GOOD FOR YOU AS IT IS FOR YOUR CHILD

Mr. Brown acknowledged that today's parents have far more responsibilities and stuff on their plates than parents did forty or fifty years ago. But he also emphasized that time spent relating to children, who live so much in the present, can offer a much-needed respite from the everyday stresses of the adult world. Shifting to the pace of children can provide similar benefits to meditation—a pause of being in the here and now—which can restore you and make your time "back at work, and in the adult world" much more productive. He also underscored how building relationships through relating can make "teaching" (and in many cases, discipline) much easier, because you have the rapport, the time, and the knowledge to guide your kids.

We'll learn how to shore up those **Teach** skills in the next chapter.

10

TEACH

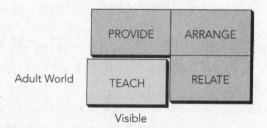

Jamari was an energetic stay-at-home mom who was craving a little "me time" when we started working together. A poet before she had children, Jamari missed writing but couldn't figure out where to find the time to work on her craft. Every waking hour was devoted to her two kids—from helping them get up and out the door on time, to chauffeuring them to and from school and after-school activities. She involved everyone in the preparation and cleanup of meals and was adamant that each kid fully participate in housework and chores.

Jamari thought she was doing everything "right"—her kids were respectful, responsible, and polite. They helped out. They were good kids. But something to Jamari felt off, and so she called. In addition to longing for some time to write, I learned through our conversation that she also wished she had more time to just be silly and play with her kids. Despite the amount of time they spent together, it rarely felt fun or relaxed. Their emotional connection actually felt a little distant. How could this be, when she dedicated so much time to them?

When I asked Jamari to walk me through her family's day (in order to see where we might find some "hidden" time), I noticed that routines were taking almost three times as long as I would normally expect. Why? Because Jamari transformed each activity into a teachable moment. Every morning, she taught the kids how to pick out outfits, how to make the bed, how to cook a healthy breakfast, how to clean up. After school, there were learning-based activities, errands, homework, more cooking, more instruction.

Jamari genuinely believed her job, as their mother, was to teach her kids to be self-sufficient. Teaching was her way of showing her kids she loved them. But even "fun" outings were treated as teaching opportunities. As a result, everything took significantly longer than necessary and created an ever-present subtle strain between Jamari and her kids—they never had the chance to relax and just *be* with each other. It also meant Jamari could never relax, and she had no time for her own interests or other important self-care activities.

Roxana, also a mom to two kids, had the exact opposite challenge. Roxana had grown up with overbearing parents and was determined to make life better for her kids by having fewer rules. She tended to avoid her role as a teacher, not because she didn't love her kids but because she was afraid of coming across as overly harsh or making them unhappy. She feared that leading with a firm hand would cause her kids to resent or even hate her. She tried to set limits but immediately backed down at the first hint of protest or unhappiness. Her goal was a more loving, connected relationship, but her approach backfired: her kids were often cranky, demanding, and out of control. The quality time Roxana craved with her kids was hard to come by because she found the time with them so draining.

When it comes to teaching your children, it's easy to fall into the trap of being an overdoer (like Jamari) or an underdoer (like Roxana). If you overdo it, time together is exhausting for both you and your kids. And if you underdo it, your kids won't learn boundaries and self-control. The reality? Both cases actually inhibit your ability to have and enjoy quality time with your children. The goal of this chapter is to help parents strike a balance—to minimize tension, battles, and power struggles—so the time you spend with your children is productive and pleasant.

IN OUR PARENT TIME SURVEY
TEACHING HAS ROOM FOR IMPROVEMENT

Parents ranked teaching values to their kids a top priority, second only to spending quality time with their kids. Yet, half of our parent respondents (50.70%) felt they spent too little time teaching kids values, life skills, and discipline.

YOU ARE YOUR CHILD'S FIRST AND LIFELONG TEACHER

You are your child's first and lifelong teacher, whether you feel prepared for it or not. It's at once a privilege, an honor, a thrill, and a burden. Some parents love this role, some dread it, and most parents find some parts of teaching easier than others.

Teaching is about preparing your children to navigate school and life, as an adult, with agility, competence, and self-confidence. All parents want their kids to be successful, and the time you invest teaching your children values, knowledge, and skills prepares them to become happy, well-adjusted adults and productive, contributing members of society.

Teach is one of the visible forms of connecting with your children—and, as with **Relate**, the time you invest in teaching can go a long way in making your kids feel loved and important. While they often seem to overlap (since kids are learning all the time), there is a clear distinction between teaching and relating from your child's point of view.

Let's break it down.

Simply stated, when "relating," you enter your *Child's World*. When "teaching," you invite your child into the *Adult World*.

THE IDEAL STATE: CALM AND CONNECTED

Perhaps the most challenging thing about managing your role as teacher is that kids are learning all the time, and you are teaching all the time, whether you plan to or not. Teaching happens when you want to ("Let's go learn how to ride a bike!") and when you don't (when your kid has a meltdown on the way home from the park after that bike ride).

Teach can be a time and energy thief because correcting a child's behavior can lead to conflicts and power struggles, which can feel exhausting and draining, stealing time from relaxing and connecting. Furthermore, as we learned from Jamari, it takes longer to get something done when teaching a kid than just doing it yourself.

Understanding and recognizing the three ways all parents teach can help to empower you to teach efficiently and effectively, without overdoing it:

Teaching by role modeling. Kids absorb and mimic the behaviors you demonstrate. Being a role model requires you to be conscious of your actions and to invest time practicing and internalizing the behaviors you want your kids to emulate. Though this takes time and conscious effort to improve on your own part, it allows you to constantly lead by example, without turning every second into one of Jamari's teachable moments. An added bonus: your kids will take teachable moments more seriously if you walk the walk and talk the talk.

Teaching by observing. Supervision involves keeping an eye on your kids when they are doing their own thing. When you take them to the playground, watch them interact with other kids; when they are nearby doing homework, pay attention to how focused or distracted they are. The more time you spend observing your child, the easier it is to guide with finesse and feel confident in being firm. When you observe, you can collect information and be ready for the right time to bring up a particular issue. Supervision not only communicates to your kids that they are safe and secure, it also gives you information to help you guide them with wisdom.

Teaching by direct interaction. Moments of concrete guidance are the most direct form of teaching. Sometimes kids seek your instruction (*"Can you show me how to . . . ?"*), and sometimes there are things you are excited to show them how to do: how to ride a bike, pour cereal, cross the street safely. And, of course, there are moments when you need to discipline or correct your children for their own well-being. Direct interactions can take all forms: levity, a quick aside, confiding heart to heart, a serious moment. It takes regular practice to get it right.

Given the anytime-anywhere aspect of teaching, parents need to embrace and be comfortable in their role as teacher.

Embracing the role doesn't mean bravado or feeling like you have to know it all. The truth is we are teaching our kids even if we are works in progress ourselves.

Done well, teaching cultivates close and loving connections with your children and builds a good, trusting rapport. It requires that you feel comfortable being the authority and are confident in what you have to offer.

Most of all, though, teaching requires striking the right balance between being firm and loving, between setting limits and granting freedom, and between doing things for your kids and allowing them to do things for themselves.

CREATE THE CONDITIONS

Writing this chapter was not easy, because the sheer amount of information and opinions about what and how to teach children is dizzying. I was privileged to interview two particularly articulate sources—each of whom has a knack for converting scientific research into exceedingly practical advice that focuses on time and energy management. Below, I'll share the most helpful information I gleaned through interviews with Laurence Steinberg, the author and professor of psychology at Temple University we met in the previous chapter, and Claire Lerner, child development specialist and senior parenting advisor at ZERO TO THREE. I think you'll agree that their approach and expertise genuinely apply to real life.

RELATE, BEFORE TEACH

One of the most important things parents can do to make teaching and disciplining more effective is to build a positive relationship with their children. Sounds obvious, right?

Relating builds the trust and rapport required to make teaching stick.

Mr. Brown, my beloved elementary school principal first mentioned in chapter 2, perfected the balance between **Relate** and **Teach**. Because he had such strong connections with every child in the building, kids listened to him, trusted him, and were more responsive to discipline. He could address misbehavior without ever making a child feeling crushed or shamed.

By investing time in relating to your child, you gain valuable insight into who your child is, how they think, and what earns their best response. And in doing so, you create a loving connection built on trust, understanding, support, and belief in their abilities to grow and change. Without that relationship, guidance and discipline—the hallmarks of teaching—can feel as if a parent is barreling in without context.

Not only is it easier to correct your child when the lines of communication are open and filled with trust, but you will likely have fewer discipline issues overall. In interviews with parents who scored particularly high in the **Relate** quadrant, parent after parent said, "I really don't have to discipline very much; my kids are really pretty easy." And experts agree. According to Laurence Steinberg, kids whose parents spend regular quality time relating with them generally do better in school, feel better about themselves, are less likely to develop emotional problems, and are less likely to take risks or get into trouble. That, in turn, reduces the number of discipline issues that come up.

The bottom line is that in order to teach your child, you must *know* your child. Do you? Here's a little assessment Laurence Steinberg offers:

- Can you name all your child's teachers?
- Do you know who your child's best friends are?
- Do you know what he or she is studying in school?
- Do you know what book your child is reading or loves right now?
- Can you name some of your child's favorite athletes, celebrities, movies, and music?
- If your child is a teenager, do you know how he or she spends time after school, in the evenings, on weekends?

If you don't know the answers, spend a little more time relating before you try to teach.

REAL PARENT VOICES

WHEN TEACH DOESN'T WORK, TRY RELATE

When Annie's daughter was around seven years old, she began spending an entire hour every morning trying on all her clothes instead of getting dressed and ready to go. Annie tried everything in the book: she cajoled her into choosing her outfit the night before, coached her that clothes don't make the person, begged her to just close her eyes and pick—"Come on, sweetie, you're holding up the works here!" Nothing worked. One day, desperate for a solution, Annie tried a totally different tack. "How about we play a game before school every morning?" That did the trick. Immediately upon waking up, her daughter got dressed, ate breakfast, and was ready to play Chutes and Ladders. It was a time gain for Mom—as the game only took fifteen minutes. But it was also a lesson: at some impasses, when children are misbehaving—the solution isn't about teaching but about relating. Her daughter just needed a little love.

THE MOST EFFECTIVE AND TIME-SAVING
FORM OF DISCIPLINE

My primary goal for this book is to help parents organize their lives to create the space to enjoy quality time with their kids. One of the biggest discoveries I made after going through thousands of pages of research was the direct connection between discipline style, or how you teach, and the ability to both create and enjoy quality time with your kids.

There are basically three styles of discipline that experts use to define the approach parents and caregivers provide. Diana Baumrind, a developmental psychologist at the University of California–Berkeley in the 1960s, first articulated these approaches, and I think they hold up well today:

Authoritarian: This is a parents-know-best approach that emphasizes obedience. Do as I say, because I said so, because I am the grown-up. In this approach, the parent holds all the power. (Think Jamari.)

Permissive: This style provides few behavioral guidelines because parents don't want to upset their children. In a sense, parents leave the kids to regulate themselves. Here, the kid holds all the power. (Think Roxana.)

Authoritative: This style combines setting firm guidelines with loving enforcement that emphasizes reason and compassion. It balances the power dynamic between recognizing the child's responsibility to cope and adapt with the parent's responsibility to respect the child's needs and feelings.

Through a time- and energy-management lens, the authoritarian and permissive approaches to parenting can feel like wins in the short run. How so? Authoritarian parents quickly shut down misbehavior with a simple harsh word or punishment. That settles that. Permissive parents get a short-term time gain through avoiding long, unpleasant power struggles by yielding to their kids' demands and pleasing them in the moment.

But as we saw with Jamari and Roxana, each of these styles can lead to a huge time-management backlash. Parents disciplining in these ways may find quality connections with their kids hard to come by, as their children feel distant and shut out, or trapped in overcaretaking, as their children fail to develop skills that foster independence, such as self-regulation, on their own.

Across the board, and across cultures, every study of child development concludes that the authoritative style leads to the best outcomes for children. Balancing limits with love and reasoning builds closeness and connection between parent and child and simultaneously leads to the healthiest social-emotional intelligence in children.

And what is the value of social-emotional intelligence? After many decades of thinking that intelligence as measured by IQ and academic excellence is what makes kids successful, we are learning that character traits, such as grit, determination, self-regulation, and social skills, are perhaps even more important.

Social skills, like getting along with others, being fair, and listening, are important skills for kids to have in every area and at every stage of their lives. They help kids build friendships and confidence and feel like they have a place in the world.

Self-regulation, an umbrella term that includes self-discipline and self-control, is a necessary skill that helps children learn to manage themselves. Cultivating self-control in your child is about teaching them to control their impulses, but it's also about helping kids to problem-solve and express themselves and about cultivating the grit and determination that will help them meet life's challenges with confidence, skill, and grace.

Authoritative parenting leads to the very best chance of kids developing these kinds of social-emotional skills. The payoff is high, as kids parented in this way tend to be happy, independent, autonomous, and self-confident, able to successfully navigate social situations and regulate their emotions. The authoritative approach ultimately leads to more time relating and less time dealing with crisis management.

Of course, parents tend to parent either in the way they were parented or in exactly the opposite way. So, if authoritative parenting is not natural to you, it's worth studying up on.

Here's a picture of what it looks like.

Find Your Authoritative Stride: Five Ways to Be Firm but Loving

Being firm but loving is no easy charge. Keeping your cool amid all the other things in life competing for your attention is a challenge. In a series of exclusive interviews, parenting and child development experts Claire Lerner and Laurence Steinberg offered up incredible insights into mind-set and behavior changes that can help you rise to the occasion and take on this marathon. Here goes:

Know that kids aren't born with the ability to manage themselves. Being a kid isn't easy. Feeling flustered or erratically moved by emotion is perfectly normal (sometimes that's even hard for adults) and tantrums are par for the course—they are simply your child's way of telling you they don't like a limit you've set or are having trouble coping—so don't fear the tantrum. Your job is not to prevent your kid from ever having a meltdown but to help them learn how to navigate the real world and their emotional landscapes. Learning to deal with life's frustrations and disappointments—not getting everything they want, when they want it—builds coping skills and resilience in young children. Setting rules and limits, based on your values and beliefs, will help your kids thrive. Setting and sticking to appropriate limits isn't mean—it's being a good and loving parent.

Remember that kids will always, always test those limits—because that's their job. Lerner assures us that having a happy child does not mean that your child is *always* happy. She warns against using a child's reaction as the gauge on whether a limit or rule is good for them or not. Don't expect to hear a three-year-old say, "Thanks, Dad, for not letting me have those M&M's before dinner. I know how important it is to eat my growing foods" or a tween to say, "Thank you for cutting off my screen time. I know there are much more enriching ways to spend my weekends." Helping your child learn to cope effectively with rules and limits is one of the greatest gifts you give, and one that pays off long into adulthood.

Show empathy. Lerner talks a lot about the importance of validating feelings because accepting feelings is the first step in learning how to manage them effectively (such as by stomping feet when angry instead of hitting). Emotions aren't the problem, she counsels; rather, the problem is the failure to navigate emotions in a constructive way. Ignoring or minimizing feelings doesn't make them go away—it just leads to more acting out. During disciplinary moments, Lerner suggests parents let their child know they understand his or her feelings while being clear about the limit and giving acceptable choices: "You're mad that I won't let you have ice cream before dinner. But that's not a choice right now. You can have a cheese stick or carrots." "You are so frustrated with that train—it is hard to make it stay on the track! But throwing the cars is dangerous. You can dump them in this container or we can try to solve the problem together." Giving your child the words to describe his feelings is the first step toward helping him manage his emotions and develop self-control. The second is to show children that they can survive the frustration or disappointment they experienced. That's what builds self-confidence and resilience.

Avoid being the fixer. One of the biggest risks in **Teach** is doing too much for our kids. Let's face it, it can be tempting to jump in to save time or to avert distress (our kids' *or* our own). It's instinctual for a parent to protect our children, and seeing them upset can be very distressing to us, which results in our trying to fix their problems to reduce their stress and make them "happy." But swooping in to fix the problem actually isn't doing you or your kids any favors. First, it sends the message to your kids that you don't believe in their ability to solve problems on their own, which can erode their self-confidence and is a missed opportunity to help them build valuable skills. Secondly, moving fast and helping your kids succeed in the moment may save time in the short run but not the long run, as children become dependent on you to fix everything, costing you *more* time because you get stuck doing for them what they can do for themselves.

Master a few quick ways to end a power struggle. Even the most loving, experienced parent sometimes runs out of time and patience to explain and debate every rule and direction. And you can't always bake in the extra time to do things at a kid's pace. But there is still a way to respect your child, stay connected, and move forward. Let's say you have ten minutes to rush in and out of the grocery store on your way home to cook dinner. You know your kid is likely to start grabbing for the chocolate chip cookies—and you just don't have time. It's all in your approach. Lerner says you can either go in like a banshee, irritated and stressed—or you can take a deep breath and be responsive instead of reactive by helping your child understand what to expect calmly, and empathically. It might look something like this:

> *"Sweetie, we will be stopping at the store on the way home to pick up three things: milk, cheese, and bread. We won't have time to go up and down all the aisles to pick a snack today. What you can do is help Mommy find these important foods!"* Then make it your child's job to point out the item on the shelf (depending, of course, on her age!). You might also make your kid the timer—see if you can be in and out in ten minutes. Engaging your child with the task gives her something positive to focus on and helps keep a breakdown at bay.

If you happen to be living with a little Clarence Darrow, who has a way of challenging every decision, but you need to move forward, Laurence Steinberg has some wonderful scripts in his book *The Ten Basic Principles of Good Parenting* to help you assert your authority as the parent and wiggle out of a tantrum or debate, without crushing your kid's soul. Here are two of my favorite ways to stop a power struggle:

> *"I hear what you're saying, and I've done my best to explain how I feel, but I think we just disagree. I'm going to have to use my best judgment."*

> *"I know we disagree, but the situation is a lot more complicated than I think you understand. Let's remember to talk about it later so that I can explain some of the different aspects of it to you."*

Finally, stay calm and be aware of your own triggers. According to Lerner, one of, if not the most, powerful and challenging influences on parenting is how you manage *your own* emotions. Often, it's your reaction to a situation that gets you into trouble. When your kid is struggling in any way (having a tantrum in the middle of the mall; clinging to you at a birthday party when all the other kids seem like social butterflies), do your best to be mindful of the feelings that are being elicited *for* you so you can manage them in a way that enables you to stay calm and tune in to what your child needs from you to help him cope. When a parent is emotional and upset, it only makes a child feel less secure and can exacerbate an uncomfortable situation. If you stay calm, your child is more likely to calm down, too.

VALUES—YOUR ULTIMATE TIME RUDDER

A simple and clear set of values can best be described as the ultimate time rudder for parenting, because the values become the foundation from which all of our choices about *when* to teach flow. They can help to guide your time together as a family and also to determine which battles—of many possible ones—are worth fighting. Your values show up in how you spend your time, what you discuss with your children, and how you reflect on and interpret the things you see in the world. Being intentional about the values you hold dear helps your children understand right from wrong and cultivates in them a sense of empathy and responsibility as they develop their own worldview so they can be productive, positive forces in the world.

Values are different from rules. They are much bigger in scope and can form the logical underpinning of rules. They should be broad enough to remember and relevant in many situations, but not so broad as to be meaningless. Determine a short list of shared values within your family and circle of caregivers. Here are a few examples:

- Always tell the truth, even when it's tempting not to.
- Work hard and try your best.
- Never do anything to hurt yourself or other people.

Do you see how values play into determining how a family decides to spend its time? A family that identifies one of their values as "taking care of others," for example, spends one Sunday a month volunteering together at a soup kitchen. A family that values "education" might regularly visit the library together and discuss topics of interest at the dinner table. A family for whom "faith" is important will prioritize religious services above a child's sports activity.

The simpler and clearer your values, the easier it is to know when to teach and when to step back. If your primary value is "Never do anything to hurt yourself or others," you may not care if your kid insists on wearing mismatched shoes to school. But to a parent whose core values include a strong belief that you "always put your best foot forward," a mismatched shoe situation may become a learning opportunity about the importance of physical presence.

HOW VALUES GUIDE TIME CHOICES

Tara and Cory have three kids, aged eleven, nine, and seven. One of their values is compassion for others. They stress with their kids that everyone is different and that no matter how different people are, they are to treat others the way they would want to be treated. The value helps to guide how they spend their time: they volunteer as a family at a local nursing home once a month, and on family trips they seek out people and experiences different from their own as a way to develop empathy and understanding.

Post your key values in a prominent place in your home. It could be a sticky note on your fridge, a paper tacked to the family calendar, or a reminder on the community bulletin board. It'll become a good point of reference for everyday decisions and discussions for both you and your children, prompting ideas for activities and providing a handy cheat sheet if you need to reinforce a rule when a certain behavior doesn't fly.

HOW TO GUIDE

Now, let's dive into the nitty-gritty of how you can actually go about teaching your kids the skills they need to know in two key areas: life skills and academics.

LIFE SKILLS

Teaching your kids life skills is about teaching them practical mechanics for managing the world: organization, time and money management, as well as the wisdom and street smarts you've picked up along the way—stuff like how to walk down a city street with confidence, how to shake someone's hand and look them in the eye, how to navigate a new city when traveling, how to parallel park, how to act on a job interview, how to dress for the first day of work.

Kids are hungry for life skills and a sense of competence. They also want to spend time with you. Think of it this way: taking the time to show your children how to do something can double as teaching and relating time.

Learn Alongside Your Kid

Life skills enable kids to function happily and well as adults. Teaching these skills to your kids saves time and energy in many ways and creates more space in your schedule for relating. But it can be a thorny area for parents because life skills are very rarely taught in schools, and parents may come into this area of teaching while lacking the skills themselves.

For this reason (and others), this is an area where teaching interactions between parents and kids can become strained and tense. Parents might feel distressed if they struggle with one area of life skills and then see their kids struggling, too. They might be at a loss about how to help them. If you struggle with how to teach skills in an area you don't know well or that may confuse or frustrate you, be honest about it. Nobody knows everything and role modeling a willingness to learn and grow is a useful parenting strategy. Plus, you can learn alongside your child. In this way, kids inspire us to be better people and never stop learning.

ORGANIZING

When kids learn how to get organized, there are fewer frantic searches for homework, soccer cleats, and water bottles in the morning. Teaching your kids how to set up systems will make it easy for them to find what they need when they need it and feel comfortable in their space. Be honest. If you struggle with organization, spend time together learning on something small, like the fridge or front-hall closet, then tackle their bedroom together. Organizing a child's room is one of the best ways to get to know her, because it's a window into what's important and what's no longer interesting. (For an age-by-age chart of the chores and household tasks kids can be expected to master, see chapter 8, "**Arrange**.")

Age-by-Age Organizing Lessons

Infant/Preschool (0–5)

Items have homes. At this stage your job is to set up systems, and your kids' job is to help clean up and put away toys before moving on to the next task. You can be cheerful in the messaging—narrating how you do this with everyday items ("I'm putting the brush back here so we can find it next time we need it!")—and involve them in putting every item back in its place.

School-Age (5–10)

Group similar items. From ages five to ten, kids can learn to arrange their own things. They can practice on clothes, books, toys, games, and school papers. You can teach them to group similar items (according to the way *they* think—not you) so they can always know where to put and find items.

Tween (10–13)

Declutter the obsolete. The tween years are a big transition time when kids' rooms get really messy as they transition (gradually) between little-kid belongings and new more grown-up items. Teach kids how to identify and preserve the most meaningful memorabilia and give away the rest, to make room for the new clothes, books, and hobbies that are important to them now.

Teen (13–18)

Care for objects. As kids get older, and more social, they begin to understand the value of organization to support a busy life (and stretch hard-earned dollars!). Learning to care for, store, and access their favorite possessions aligns with their motivations to look good, feel good, and always feel ready to go-go-go.

EXPERT ADVICE | **MAKE ORGANIZING FUN**

Parenting expert and counselor Annie Pleshette Murphy turned cleaning the house (a necessary life skill!) into a game with her children. She took on the persona of "the Queen of Mean," rolled out her most shrill British accent, and barked orders. "Scrub the bathtub—now!" "Fold towels into thirds, and I want to see perfect edges!" The kids loved it, they learned something along the way, and the work got done.

TIME MANAGEMENT

Time management is the art of accurately calculating how long things take, how to plan an appropriate amount of time for tasks, and how to find more efficient ways to get them done. Once your kids learn the skill of time management, they'll be more successful (and less frazzled) in and out of school. If you are always rushed and running late, acknowledge that you struggle and commit to learning together.

Age-by-Age Time Management Lessons

Infant/Preschool (0–5)

Time consciousness. Talk about schedules and timing in everyday conversation to help your child get a feel for time. "We're reading for thirty minutes." "I'll pick you up in one hour." "Dinner is at six p.m." Use tools to reinforce your words—a clock on the wall, the timer on your cell phone to go off when playtime is over. See if you can get your hands on a cool device called a Time Timer, which helps kids visualize the passage of time. Young children don't really know what five or ten minutes actually means, but a Time Timer lets them see time elapsing.

School-Age (5–10)

How long things take. The gateway skill to good time management is understanding how long things take. Help build awareness during everyday activities. You can even make it a friendly competition: who can more accurately calculate the duration of a task? Use the timer on your smartphone to track the truth.

Tween (10–13)

Balance a schedule. Middle school is a key stage to fortify time-management skills. Kids shift from a single classroom to multiple classes and teachers who may not coordinate with each other. Teach them to use a calendar to block out the week and divvy up their non–school hours among homework, friends, family, and time for oneself. Show them how to break big, long-term projects into doable daily steps to avoid missing deadlines.

Teen (13–18)

How to do things more efficiently. Life gets busier (school, college applications, part-time job, socializing) and the stakes get higher: Grades impact college applications. Teens want to feel competent, so coaching them in some cool hacks on how to do things more quickly, better, and faster is very motivating.

MONEY MANAGEMENT

Of all the life skills, financial literacy seems to be the most elusive—a topic children are often shielded from. If your own parents didn't teach you money management, or if you learned late in life, you may be at a loss about how to teach your kids. So pick up a book or two written for kids on the topic—and learn as you teach. My all-time favorite is *The Sink or Swim Money Program*, by John E. Whitcomb, which has some radical approaches. Experts agree that money lessons need to be started as soon as kids begin developing executive function—at age three—and continue through young adulthood. Lessons should commingle the concept that managing money is both a habit and an attitude, as well as a technical skill. The Consumer Financial Protection Bureau (CFPB) suggests that there are three stages and ages to money lessons, which I've shared below.

Age-by-Age Money Lessons

Preschool (3–5)

Money concepts and attitudes. Introduce kids to money as a resource and demystify it by talking about it in everyday life. Teach them to identify coins and the basic math: five pennies to a nickel, two nickels to a dime, ten dimes to a dollar, and so on. Teach kids where money comes from and help them grasp the connection between money and things. Start by giving them a toy cash register and going imaginary shopping at the grocery store. Then head to the supermarket with a list and budget in hand. Involve your kid—can the two of you stick to it?

School-Age (6–12)

Budgeting and planning habits. Give kids a chance to learn about spending, saving, and using money to achieve various goals. When shopping, narrate the thought process behind your choices (*"I'm choosing this pasta over that one, because*

they are both good but one's on sale." "I'll pay a little more for
these brand-name trash bags because the cheaper ones rip and
we have to double them up anyway"). Experts recommend
giving kids a chance to earn an allowance, through chores,
and setting up a three-jar system—Spend, Save, and Share—to
practice divvying up dollars for different purposes. Have them
set goals for each and use clear jars so they see their money
adding up.

Teen And Young Adult (13–26)

Financial systems and responsibilities. These are the years to
train your children to make independent financial decisions,
starting with managing a budget. John Whitcomb suggests a
graduating series of budgets to put your kids in charge of
leading up to making their entire clothing budget for the year.
Bring your kids to a bank to set up their own account(s) to
manage—maybe replicating the Spend, Save, and Share jar
system you taught them. Teach them about interest rates, the
parallels between credits cards and loans, and the importance
of paying on time to minimize interest and build credit.

Be confident that you have valuable knowledge, skills, and
experience to offer your children. You may feel you haven't
figured out the world well enough yet to impart wisdom to
your kids in all of these areas, but in a pinch, remember that
you're farther down the path than they are. Using your values
as a guide, you do have valuable knowledge to share.

ACADEMIC SKILLS

In his book *Our Kids: The American Dream in Crisis*, Robert Putnam writes that regardless of a child's race, socioeconomic circumstances, or family structure, parents who are involved—and who know what's happening with their children in school—result in a child's greater academic success.

But what exactly does "being involved" mean? Is it doing your kid's homework with them, or (gasp!) *for* them so that they get good grades? Is it about supplementing your child's education with more study at home? Is it about being on the PTA, volunteering frequently at your kid's school—which parents who work outside the home feel guilty about being unable to do, and stay-at-home parents often feel burdened by? Here are some answers that can help you manage your time.

Be your child's learning coach. Beyond the specific subject matter, one of the primary purposes of homework is to help your child learn how to manage his time, monitor his own learning, and make sure that his standards for his own work meet those of his teachers. In other words, learning how to learn is a skill that will help your children excel not only academically but throughout their career and lives. Don't do your child's work for him but do serve as his learning coach by being aware of what is expected and offering the time, space, and support to work on those assignments.

Get to know your children's teachers and understand their expectations. Getting involved with your child's education starts with getting to know your child's teachers and attending school events and functions. It opens up the lines of communication and awareness that enable you to support your child's education. It means that from preschool through high school, you take the time to find out what the standards are and make sure your child is striving to meet those standards. Don't be afraid to ask teachers how much time your child should allocate to specific assignments, or even for clarification on how your child is being assessed (creativity, neatness, accuracy, and so on). You should also know where your kids are excelling and where they are struggling. Help to communicate that information back to school.

Model good habits. Starting when children are young, set a regular schedule that the entire family can participate in: while kids do homework or read books, parents do their own quiet activity nearby and stay available for questions. Make sure you create a quiet space and environment to support the routine (this includes turning off the television—indeed, all electronic devices—except those required to do the homework). If you are at work when your kids are doing their homework, schedule a regular call/FaceTime conversation before they begin, to stay connected and be aware of what's on their plates. You can review the work when you get home.

REAL PARENT VOICES

MAKE STUDYING A FAMILY VALUE

Cary and Tiffany have three kids, aged thirteen, ten, and eight. And one of their values is "finish what you start." Here are two ways it plays out: 1) All three kids sit together and do their homework, waiting until everyone is done, before they are excused. If one child finishes before the others, he sits and reads or does something quiet (no TV or technology allowed) until the others are finished. 2) When a child is interested in an activity, he's allowed to sign up for it. If he discovers he doesn't like it, he doesn't have to sign up again—but he does have to finish the duration of that first sign-up.

Age-by-Age Academic Support

Infant/Preschool (0–5)

Lay the groundwork for enjoying learning. The American Academy of Pediatrics warns parents against trying to give their kids too much of a head start. Instead, focus on just talking, reading, and play. These things are the foundation of a love of learning, trust, and communication.

School-Age (6–10)

Monitor good work habits. Ask every day if your child has homework and establish a regular time and proper setting for her to get it done. Provide supplies and ensure she has eaten, is rested, and is energetic. Check to see that your child has completed the assignment and make sure she knows to ask for help at any time if she needs it.

Tween (10–13)

Get some outside help. Your kids need help at this stage to learn how to manage their more complex schedules, with multiple classes and teachers, but ironically, this is a time when kids have a hard time taking advice from their parents. Consider outside assistance—from a teacher, a local teen, or a tutor—to help your kid master the skills they need, including tracking their assignments, managing competing deadlines, and mapping out the steps of long-term projects.

Teen (13–18)

Let your kids take ownership. Assuming your kids have learned and mastered good study habits, you can begin to pull back in this stage, according to experts, only offering help if it is explicitly asked for. It's fair game to continue to provide the quiet study space, company, and supplies, and to build in family activities around topics they're learning about in school. If your child is studying the Civil War, for example, a family trip to Gettysburg can be an interactive way to reinforce what your child is learning.

Expect the push-pull puzzle of your growing kid. Keeping the lines of communication open while you teach your child is tricky business, as your role as guide will change many times over the course of your child's development. It can be vexing to keep up. What works one month might not work at all the next. That's just what it means to be a parent.

If you've ever had (or been) a teenager, you know what I mean. One day your kid hangs on your every word, the next she'll avoid sharing a sidewalk with you at all costs.

The "terrible twos" are sometimes known as the "first adolescence," when kids want to do everything by themselves, regardless of their own skills or ability or safety. Their demands don't make much sense ("I want *that* red cup, not that red cup!"). It's the first time your child gets a taste of his or her own independence and wants more of it. Now!

This fierce scramble will happen several times throughout childhood, each time manifesting itself in a different way.

It's not easy to keep pace, but it's up to you to keep up. And to keep the lines of communication open and to understand your role, so that when it really counts, you are able to support your child in the way she needs it.

Laurence Steinberg, in his book *The Ten Basic Principles of Good Parenting*, offers the best guide to keeping up with your child's stages of development I've come across—it focuses not just on what your kids need but on the changing role you play as a parent at each stage of childhood. Understanding where your child is on the spectrum of emotional development will not only make them less of a puzzle but will enable you to be a more responsive and attuned mom or dad.

For each stage of development, Steinberg says, there is always a central question that you should ask yourself, that will help you figure out what your child needs from you.

Infant: *How can I help my child feel more secure?* Babies are very dependent and rely on you to be there, to do things for them, and to teach and guide them directly. Your infant's needs revolve around developing a sense of security. You can make him feel this way by being calm, soothing, predictable, and affectionate.

Toddler: *How can I help my child feel more in control?* When your child moves from infancy into toddlerhood, her emotional concerns shift from security to independence. She is developing a sense of herself as a separate person who thinks she knows what she wants and can make her own decisions. Your role is to help your child feel in charge without actually giving up your authority as a parent.

Preschool: *What can I do to help my child feel more grown up?* During early childhood, children are beginning to learn about the world outside of home and starting to envision themselves as grown-up participants in the larger society. Despite these daydreams and fantasies, though, preschoolers feel small and powerless, and they know that there is a huge gap between what they want and what they are capable of. Your role is to help your preschooler feel that his dream of becoming a grown-up is an achievable one.

School-Age: *How can I help my child feel more capable?* Once kids enter school, they are expected to learn a huge number of things—many different academics, study skills, social skills, extracurricular activities—and develop relationships with classmates, teachers, and people in the outside world. The child also knows that her teachers, her classmates, her friends, and her parents are frequently evaluating her performance. What does she need at this point? She needs to feel competent. Your role is to help her identify what she's good at and to become better at the things she needs and wants to master.

Tween: *How can I help my adolescent feel more independent?* The emotional needs of your twelve- or thirteen-year-old parallel those that were central when he was a toddler, when independence was on his mind, but in a way that is much more psychological than before. He needs to become an intellectually and emotionally separate person from you, one with his own beliefs, values, and opinions. Your role is to help him become more of an individual without severing your relationship with him. (While the whole point of emotional development at this stage is for your tween to not feel dependent on you, you play a huge role in helping this independence to develop.)

Teenager: *How can I help my teenager understand himself or herself better?* Around fifteen or sixteen, kids start to think more deeply about who they are and where they are headed. In many of the same ways that the emotional needs of toddlers (feeling in charge) give rise to the emotional needs of preschoolers (feeling grown up), the emotional needs of young adolescents (*being* in charge) give rise to the emotional needs of older teenagers (*being* grown up). Your role is to help your teenager figure out what kind of person she is and what kind of person she wants to become.

ADOPT A GROWTH MIND-SET

Teaching is a marathon, and like all marathons, there will be good miles and bad miles. It's essential that you develop a sense of optimism and hope that keep you moving forward. The key lies in adopting an inherent belief in both your own and your kid's capacity to learn and grow.

Psychologist Carol Dweck of Stanford University is best known for her research on human mind-set. She discovered that children and adults think about success in one of two ways:

A *"fixed mind-set"* assumes that our character, intelligence, and creative abilities are static givens that we can't change in any meaningful way, no matter how hard we try.

A *"growth mind-set,"* on the other hand, is based on the belief that basic qualities are things you can cultivate through your efforts. Success and failure are not personalized but rather are tied to effort, with the belief

that challenges are simply a springboard for growth
and expanding existing abilities.

Kids and adults with a growth mind-set go farther in
life, regardless of their IQ, innate talents, or life circumstances,
because they believe in their ability to grow and don't personalize failure or success. They attribute both to effort—and feel
in control of that drive.

Adopting a growth mind-set helps parents create and
contain the time to teach. It creates optimism, reduces stress
and pressure, and allows a parent to take the learning process
in stride, accepting a child (and their momentary failings) not
as a reflection of the child (or parent) but as a reflection of
knowledge and effort. It also allows a parent to be more forgiving of themselves as they bumble through the journey of
parenting and to develop a parenting philosophy that inspires
confidence and helps their child fulfill her true potential.
(Recall from the previous chapter that your job is not to solve
your children's problems, but to help them become super
problem-solvers.)

The old cliché that "kids teach us as much as we teach
them" happens to be true. Our children can inspire us to bang
out our own dents, so that we can better lead by example.
That's the primary way we teach our children—through role
modeling and investing the time in practicing the behaviors
we want our kids to emulate (without turning every second
into one of Jamari's teachable moments). It's not by what we
say but how we act.

And, as we'll discuss in the next part of this book, how
you act is particularly important when it comes to taking care
of yourself. Do you set a good example for your children

when it comes to getting enough sleep, maintaining your relationships, exercising, and making space for joy? Those self-nurturing activities, which ensure you maintain a sense of self, are equally important to the task of raising a human being.

PART IV

BEING A HUMAN BEING:
FUELING YOUR S.E.L.F.

11

SLEEP

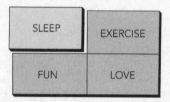

My client Rob complained that he felt dull, slow-witted, tired, impatient, and permanently stuck in a bad mood. A married dad with two girls in the throes of adolescence, life at home had gotten pretty intense. He and his wife were doing their best to console and guide their kids through traumatic social slights, school anxiety, and almost daily battles over rules and independence.

All that stress was on top of normal demands in his professional life. A lawyer with his own practice, Rob's days (and some evenings) were packed with client work and courting new business. During our initial session, I asked him (as I ask every new client) about the structure of his day, including sleep. He revealed that he was only getting about four to five hours a night on average. Why? The only time he had for himself was after everyone else went to bed, he explained. And after a long day, he relied on binge watching TV series (punctuated by trips to the fridge for sugary snacks) to decompress.

A large number of the parents I coach fall into this trap—staying up way too late because it's the only time of day they feel they can take for themselves, since no one needs anything from them at that point. While the impulse for time for oneself is healthy, this particular method usually backfires as lack of sleep takes its toll. The solution is to integrate more self-time moments throughout the day, so that you get rejuvenated in a variety of healthy ways during waking hours.

Rob doubted his ability to change his habits, but, after a little coaxing, he agreed to adjust his bedtime and build in more moments to recharge throughout the day. Rob was a runner, so he understood the concept of periodic refueling, comparing it to water stations and gel packets on a long-distance run. Instead of leaving late night as his only "me time," Rob began refueling in small ways throughout the day: he started swimming a couple of mornings a week, actually stopped working to eat a healthy lunch, and left his office to get fresh air and sunshine on a mid-afternoon walk. It worked. As to breaking a long-standing habit of flipping on the TV instead of heading to bed at a reasonable hour, he discovered that the trick was getting in bed before midnight (which prevented him from getting a second wind).

After about six weeks of trial and error, Rob built himself up to a fairly consistent seven hours per night. Was every night perfect? Of course not. But the positive benefits of daytime rest and more sleep each night were immediate and profound.

He discovered a counterintuitive truth: when you are sleep-deprived, you waste time all day long. Most likely, you *do* actually have the time to sleep . . . it's just being stolen away by seemingly simple tasks that take four times longer when you're fatigued: making a shopping list, editing a paragraph, or writing a thank-you note takes longer when you are functioning in slow motion.

It's time to talk about the other major component of raising a human being: *being* a human being. In this section of the book, we'll explore the four areas where parents need to spend time to build and sustain a consistent practice of self-care.

Just as your child's overall well-being is a priority, yours is, too. However, parenthood has a way of eclipsing our better judgment about self-care in favor of self-sacrifice. Just as the four quadrants in "Doing Your P.A.R.T." were equally important, so, too, are the quadrants in S.E.L.F. When we get enough rest and exercise, when we take time to strengthen our relationships with others and stay connected to the hobbies and activities that fuel us, we are happier, more fulfilled, and better able to give our kids the time and attention they need and deserve.

IN OUR PARENT TIME SURVEY
MOST PARENTS AREN'T GETTING ENOUGH SLEEP

A total of 66% of parents reported getting too little sleep.
Some 34% said they got the right amount.

BETTER SLEEP MAKES FOR
BETTER PARENTS

It's been well-established that the amount and quality of rest you get influences your state of being. Study after study cited by the American Psychological Association show that adequate sleep boosts mental function, patience, productivity, and happiness across the board.

And yet, the American Academy of Sleep Medicine

(AASM) says that fifty to seventy million American adults suffer from a sleep disorder, and the Centers for Disease Control and Prevention has proclaimed insufficient sleep a public health problem. According to Gallup, 46 percent of adults with children under the age of eighteen sleep less than six hours per night. Clearly, that's not enough.

It's no joke. According to studies both conducted and reported by the AASM, lack of adequate sleep can lead to:

Weight gain: Too little sleep causes the body to crave fast-burning carbohydrates and sweets that can lead to weight gain. If you're relying on "quick fix" foods, your kids are probably eating the same things. One study reports that kids of parents who get less than five hours of sleep were 1.3 times more likely to be overweight.

Clinical depression: Research has shown that averaging less than six hours of sleep per night increases the risk for major depression, which in turn can syphon energy and interest away from spending quality time with our families.

Lower wages: In a 2015 study, researchers discovered that a one-hour increase in average weekly sleep increased wages by 1.55 percent in the short run and by 4.9 percent in the long run.

More sick days and colds: A University of California–San Francisco study found that people who sleep six hours a night or less are four times more likely to catch a cold than those who sleep more than seven hours a night. People who slept less than five (or more than ten) hours per night took 4.6 to 8.9 more sick days than those who kept to the optimal sleep length. As anyone can attest, sick days are not very conducive to quality time for our kids or for ourselves.

Poor judgment: Sleep deprivation can have similar cognitive and physiological effects to being intoxicated, not a safe state to be in while caring for kids. According to a study conducted by the School of Psychology at the University of New South Wales and published in *Occupational and Environmental Health Medicine*, chronic lack of sleep can produce effects similar to that of alcohol consumption, with decision-making, reaction times, and general awareness all suffering significantly.

Short tempers: For long stretches of parenthood, parents suffer from interrupted sleep when they aren't able to get more than two to four hours at a time, which a study published in the journal *Sleep Medicine* showed can be as physically detrimental as no sleep at all. These effects accumulate, leading parents to develop feelings of anger toward their kids and then guilt about these negative feelings. How many times have you heard a parent complain, "This kid is trying to kill me!"

You may think you can be more productive by burning the midnight oil, and for a short time, you can be. But over the long run, it's a recipe for exhaustion, irritability, and even cognitive impairment. At a basic cellular level, our bodies require sleep—to rejuvenate our skin, muscles, joints, and brains.

I probably don't need to convince you of the need to get enough sleep—I'm sure you already wish you could have more shut-eye. What you do need is a practical approach to getting the sleep you need, more often than not, as well as the ability to recover when life, and parenthood, derail a full night's rest.

No matter your child's age and stage, prioritizing sleep will help you model healthy sleep habits for your kids and be a better parent.

BECOME A SLEEP NINJA

The solutions to sleep problems as a parent don't come easily because parenthood forever alters your relationship to sleep: From those early, hazy days as the parent of a newborn, to waiting up for a teenager after curfew, it is guaranteed that your sleep will be interrupted. It's as certain as death and taxes.

It is unrealistic to claim that I have a solution to ensure all the sleep you need, all of the time.

But there are ways to tweak your mind-set, habits, and schedule so that you become a "sleep ninja"—meaning you are a master at getting the sleep you need and also employ strategies for recovery when your sleep is significantly compromised, to boost your ability to be patient and present.

If we see sleep as a responsibility we must find time for, we are more likely to carve out the space for it. Unlike other tasks, when you are sleeping, you may think you're not actively doing anything—but no! You *are* restoring your body and mind in a way that no other activity can.

When you aren't getting the rest you need to be at your best, you need a practical plan of attack. The goal is to make getting more sleep as simple and systematic as possible, by targeting a handful of extremely common problem areas that affect parents' ability to get shut-eye. (If you suspect you have a more serious sleep problem, such as snoring, sleep apnea, or extreme insomnia, talk to your doctor and see a sleep specialist.)

Below are five concrete touch points that you can examine to build healthy sleep habits, no matter what the age and stage of your children. Though you may only need to make one or two adjustments at any given time, come back to this list every time you get off track, to keep pace with your changing needs throughout the child-rearing years.

1. Adjust your sleep schedule.
2. Renovate your bedtime routine.
3. Surrender to sleep.
4. Recover when sleep-deprived.
5. Synchronize your sleep with your kids' schedules.

1. Adjust Your Sleep Schedule

The sleep-deprived among us must create and stick with a sleep schedule. Consistency is the most important thing when you are on a mission to reset the internal biological sleep clock known as the *circadian rhythm*. Going to sleep and rising at the same time every day—weekends too!—will take hold, usually within four to six weeks. Rob found that after six weeks of forcing himself to adhere to his new sleep schedule, he got tired around the same time every evening and naturally woke up at the same time each morning.

Change your mind-set. Here's an interesting question I ask clients who stay up too late. Do you think of sleep as the *end* of one day or the *beginning* of the next? People who think of sleep as the "end" of the day often have trouble letting go at night—like the kid who refuses to leave a party for fear of missing out. Try flipping your thinking—when you view sleep as the *start* of your next day, you feel excited to charge up your batteries and fill your fuel tank for the next day's adventures.

Determine how much sleep is enough. The first step to ensuring you get enough sleep is to determine how much you need. We all have one friend who is high functioning on little sleep and another who could nap anytime and is adamant about getting their eight hours a night. Pinpoint what's right for you:

- **Aim for seven to nine hours a night.** Every individual needs a different amount of uninterrupted sleep per night to feel well rested the next day. But every source I've come across, including the National Institutes of Health (NIH), agrees that the magic number for the average adult falls between seven and nine hours. The science is clear that under seven hours of sleep is unhealthy. When healthy adults are given an unlimited opportunity to sleep, they average between eight and eight-and-a-half hours a night.

- **Count backward from your desired wake time.** The simplest back-of-the-envelope way to pinpoint your ideal bedtime is to count backward in ninety-minute increments from your desired wake-up time. If you've read anything on the science of sleep, you may have heard about the different stages of sleep, including deep REM (rapid eye movement) sleep. An average full sleep cycle is ninety minutes—and a healthy night of sleep is five or six cycles. (Five cycles is seven-and-a-half hours; six cycles is nine hours.) Say you have to wake up at 6:15 a.m. and want to get at least five cycles. Counting backward—your goal is to be in bed, ready to sleep, by

10:45 p.m. Dr. Michael Breus, a sleep doctor, says the goal should be to wake up, naturally, five to ten minutes before your alarm goes off. If you find yourself waking up significantly earlier, shift your bedtime to a bit later (and vice versa, if you are sleeping through your alarm). Try tinkering with your bedtime in fifteen-minute increments (earlier and later) until you get it right.

- **Leverage sleep-cycle math when you are in a pinch.** Parents' sleep does not always go the way they want it to. We know this. On nights where things don't go as planned, and you simply *have* to get by on significantly less than your ideal, you can still take control of how rested you feel upon waking up with a simple calculation. Let's say your kid wakes you up at 1:00 a.m. with a nightmare, and by the time you settle her back down, it's 1:30 a.m. You still have to get up at 6:15 a.m. Calculating back from 6:15 a.m. in ninety-minute intervals reveals that if you stay up a little longer—and get back to sleep at 1:45—you will get a full four cycles. Waking up between cycles, rather than in the middle of a sleep cycle, will leave you more refreshed. And if you're just too groggy for math in the middle of the night (it happens!), a handy website called sleepyti.me will do the calculations for you. Check it out—it's my favorite hack.

Add something fun to wake up to. It can be hard to let go of the day, but more enticing if you project yourself forward to the next day. Reward yourself for the effort of getting enough sleep by injecting something pleasurable in your newfound morning time. Relish the first half hour (before your kids wake up) to savor a cup of coffee or dedicate the extra calm in the morning to some true quality time—over breakfast, playing a game, or chatting while you help your kids get ready. Choose something rewarding, delicious, and wonderful.

Adjusting your sleep schedule can be a slow and uncomfortable process. Start by applying even one of these tactics for an entire week. You'll probably be tired for a few days—but if you hang in there and stick to the plan, it will pay off.

2. Renovate Your Bedtime Routine

It takes the average person fourteen minutes to fall asleep once the lights are out. A forty-five-minute bedtime routine would mean thirty minutes of relaxing activities before you turn the lights out.

Establish a soothing routine with sensory indicators that cue your body that it's time to sleep. Many people gravitate toward mindless activities in an effort to unwind. Like Rob, they turn to TV, go on the Internet, and consume mindless snacks. And too many parents—moms especially—spend the evening puttering around the house doing chores, thinking that will help them relax. For most people, those activities don't actually unwind you.

Know the difference between an "evening routine" and a "bedtime routine." The website Baby Sleep Science, one of the most useful and practical sources I've found for help with sleep challenges, offers insights for getting your kids to sleep that apply equally well to adults. The site distinguishes between an "evening routine"—what you do to relax at night in general, which can be flexible and varied (sometimes a movie, sometimes playing evening games with your kids, etc.)—and a "bedtime routine," which is the series of specific activities you do between the end of your evening routine and getting yourself into bed, ready to fall asleep. *The bedtime routine should be the exact same steps every night, in the same order.* Begin the ritual at the same time every night and aim for forty-five minutes to one hour before you want to be asleep.

Choose three or four soothing activities and sequence them. Train your mind to make a habit of rest, by making subtle changes to the things you do before bed to give your body and mind the cues it needs to easily drift off to la-la land. Three or four simple and engaging activities will do the trick. Here are a few ideas to get you started:

- **Unplug.** Set an alarm to go off at least sixty minutes before bed, cuing you to shut down all devices. No more email, social media, online shopping, or cat videos. While we often turn to screens to unwind, research shows that the light they emit actually stirs us up. Cover all electronics in your bedroom (alarm clocks, laptops, cable boxes, etc.). One study by researchers at Harvard Medical School found that it took people who read an e-book on an iPad, rather than a printed-on-paper book or Kindle, at least ten minutes longer to fall asleep.
- **Turn down the lights.** Any sensory trigger that shifts the environment can announce to every cell in your body and mind, "We are entering wind-down mode." Dim the lights, put on some mellow music, light candles, or use an aromatherapy diffuser, which sends scent signals that it's time to chill out.

- **Do something creative and absorbing.** Activities such as playing guitar, drawing, or knitting are productive forms of expression that help relax and refocus the mind on something other than your work-a-day worries.
- **Stretch and move your body.** A walk after dinner, sitting on your back porch after the kids fall asleep (with the monitor nearby if they are young), or doing yoga or deep stretches can help to relax the body and work out the kinks from the day.
- **Relax with food or drink.** Enjoy a cup of tea, some warm milk with cinnamon, or a healthy snack. Rather than mindlessly consuming the treat while watching TV, savor the taste.
- **Connect with a loved one.** Spend focused time with another adult—connect to your partner, friend, or relative on the phone or Skype to talk about your day. Connecting to other adults—the topic of chapter 13—can nourish your soul.
- **Put on your pj's.** Some people start their evening ritual by bathing, grooming, putting on their pj's or loungewear, and brushing their teeth; others save this self-care for right before getting into bed. The purpose is to relax, cool off, and tell your body it's time for sleep. The NIH actually recommends bathing before bed because it helps your body temperature cool down, relaxes you, and makes you feel more ready to sleep.
- **Put the house to bed.** Walk around the house locking the doors, turning off lights, and closing shades. Straighten the sofa pillows and bookshelves. Prep for tomorrow by laying out your clothes for the next day and setting up the baby bag, backpacks, after-school gear, and briefcase by the front door.

- **Put a bow on the day.** Reflect on the day through prayer or journaling. Think about what you learned and what you are grateful for. Get centered and focus on the accomplishments. If you feel upset with yourself, forgive yourself and feel grateful for recognizing an opportunity for growth.
- **Give yourself a bedtime story.** Reading can be relaxing—but gravitate toward novels, short stories, poetry, or something peaceful that transports you. The news, business, or how-to books are often too stimulating and intellectually demanding to be conducive to sleep. If you prefer to listen to audiobooks, set the timer in your preferred app (such as Audible) to fifteen or twenty minutes, so it doesn't continue all night long.

3. Surrender to Sleep

So you finally made it to bed, the kids are asleep, you've done your own routine, and you've turned off the lights. You're exhausted, but your mind won't stop racing. How do you actually release into a deep sleep, so you get the full pleasure and benefit of a restful night?

Here are ways to clear your head and surrender yourself to the pleasures of sleep:

Unburden your memory. Are you lying awake cycling through your to-do list? Is your mind brimming with ideas for a big project or things you need to remember? One of the best sleep aids for overloaded parents is a single, reliable notebook system that you use to capture every thought, task, and idea all day long. If you trust your system, it relieves your brain of the burden of having to remember things—and makes it much easier to go to sleep at night, knowing everything is accounted for. If keeping that notebook by your bedside comforts you and allows you to write down thoughts that float through your mind, do that. But be careful. For many people, the "bedside notebook" can act as an *enabler*—a bad influence that sends your mind a message that it's okay to *never* shut down.

Use essential oils. Aromatherapy really works. Lisa, a mom of three, has a soothing evening ritual that helps her unwind after putting the kids to bed. During her evening shower, she fills a pitcher with warm water, adds a few drops of lavender oil, and pours it over her head, like a rainfall of warm lavender oil. (If lavender oil doesn't appeal to you, jasmine oil is also known to be conducive to sleep.) Enhance the experience by spritzing your pillow or using a bedside diffuser.

Think about relaxing imagery. There are a variety of clever ways to "trick" or lull yourself to actually go off to dreamland. Here are a few:

- **Imagine yourself falling.** Not the kind of tripping down stairs that jolts you awake. While lying down, with your eyes closed, just picture yourself actually falling backward, perhaps through the sky, on your back. It's amazing how you actually "fall" asleep. I read about this technique years ago and have been using it ever since.
- **Imagine breathing out to the ends of the universe** and breathing in from there back into your body. Mindfulness and meditation expert Jon Kabat-Zinn suggests following the breath as it moves in and out of the body and feeling yourself sink deeper and deeper into the mattress, descending farther with each breath.

- **Imagine being massaged by a swirling cocoon of light.** Author Brian Weiss recommends imagining a light, in whatever color it occurs, spiraling around your body. It starts at the top of your head and travels down to your toes with each inhale, and back up to your head with each exhale—like a full body massage of light.

Make your bedroom incredibly inviting. Evaluate your bedroom to make sure it is a comfortable and conducive place to relax and fall asleep. Here are a few small changes that make a big difference:

- **Invest in a comfortable bed.** You spend a lot of hours here, so invest in the best-quality mattress you can afford and keep it in good condition by rotating it regularly. An egg-crate foam–topper for your mattress can upgrade the comfort quality of even an inexpensive bed.
- **Memorize the difference between percale and sateen.** Get the highest-quality sheets and pillows you can afford. Buying sheets can be a dizzying experience—thread counts, country of origin, fabrics—but there's one thing worth memorizing: the difference between sateen and percale. These terms refer to the kind of weave. Both feel luxurious to the skin, but percale creates sheets that are cool to the skin, while sateen is warmer, cozier. Know which you prefer, and hopefully your bedmate agrees!
- **Get the air temperature right.** Experts say a cool sixty-three degrees is optimal for sleep. Open the window or turn up the AC to get as close as you can to that ideal. Moving air—care of a fan—also helps many people sleep better.
- **Use white noise.** Of course, parents need to keep an ear out for their little ones—and may have the monitor on—but the quiet, soft sounds of a waterfall, rain falling, or

calming white noise and moving air can make sleep come and stay more easily.

- **Don't do office work in your bedroom.** I subscribe to the belief that the bedroom should be associated with sleep, relaxation, sex, and getting dressed. Nothing else. Make sure your bedroom is a sanctuary: a refuge from the outside world. Same goes for keeping kids' stuff out of the bedroom. Piling it up with toys, games, and clutter can make it very hard to turn off and go to sleep.

4. Recover When Sleep-Deprived

There is no perfect system to getting the perfect night's sleep, and there will *always* be some sleepless nights, especially as a parent. So if sleep deprivation is an unavoidable part of a parent's reality, learning to recover and keep yourself going to make up for lost z's is an essential concept.

Combat the temptation to indulge in caffeine or sugary foods. Though artificial energy may seem like your only hope to get through the day, sugar and caffeine will only make it harder to fall asleep. Opt, instead, for healthier forms of quick energy. You probably know the basics already: splashing cold water on your face, doing jumping jacks, going for a walk outside, pausing for a quick dance party. Here are a few techniques you maybe haven't tried to help you regroup:

Tap your thymus. "Your thymus is located at the center top of your chest, below the collarbone, between your breasts. When tapped, it triggers the production of T-cells that boost energy, relieve stress, and increase strength and vitality," says Marian Buck-Murray, a nutrition coach and Emotional Freedom

Techniques (EFT) practitioner in Maplewood, New Jersey. For an instant boost of energy, Buck-Murray recommends tapping your thymus with your fingertips for twenty seconds while taking slow, deep breaths in and out.

Drink (cold) water. Whether trying to rouse yourself after a sleepless night or beat sluggishness during the day, dehydration is a major cause of fatigue and is only compounded by sleep deprivation. So stay hydrated. And throw in a few ice cubes. "Unlike warm drinks, which tend to relax you, cold beverages can increase alertness," says Janet Kennedy, PhD, a New York City–based clinical psychologist who specializes in sleep disorders.

Discover your favorite yoga poses. I'm not suggesting you do downward facing dog in the middle of your conference room. I'm thinking of quiet, unobtrusive moves that can be done anywhere. Gravity poses, in particular—when your back sinks into the earth and your legs enjoy the benefits of the full force of gravity—are especially energizing and relaxing, especially in times of stress.

Nap smart. My client Sara, an executive, confessed her desire to shut her office door and take naps during the workday—but she lives in fear that a colleague might walk in while she's dozing and think she's slacking off. Yet, the science proves that napping boosts productivity: naps are healthy and make you more effective. Dr. Damien Léger, who runs the sleep-research center at the Hôtel-Dieu hospital in Paris, says sleep is not a luxury, it's a right—and he's on a mission to destigmatize workplace napping. He even recommends napping rooms in workplaces. (Wouldn't that be nice!) The key to productive napping is to know how long to nap for. Dr. Léger, and the NIH, say twenty minutes is the ideal maximum, to prevent you from waking up groggy and disoriented.

How to Rest in Twenty Minutes or Less

So many parents worry that if they take a break, they might crash—permanently. Take Victoria, a mother of three, who somehow always managed to have everything in tip-top shape: never late, everyone dressed, school forms filled out on time, and so on. She told me the only way she makes it happen is by being in constant motion from the time she wakes up until she falls facedown on her pillow (and sometimes in her soup). "I can't stop to rest," she told me. "If I did, I'd never be able to get myself going again."

I get the sentiment, but I don't buy it—and neither does the research. To go the distance, it helps to take short breaks throughout the day. These little bursts of rest constituted some of the "me-time" Rob took to fuel his energy all day long.

My quest for recovery tools for sleep-deprived parents led me to the revolutionary work of Dr. Matthew Edlund, now known by many as "the Rest Doctor." What most amazes me about Edlund's methodology is the idea that rest is not only to be used as a rescue valve for lack of sleep but as an essential element to be built into the cadence and rhythm of every day for peak performance.

Edlund first became intrigued with sleep and sleep deprivation during his time as a medical resident. As he learned more about the science of sleep, he discovered that rest was as important, if not more important, than nighttime sleep. Rest is not a waste of time but a biological need—a process for restoration and rebuilding. It has tremendous power to restore our cells, alertness, and ability to be conscious and engaged. Most interestingly, he's made the case for why "active" rest (directed, conscious forms of rest) is better than "passive" rest (lying on the couch watching TV, scrolling through your Twitter and Facebook feeds, etc.).

In Edlund's book, *The Power of Rest*, he suggests four types of rest to revive and restore your energy. He recommends weaving one-to-three-minute periods of rest into your day based on a framework of cycles he's dubbed FAR (food, activity, rest). Stop to think about that for a minute. By cycling your day between food (e.g., breakfast), then activity (e.g., walk kids to school or write a report), then rest (e.g., one-to-three-minute pauses, as described below), you will steadily fuel your performance all day long so you can be present for each thing you do. I like his FAR framework better than what we tend to do, what I am going to call FAEF (food, activity, exhaustion, more food), which doesn't even sound good. Here are Edlund's four types of "active" rest that truly rejuvenate you in one to three minutes each.

- **Physical rest:** A proven way to improve mental alertness, motor skills, and mood is to give your muscles and mind a chance to relax. Take a moment to just sit (or lie on the grass, or on the sofa). It's recharging just to be still, even if you can't sleep. Edlund says naps as short as six minutes are beneficial.

- **Mental rest:** If you have been focusing on something for a long time, combat mental fatigue by shifting your focus. Whether you are overthinking a parenting problem and can't figure out what to do, or rereading the same paragraph at work without absorbing it, give your brain a brief respite. If you are at the office, look at a sedentary living thing (plant or desk flower) or an image you like for twenty to thirty seconds. Consciously shifting your attention for a short period has been shown to improve focus and positively impact blood pressure, heart rate, and body temperature.

- **Social rest:** Humans seem to have an instinct for this, knowing that human contact, even for an introvert, can be energizing. It's why people tend to congregate at the water cooler or chat with neighbors on the front stoop. Taking a conscious break to chat for just a couple of minutes has proven to be an extremely effective shot in the arm: it can reduce stress and provide hormonal and psychological benefits.

- **Spiritual rest:** Brain scans have shown that people who meditate or pray are able to physically expand their brains' frontal lobes, the section that controls concentration, attention, focus, and problem analysis. While longer chunks of meditation and prayer (twenty-plus minutes) may be a more common recommendation by hard-core enthusiasts, Edlund says that taking even one minute to pray, meditate, or imagine something existential—like moving through time and space—can calm and recharge.

And as a parent, learning how to inject "active" rest into your schedule is a game changer. Power naps, along with the one-to-three-minute activities Edlund recommends, help to restore, rebuild, and rewire your body and mind. Active rest keeps you conscious and attentive to what's going on around you and lets you have fun doing ordinary things. Best of all, these relatively tiny rest stops (seriously: maximum of twenty minutes!) won't break your momentum—they will just make you powerful and more present in each thing you do.

5. Synchronize Your Sleep with Your Kids' Schedules

I started out this chapter saying that as a parent, you need to become a sleep ninja, because as long as your kids are living at home, your sleep schedule is not something you can always control. The sooner you accept that—and find ways to get the sleep you need anyway—the better off everyone will be.

That said, we all know if your kids aren't sleeping well, you aren't, either. And kids' sleep schedules are dynamic. They are ever-evolving, as they go from sleeping around the clock in short intervals in infancy, through the teenage years, when changing hormones and biorhythms literally beckon them to stay up well past midnight.

If you want good sleep as a parent, you have to flex your own sleep schedule around your kids' changing cycles. This means you can't always sleep on the schedule you want (or got used to), but you can always be strategic and committed to getting the rest you need. By coordinating your sleep schedule with your kids', you have the best chance of everyone getting the rest they need.

If you look at the national scientific sleep recommendations by age, you will see that if you're able to get your kids to sleep enough, you'll have ample hours for adult self-time after your kids are in bed and get a full night's rest, too. I know, I know: it's never as easy as it "should" be. Kids struggle with sleep issues, bedtimes vary when you have more than one child, and depending on your job, your own work hours may require you to go to sleep or wake up much earlier than your kids. And let's acknowledge that more than 90 percent of adolescent children don't get the recommended amount of sleep on school nights (most adolescents get 6 to 7 hours of sleep, although they really need 9.25 hours—and bedtimes between ten and eleven p.m. have been correlated with higher GPAs, according to new research published in the *Journal of Sleep Research*).

There are hundreds, if not thousands, of books in print that advise parents how to get their kids to sleep. I couldn't begin to do justice to the knowledge out there in that department. But I can advise you—from a time-management perspective—that the first goal is to organize your family's schedule and routines around making sure everyone gets a good night's rest.

For example, if your toddler goes to sleep at eight p.m., you might aim to start a calming routine for yourself at nine thirty, with the goal of being in bed, with the lights out, by ten p.m. One dad, knowing his twelve- and fourteen-year-old would be up until one a.m. if they could, took it upon himself to create an "Internet off switch" that he could control from his smartphone. Every night at ten he turned the Wi-Fi off, and they all began their wind-down routines. The result? The kids began to do their homework much more efficiently, and the whole family settled into a consistent sleep routine.

Knowing how much sleep your child needs to be healthy and alert empowers you to structure your own sleep routine accordingly, whether it's accommodating an infant, who naps three times a day; or a toddler, who needs an afternoon nap (to avoid morphing into the Incredible Hulk at five o'clock); or your teenager, whose evolving circadian rhythms drive him to go to bed later and wake up later.

It's important to remember that all of these stages are temporary. While you might not get the sleep you need one week, things may settle down the next week before they change again. No sleep cycle lasts forever.

SCIENCE OF SLEEP: Sleep requirement by age	
Age	Recommended Amount of Sleep
Infants aged 4–12 months	12–16 hours per 24 hours (including naps) Ideal bedtime: 6:00–7:30 p.m. Average wake time: 2–4 hours
Children aged 1–2 years	11–14 hours per 24 hours (including naps) Ideal bedtime: 6:00–8:00 p.m. Average wake time: 5 hours
Children aged 3–5 years	10–13 hours per 24 hours (including naps) Ideal bedtime: 7:00–8:30 p.m. Average wake time: 12 hours
Children aged 6–12 years	9–12 hours per 24 hours Ideal bedtime: 7:30–9:00 p.m. Average wake time: 12 hours
Teens aged 13–18 years	8–10 hours per 24 hours Ideal bedtime: 10:00–11:00 p.m. Average wake time: 12 hours
Adults aged 18 years or older	7–9 hours per 24 hours

This table reflects recent American Academy of Sleep Medicine (AASM) recommendations that the American Academy of Pediatrics (AAP) has endorsed. The Baby Sleep Science website has even more detail about average nap and wake times for babies and toddlers.

MAKE SURE SLEEP IS NOT YOUR ONLY FORM OF SELF-CARE

Many parents struggle with staying up too late for the same reason Rob did: those late-night hours can feel like the *only* time of day to indulge in "me time." But don't fall victim to that thinking. The time you should be sleeping is *not* the only time for you.

By allocating time for other kinds of self-care—as we'll discuss in the next several chapters—your time allotted for sleep becomes established and sacrosanct, a real energy booster. Just the way it should be.

12

EXERCISE

My client Cicely was a single mother with a four-year-old son. Although she'd always been committed to fitness, enjoying spinning and yoga classes several times per week, she told me she had found it almost impossible to fit regular exercise into her schedule since her son was born.

Cicely missed yoga especially, which she found to be a different kind of stress relief. Lately, she'd been using vacation time to take a Monday afternoon yoga class with a friend and found it had made an enormous difference. "I could feel its effects throughout the week," she told me. "I actually had more breathing room, I stopped thinking about my to-do list, and I've had more little quality moments with my son."

Given how much she loved her yoga practice, I asked if she'd ever tried yoga from home. Cicely said she had, but that without the change in environment, it didn't give her the same sense of relaxation.

I suggested she set up a space in her home that could be just hers, and just for yoga. I also posited that yoga didn't have to be something she did for ninety minutes at a pop. Why not make it a bit more achievable on a regular basis? Perhaps a class once a week, supplemented by ten minutes every morning (a reasonable duration, given her active and curious four-year-old). That thought—adjusting the duration of exercise—had never crossed her mind.

I checked in with Cicely about two months after we first met. She was a woman transformed. She was doing yoga every day at home for ten minutes and going to a yoga class once a week (and not using vacation time to do it!). Once she'd built yoga back into her life, she felt like she was being a better professional and mom. An attorney, she was calmer, was able to think more clearly, and was so much more productive that she was able to take a lunchtime yoga class.

Cicely never put pressure on her son to join her yoga routines, but he often ambled over to join her, because doing his imperfect downward facing dogs was fun. It was quality time together that they both enjoyed. This was the biggest lesson Cicely learned. A combination approach worked for her—one yoga class a week, plus regular practice in a beautiful dedicated space in her home.

Her breakthrough came from breaking her all-or-nothing thinking and realizing the power of small chunks of time, done consistently.

IN OUR PARENT TIME SURVEY
MOST PARENTS AREN'T GETTING ENOUGH EXERCISE

18% of parents reported almost never exercising.
31% only get to exercise once in a while.

For many working parents, it can be hard to justify paying a babysitter so you can sweat. (It goes part and parcel with the "put everyone else first" attitude that also leads parents to neglect doctor visits and other commitments that are essential to good health.)

If you have any extra time, you may feel compelled to work more hours rather than taking time for your own fitness. According to a recent WebMD survey, 42 percent of parents are more concerned with their children's financial security than with their own levels of physical activity.

Whether you were an athlete or a reluctant gym-goer before you had kids, the only way you're going to find time to exercise is to believe that it's important and to commit to carving out the time for it.

REGULAR EXERCISE HELPS YOU BE A MORE PRESENT PARENT

A regular exercise regime benefits your kids in a gazillion ways—giving you energy, perspective, stamina, and joy. More than anything, exercise makes you feel good about yourself. When you move your body, no matter what else is going on, you've succeeded in making time to do something for yourself that gives you the fuel you need to nurture your kids and take care of everyone else.

The Mayo Clinic says exercise helps you be there for your kids in at least six ways:

1. **Controls weight.** When we are fit, and feel good, we have more energy to run around with our kids.
2. **Combats health conditions, depression, and disease.** This ensures, in the most fundamental way, that we are there for our kids.
3. **Improves mood.** Physical activity stimulates brain chem-

icals that leave you feeling happier and more relaxed, giving you more resilience for dealing with children.

4. **Boosts energy.** Regular exercise improves muscle strength and endurance by delivering oxygen and nutrients to your tissues and helping your cardiovascular system work more efficiently.

5. **Promotes better sleep.** As we know, sleep is the nectar of the gods to parents, who often struggle to get enough z's.

6. **Puts the spark back into your sex life.** Regular exercise may enhance arousal for women, and men who exercise regularly are less likely to have problems with erectile dysfunction.

What's more, there is a clear correlation between your exercise habits and your kids' lifelong exercise habits: studies find that parents' commitment to exercise is a strong predictor of kids adopting those same habits. According to the President's Council on Fitness, Sports, and Nutrition, only one in three children are physically active every day, and 12.5 million children and adolescents are classified as obese. Three out of four children ages five to ten get less than an hour of physical activity a day! When you exercise, you *are* taking care of your kids by setting an example of fitness and self-care.

REDEFINE WHAT IT MEANS TO EXERCISE

I once had a conversation with a stranger on a plane that was the greatest gift to my own attitude about exercise. As we flew from New York to Los Angeles, we chatted away, and when the topic of exercise came up, I confessed how much I hated working out. We were gossiping like old friends by that point and I expected her to commiserate. Her response took me totally by surprise. "Oh, I *love* exercise," she said. "Exercise gives me a chance to marvel at how my muscles work." Whoa. I'd never thought of it that way. That one mind-set shift permanently changed my perspective. Twenty years later, anytime I'm feeling lazy or unmotivated to go to the pool, or a Pilates class, or out for a walk, I conjure that image and get up and go, excited at the opportunity to marvel at my muscles in motion.

What if you viewed each exercise session, short or long, solo or with your kids or family or friends, as an opportunity to enjoy being in your body, no matter which type of activity you choose to do or with whom you choose to do it?

Many people think exercise means three times a week, out of the house, at the gym or a class. And it can be difficult to break out of that notion—even if it's a healthy one! As a parent, you may have adopted an all-or-nothing mentality: you know it's impossible to exercise as much as (or in the way) you once did, so you stop. My client Alyssa, the mother of a two-year-old, struggled with weight and exercise for years. Prior to having a baby, she developed a healthy eating and exercise routine and lost forty pounds. Once she became a mom and her gym sessions became sporadic at best, she didn't enjoy working out anymore because she felt defeated before she began. What was the point of even trying, she wondered, if she never knew when she wouldn't make it back to the gym for a month? She felt frustrated at no longer being able to control her workout schedule.

Here's the big idea: Exercise doesn't have to happen for an hour each time you do it. It doesn't have to happen at a gym. It doesn't even have to happen every single day. It's time to expand your definition of exercise. And if you used to play basketball, or tennis, or endurance sports (like running marathons or cycling) that require large chunks of time to do, it's time to change your approach.

Small bits of time can make a huge difference and can fit into your life in multiple ways. Below are some of the quickest workouts that yield the biggest results.

High-Intensity Interval Training (a.k.a. HIIT)

Interval training is popular because it trades duration for intensity. According to research, shorter can be better. "The return on investment of interval training is fabulous, and it keeps exercise interesting," says Richard Cotton, the national director of certification and registry programs at the American College of Sports Medicine. "Even walkers can incorporate interval training by walking for three minutes and jogging for one minute and repeating that pattern for thirty minutes." Studies have shown that interval training can help people burn more fat and increase fitness levels even after just fifteen to twenty minutes of exercise. CrossFit groups offer access to Workout of the Day (WOD) ideas and videos, which usually take only twelve to fifteen minutes to complete.

I spoke with Dr. Geoffrey Colon, a professor at the School of Health Promotion and Human Performance at Eastern Michigan University. He's a huge advocate of HIIT for parents because it gets the blood flowing and the muscles pumping in a short amount of time. According to Colon, you can convert any form of exercise into HIIT by alternating patterns as you work out. For example, walk, then sprint. In the pool, do a few easy laps of the breaststroke, then pick up the pace doing the freestyle. On your bike, cruise at a calm pace, then power push up hill. Focus on the high-intensity burst for one to three minutes followed by a lower-intensity interval of about two to five minutes. He says the duration should be fifteen to thirty minutes, three or four times a week.

Three Types of Movement

Exercise scientists and fitness experts say there are three distinct and necessary types of movement to mix into your lifestyle for overall fitness: stretching, cardio, and weight resistance. You can fit these different kinds of exercises in, maybe with more frequency and less effort than you expect, by taking advantage of everyday activities.

- **Stretching:** Putting groceries away, reaching to the top of a closet, or a five-to-ten-minute quick stretch or yoga session in the morning, or as part of your wind-down evening routine as a family.
- **Cardio:** Racing, running, chasing, jumping jacks during TV commercials.
- **Weight resistance:** Lifting groceries (or toddlers!), lifting weights during TV time.

Informal Exercise (a.k.a. Mindful Movement)

With informal exercise, you can build in exercise simply by paying attention to any kind of movement, all day long. It doesn't have to be "formal" or require you to set aside a big chunk of dedicated time apart from your kids. Here are some ideas for mindful movement. You may spend most of your day at a desk or spend hours of your life commuting. Try paying attention to when and how you move. Cultivating this awareness may help you work in more physical activity and bolster your confidence by revealing that you're able to be more active than you might think.

While walking around during the day:
- Pay attention to your posture.
- Walk from your core.
- Sit and stand mindfully, engaging your quads, glutes, and biceps.

While at work:
- Isometric exercises require you to contract and hold a position. That's easy enough to do in your desk chair.
- Sitting on a big, rubber balance ball makes you hold in your abs.
- Walk and talk during conference calls. Bonus: it gets you away from your computer, reducing the temptation to multitask during calls.
- Send print jobs to the printer farthest from your desk to get your body moving.
- Leg lifts are effective and easy to do from a desk chair. You might also look up Carrie Rezabek's series of office workouts that you can do in no time. Try this:
  - Sit straight on a chair with your feet and legs together, abs engaged, and arms extended at shoulder level in front of you, palms down.
  - Draw your shoulder blades together to make them "kiss"; relax your shoulders. Do five reps.
  - Keeping your arms extended, make ten apple-size circles with your hands. Do the combo eight times.

While doing errands and chores:

- Take the stairs at the mall, in your apartment building, and at the office.
- Stretch and bend while cleaning the house.
- Park in the spot farthest from the grocery store rather than battling to get a spot up front.
- Mow the lawn.

While playing with kids:

- Do deep knee bends or lunges when kneeling down to talk to young kids.
- Race your kids to the bus.
- Use your whole body while playing with your kids.

Fidget your way to fitness:

- Parents and teachers may once have urged you to sit still, but wiggling, tapping your toes, and otherwise fidgeting as much as possible at your desk is in fact good for your body.
- In one recent study, college students who fidgeted showed healthier blood flow in their lower legs than those who didn't. Even better, a 2008 study found that among office workers, those who frequently fidgeted burned as many as three hundred calories more each day than those who stayed still.

Exercise in Ten Minutes

Colon says any activity in which more than two minutes of movement occurs can be considered aerobic. Live Science reported that 43 percent of people who participated in bouts of ten minutes or less of physical activity, multiple times a day—the so-called active lifestyle approach—met the federal guidelines for being active.

Here are a few ideas from Colon to squeeze in ten minutes of exercise at home:

- Jump rope for one minute, do thirty seconds of push-ups, jump rope for another minute, do thirty seconds of ab crunches. Repeat the cycle for ten minutes. (Push-ups can be modified with knees on the floor or wall push-ups.)
- If you live in a multilevel home, walk up and down the stairs for ten minutes nonstop. Want a bigger challenge? Do ten push-ups whenever you get to the top or bottom of a set of stairs.
- A thirty-minute television show includes eight to ten minutes of commercials. Use the commercials as exercise time—make it an activity for the whole family.
- Do jumping jacks for one minute, then march in place for one minute with high knees and exaggerated arm swings. Repeat for ten minutes.

Find guided workouts on YouTube or through your cable's On Demand service. Here are some fun examples to jump-start your search:

- Fitnessblender.com offers free HIIT, Tabata-focused, body-weight intervals and weight training workouts (with or without actual weights) that are as short as five minutes.
- Check out the Seven-Minute Workout Challenge or the Scientific Seven-Minute Workout.
- The Eight-Minute Plyometric Workout aims to work your muscles and raise your heart rate to help you burn calories faster.

- The ten-minute belly dancing ab workout led by Rania Androniki Bossonis sculpts almost every single muscle in your core, even the hard-to-target, deep transverse abdominals.

Exercise in Twenty to Thirty Minutes

You can get a great workout in, in just ten minutes. But if you have more time, all the better. Here are some additional workout ideas from Colon:

- Try walking for twenty to thirty minutes while holding two- to five-pound dumbbells. "That's my favorite and most efficient workout," Colon told me. If you're doing it on a treadmill, set the speed to 3.5 to 4.5 miles per hour. While walking, perform upper-body exercises in thirty-second intervals: jabs (chest/arms), shoulder presses, bicep curls, overhead triceps extensions, and upright rows are all great. Doing this simple workout three to five times a week will do great things for your overall fitness.
- Using the Xbox or PlayStation systems, choose the interactive fitness software. It gives you immediate feedback and keeps track of your progress.
- Use YouTube or your cable box and search for on-demand twenty-to-thirty-minute workouts. As of this writing, some excellent workouts that do not require a gym, and can be done at home, can be found on Popsugar fitness, health.com, *Shape* magazine, and mensfitness.com.

MAKE IT SOCIAL

Lots of people prefer to work out on their own, but for many parents, having an accountability partner can be the difference in saying they're going to exercise and actually exercising.

Accountability takes all forms, whether it's a friend you *have* to meet for a six a.m. walk (or leave out in the cold), joining a group exercise class, or connecting to your fellows-in-sweat through a Facebook group that encourages its members to submit weekly progress pictures and reports. Do whatever you find most motivating.

My client Emma was a new mom who struggled with finding time to work out. She felt guilty leaving her young son in order to do something just for herself, and even if she did move beyond that feeling, she never felt like she had the energy. But she was a bear when she didn't exercise. For someone who had been committed to fitness before having a kid and throughout her pregnancy, not having time to regularly move her body was taking a toll on her mood at home and productivity at work. She didn't feel like herself.

Emma also put a huge premium on alone time—it was important that exercise wasn't the only time she got to spend on her own self-care. She liked to read and be creative . . . and occasionally, just sit. Imagine that! Emma didn't always have a plan for her prime time for productivity, when her young son was sleeping. Should she sleep, too? Or wash dishes? Or call her mother? Or fold laundry? Or do planks in the living room?

I asked Emma about her schedule. Together, we figured out reliable times when she could commit to exercise. Sometimes, that meant working out while her young son was sleeping—but not all the time. Here's what we came up with:

One day a week, on Thursday mornings, Emma committed to going to an exercise class. It was a throwback to the child-free days of yore, and well worth the cost of a sitter, in both mental and physical health gained.

She made a deal with her sister-in-law to come over for a couple of hours once every two weeks. She'd use that time to get out to a class or do some other type of exercise out of the house, while her sister-in-law babysat.

We created a workout area in her home where she could do a ten-to-thirty-minute workout several times a week, usually at night, after her son's bedtime. Emma agreed that finding time for a ten-minute workout at home was much more realistic than attending a class every day. We had to change her mind-set about what it meant to be active.

When I checked in with Emma a few months later, she had great news. Not only were the Thursday morning classes and biweekly sessions (care of her sister-in-law) a success, she'd also made great strides on her plan to work out from home because she'd found a way to hold herself accountable.

Emma had recruited her friend Cindy to be her workout buddy. They didn't work out in the same space (Cindy exercised at her house), but they would do the same workout at the same time. They organized a series of workouts—using resources she found online on YouTube—and committed to sticking with the same schedule. Three nights a week, Emma sweats it out in her living room while Cindy gets active in her basement—then they text each other when they're done. Just knowing Cindy is waiting for her text makes Emma more likely to exercise. (It also helps that she keeps her weights and sneakers under the couch, so all she has to do is move the coffee table and press Play!)

Best news of all: it was working. Emma felt less frustrated and more productive at work.

MAKE IT EASY

No matter what workout regime you choose, you want to make it as easy and automatic as possible to implement and stick to. Remove obstacles standing in your way. Sometimes all you need to get back on track is a small tweak to your regime, not a total overhaul. I've found that there are three common, small tweaks that are often all it takes to make your best-laid plans a reality.

If you used to exercise but have fallen off track, or keep planning to get moving but rarely follow through, do a quick assessment of your main logistical hurdles to see what small changes you can implement to get back on track.

Have your exercise space and gear ready to go. Once you've set aside a time and place to exercise, remove the hassle of needing to gather equipment at the last minute. Set up an exercise area in your home that is always inviting and ready to go. Put out your workout clothes the night before so you see them upon waking. Keep your gym or swim bag prepacked and placed by the front door so you can just grab and go. Store your free weights in a cabinet in the kitchen, so when you have a free ten minutes you can pump some iron—without having to run to your designated workout area. Keep a resistance band in your office and hang it under your coat or in your desk drawer where you will see it—a reminder to do even a few minutes of weight training when you get the chance. Keep an extra pair of walking or running shoes in your office, so if you have time and the weather permits, you can do a quick power walk to get some fresh air.

Change the location. One client, who was a fitness buff, had a longtime membership at a gym five miles away, which happened to be less expensive than the gym around the corner from her house. When her kids' schedules changed, it was just too much to get to her old gym, and her workout routine went to the dogs. Though the gym next door was more expensive, by switching, she actually started working out again. Find a gym closer to your house. Or closer to your office. Or, quit the gym and (if you have the room) work out at home. Factoring in travel, exercise, and showering, a thirty-minute workout is often a sixty-to-ninety-minute time investment.

Find a new time to exercise. If you used to work out in the morning (or evening), but now that time is devoted to kid care, expand your blinders and experiment with a new time. What about lunch hour at the office—even doing ten sprints up and down the stairs instead of taking the elevator every day? Can you tweak your commute and bike to the office? Or hop off the bus or train one or two stops early and walk the rest of the way home or to work? Why not park a mile away from where you need to go and speed walk to and from the car? (Bonus, that walking time can be a great transition time between work and home mind-sets.) Maybe you can leave work thirty to forty minutes early twice a week to get a workout in on the way home. Get creative. There is more time for exercise than you think.

ADAPT YOUR EXERCISE ROUTINE TO YOUR KIDS' AGES

As your kids go through ages and stages—and their time demands impinge on your schedule—you need to adjust your workout to adapt. Not give up, but adapt.

Below are a variety of ways to fit in exercise at every age and stage of your kids' lives. Just remember to never get too attached to one routine. Murphy's Law: As soon as that happens, it'll change.

Even without a formal workout, keeping pace with energetic kids offers tons of opportunities to be physically active. You can find ways to integrate exercise into your family life and parenting activities, role modeling the importance of an active lifestyle and keeping the whole family healthy. Here are activities you can do *with* your child at any age. You benefit and so do they.

Sharing Exercise with Your Kids Age-by-Age

Infant (0–1): Make exercise part of your daily routine.

With a new baby, you'll be reeling from the changes a tiny human has wrought on your schedule. Be gentle with yourself as you find new ways to integrate exercise into your family routine:

- Invest in a running stroller or a baby carrier and hit the streets (or trail). The fresh air will benefit you both.
- Lie on your back and lift your baby up and down or swing them around the room super-baby style.
- If you have a piece of exercise equipment or a digital library of DVDs, allow your infant to sleep in a bouncy chair or a bassinet while you bust a move. Most tiny

babies can sleep through anything at this stage, and this ensures that they are never out of your sight.

- When your infant is having tummy time or playing on the floor, use that time to work your abdominal muscles or do leg lifts.
- When your baby is learning to crawl, you crawl, too!

Toddler/Preschool (1–5): Introduce your toddler in your exercise routine.

Toddlers move, a lot. They also like to mimic their parents ("I'm doing push-ups just like Mama") and happen to be the perfect size to act as a free weight! These ideas for engaging your toddler will make it easier for you to actually get in a workout:

- Use your growing child as a universal machine! While lifting your toddler, you can do deep knee bends.
- When your toddler starts walking, follow them around the room. Toddlers are busy bodies. They always manage to get in their ten thousand steps a day!

School-Age (5–10): Play actively with your kids. Make it fun!

Before kids get too involved in organized sports (and the pressure that can accompany sanctioned competition), make "moving your body" a fun thing for kids to do. Here are some activities that promote adventure and exploration:

- Walk with your kids to school or the bus stop every day. Make walking more fun by making it a game: doing a treasure hunt, counting birds, looking out for cats, finding license plates from a different state, or racing to your favorite landmark.
- Play freeze tag or another game that works with just two people or involves the whole family.

- Go to a park at least once a week and be that crazy mom or dad doing pull-ups on the jungle gym or step-ups on the slide.
- Go for a nature walk, go for a walk around the neighborhood, or take a hike in an area you haven't yet explored.
- Make a deal with your kids: if they go to your gym's day care for an hour, you'll take them swimming in your gym's pool after your workout.

Tween (10–13): Help your kids to develop their own healthy exercise habits.

By the tween years, kids may be more engaged in organized sports. As adolescents, they may also be more aware of their own bodies and what they can do physically. Give them ideas about how they can exercise, all with an eye toward health and healthy body image:

- Take a dance class or a spin class together.
- Instead of driving, walk as much as possible to do errands or shopping.
- Keep an activities box in your car with balls, bats, a kite, a beach bucket, and a shovel so that you're always prepared.
- Walk the dog as a family. New research from the North American Association on the Study of Obesity shows that dog owners have more fun losing weight and were able to keep it off longer than people without dogs.

Teen (13–18): Use exercise as a way to connect.

The teenage years can be a challenging time for kids and parents to maintain open lines of communication. Make exercise common ground where you can connect.

- Start running together or commit to a particular fitness goal like a 5K or charity bike ride that you can train for as a parent-kid team.
- Cheer on your child during their organized sports. Learn the game alongside them, which is another way of modeling the value of practice versus perfection. Show them that when it comes to exercise, it's just about *doing* it and enjoying it.
- Yard work! Research shows that gardening is as good as weight training when it comes to preventing osteoporosis. It also gets kids outside and connected with nature.

REAL PARENT VOICES

TEN-MINUTE CIRCUIT WORKOUT TO DO WITH KIDS

Kristen Howerton, a professor of psychology, blogger, and mom of four, identified a handful of moves that are simple enough for kids to keep up with, and challenging enough for parents to feel like they're getting a workout, too. This is not Kristen's only workout—she still savors her own workouts as a time to decompress. But she also knows how important it is to include her kids in the exercise spirit.

She suggests mixing it up. For each ten-minute workout, have one kid pick any three of the exercises. Then everyone does the circuit: three sets of ten repetitions of each move, aiming for their best form.

1. **Planking**
2. **Squats**
3. **Push-ups**
4. **Crunches**
5. **Lunges**
6. **Side leg raises**
7. **Burpees**

What's most important is that everyone has fun, Kristen says. "If your kids are having fun exercising, then they always want to keep going. And, of course, we always have some music blasting. Music makes exercise more fun."

KICK-STARTING YOUR MOTOR

Even once you get an exercise groove going, the reality of being a parent means that there will be many times when your exercise routine falls off track: when your kids get sick, when your work gets crazy, or when the family schedule is upended during the holidays or over summer vacation. And we all know that when you haven't exercised in a while, lethargy sets in, and it's just so hard to start again. Learning how to kick-start your motor every time it goes cold is another essential strategy for parents to build into their arsenal.

Don't beat yourself up. Don't curse the gods, or your boss, or the difficulties of parenting. Just accept that you needed to take a pause—recommit to your belief in the value of self-care, get excited about the chance to marvel at how your muscles work, and get back on the treadmill (or free weights, or power walks). And have faith in the process—getting going again may initially feel like torture, but within a week, like clockwork, you'll get your groove back.

13

LOVE

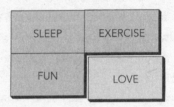

Adele, a thirty-eight-year-old graphic designer with a four-year-old son, was desperate to build some grown-up time back into her life. A creative type who always got through life's adventures by just figuring it out as she went along, Adele confessed to entering parenthood without the slightest clue about how the experience would change her marriage, her time for friends, her body, and her relationship with herself.

Once her son was born, she went from being a charismatic social butterfly to feeling perpetually sleep-deprived, unattractive in her post-baby body, and having little to talk about but being a parent. She and her husband didn't make as much time as they knew they should for their relationship, but babysitters were costly and even when they did opt to pay the cash for a night out, they felt so disconnected they often just stared blankly at each other across the table. "I've been in full-on **Provide** mode," Adele told me. "First I was pregnant, making a baby, then I was making milk, then I couldn't wear nice clothes anymore because I was always covered in poop and vomit. None of this is conducive to romance!"

She told me they weren't organized or prepared for how parenting would impact their romantic relationship. Before parenthood, their daily lives were independent—each pursuing their own careers, and only having to make a few simple decisions together daily (dinner, movie, weekend plans, etc.). It was very different from their new lives as parents, where they faced dozens of decisions together all the time: feeding the baby, putting the baby down for a nap, identifying activities and caregivers.

In their four years as parents, Adele and Brad had never really worked out how to talk about all of the daily decisions, so instead, they each fell into doing parenting their own way. It became parallel parenting under the same roof, and though their son got lots of love and attention, coordination between the parents was absent, which meant neither Adele nor Brad felt recognized enough for their individual contributions to the parenting workload.

Adele was the poster child for the well-meaning parent trap that sociologists Melissa Milkie, Suzanne Bianchi, and John Robinson identified in their seminal 1975–2000 study, "Changing Rhythms of American Family Life". Since the birth of her son, Adele's "all in" approach to parenting had thrown her way out of balance, eclipsing her time and energy for anything other than her son, her work, and any sleep she could muster. As Adele put it: "I've spent four years on the *raising* of a human being, and none on *being* a human being."

It was no way to live, and Adele knew it. "I wouldn't recommend this approach to anyone," she said. She felt depleted, which wasn't good for her son, her marriage, or herself.

LOVE DEFINED

Love in this chapter refers to adult-to-adult relationships, including romantic partners, friends, extended family, or a broader community. Close adult relationships sustain us. These **Love** connections with other adults are nourishing and satisfying in a different way than the love and affinity you feel for your children.

The landmark seventy-five-year Grant Study at Harvard found that strong relationships are the most important ingredient to well-being over a long life. "The clearest message that we get from this seventy-five-year study is this: good relationships keep us happier and healthier," said Robert Waldinger, director of the Harvard Study of Adult Development.

Intellectually, and even emotionally, healthy, rich adult relationships have huge benefits to parents. Friendships, romances, and partnerships boost your happiness, resilience, and sense of belonging while reducing stress, offering stimulation, and giving you a break.

Being nourished, on a regular basis, by other adults helps you go the distance and also helps you be a more engaged parent. When you make time for adult relationships, you'll find many benefits:

- It's easier to give, because you are also receiving (from other adults).
- It's easier to empathize with your children when your own tank is filled up.
- It expands your *Child's World*—with additional adult influences and perspectives that stretch their minds and open up more possibilities.

- It provides critical modeling for your children, on how to sustain and care for friendships and relationships.

Whether you are an introvert or an extrovert, you need human contact and healthy adult relationships to sustain you as a parent.

WHAT MAKES IT HARD

Yet, as Adele and Brad learned, the responsibilities of child rearing can take every waking moment if you allow it to. Here are the big things that make being a parent and maintaining Love relationships so hard:

Added responsibilities change relationships. Having a child changes your relationship with your partner or spouse. Like Adele and Brad, you may struggle to adapt to the near-endless list of tasks that come with child rearing—and you may be surprised by how many values show up in those every-day choices about what to give your toddler for dinner or how much television you allow your children to watch a week. All these decisions can put a strain on your primary romantic relationship. Parenthood also puts a strain on other important relationships in your life: your friends, your siblings, and even your own parents. The added responsibility of caring for another human being—permanently—requires adjustments across the board. Change is hard, because either you don't realize it needs to happen or you resent the idea that it must.

You feel less attractive/interesting. What parent hasn't experienced this scenario: you're out to dinner (at last!), and forty-five minutes into the evening, you find yourself talking about a funny thing your kids did at bedtime, or a nightmare scenario at school, or the outrage of your morning routine. You look at yourself and think: why am I talking about this? Being a parent ensures that you always have something to talk about at a cocktail party, but talking about your kids all the time (just like talking about your work all the time) interferes with the primary benefit of adult relationships: the chance to connect with the people who know you for more than being a parent! Chances are, the important people in your life are most interested in hearing about *you*—your ideas, experiences, thoughts—not your Saturday morning routine with the kids.

You're planned out. So many parents are overwhelmed by the barrage of logistical arrangements for their kids that they don't make plans with friends or family because it takes too much extra effort. When life (and work) requires so much planning, it's understandable why some parents resist having to "schedule" any self-care activities (including quality time with people they love). But of course, with no planning comes no time for adult relationships.

You're peopled out. Kids demand a lot of our time and emotional energy. If you get any time away, you may just prefer to be alone to stare off into space or go on a solo bike ride or read a book. When you are in this frame of mind, spending time with anyone—friends, spouse, family—feels like work you can't bear to take on (after all, no relationship is perfect—it will require something of you). This "peopled-out" feeling can make you feel even more isolated than you may be feeling already. It can feel like we have no choice but to skip out on time with our children in order to get any time with adults. Is that true, or is there another way?

Each type of relationship comes with its own opportunities and challenges. No one person can fulfill all of your needs—a mixture of adult relationships, including romantic ones, friendships, and extended family, will take the pressure off any one person to be your everything and provide a strong network of love and support that makes it easier to nurture your kids. Let's look at a few tips on how to make and contain the time for different types of relationships in your life.

SPOUSE/ROMANTIC PARTNER

Of all the couples I interviewed, those who kept their relationships strong worked conscientiously to nurture their love relationship separate and apart from their role as co-parents. Allowing family life and logistics to dominate all of a couple's time together is a relationship killer, drifting you both further and further apart from the unique spark and connection that sustains you. Yet, coordinating as partners on the logistics of family life is just as essential to making the romantic part work, on both a practical and an emotional level. It's a delicate and essential balance that needs to be tackled head-on.

My client Nate said his marriage ended in divorce because of what he called "the unspoken dialogues." He and his wife didn't talk about the workload of parenthood (who was doing what, when), what tasks really needed to happen (and what didn't), what values the children ought to be taught, and how they planned to give each other a break. Nate believed the failure to discuss the little things, out in the open, resulted in the disintegration of their marriage. He called them the "unspoken dialogues" because while they may never have been discussed, the dialogues absolutely happened: in side glances, winces, eye rolls, assumptions, hurts, and looks of shock and frustration.

Couples Who Share the Workload Have More Sex

Whether you've been married for two years or twenty, if you need any motivation to get the chore thing right, here it is. A briefing paper for the Council on Contemporary Families found that "couples who reported sharing housework fairly equally, with the man doing more than a third and up to 65 percent of the housework, reported having sex significantly more often than did couples where the woman did 65 percent or more of the housework."

An August 2017 study in the *Journal of Marriage and Family* concurred, finding that among couples who share their chores more evenly, there is more sexual gratification. The workload that occurs outside of your romantic relationship (e.g., getting the kids ready for school, food shopping, handling transportation, planning a child's birthday party) will affect your energy and interest in romance. When you get in sync regarding the workload and the house rules, and acknowledge each other's need for breaks, you give each other the gift of time. Bonus: you also are likely to have more sex.

Hit the Reset Button

When I suggested to Adele that the first step to reconnecting to her husband might be to work out the time dilemmas that had been causing so much tension, she sighed. I would love to, she told me, but there were so many years operating out of sync, she didn't even know how to start. My suggestion: hit Reset. Say, hey—we went into this whole parenthood thing with a lot of love, and without a clue, and got blindsided by how much joint decision-making we'd have to do. Now that we know, can we hit Reset and work out a way for us to coordinate and share this workload, and the time we need for ourselves together?

Once you hit Reset, try some or all of these tips to stay connected:

Daily glue. Aim for a regular cadence of daily touch points with your partner. The happy couples I interviewed averaged three to five touch points a day, often for only five or ten minutes at a time, whether it was a quick call or text, or an in-person chat at the end of the workday. Among kids, work, and home logistics, these nurturing touch points are grounding connections that make you feel you have someone on your team who "gets" your day-to-day existence. It also means you have less to catch up on when you get home (opening up more time for connection).

Do the dishes together. Of all the chores to share, many couples I interviewed opted to do the dishes together: it's a reliable time to catch up, and sharing the task can warm you up for intimacy later. If your kids have early bedtimes, maybe you both put the children to sleep, and then come back to the kitchen for a glass of wine, or tea, and relaxing cleanup. Older kids can occupy themselves with homework or individual play while you clean up.

Form a babysitting swap. Babysitting is expensive, and you might feel bad leaving your kids for an evening when you've been working all week. But what if they get to hang out with their friends while you have a night on the town? Undoubtedly, there are parents in your neighborhood or your child's class at school who would also love a night out with some regularity. Approach your kids' friends' parents to see if they'd like to form a swap: you watch each other's kids (at your house or theirs) while the other couple goes out, and vice versa. It's a win-win.

Find creative times and places to spend time together. Kids make it harder to keep track of time. But that doesn't mean you can't have fun—or enjoy time with your partner. It just means you need to get inventive and find new activities that satisfy in shorter bites. Here are a few ways to diversify your portfolio:

- **Day dates.** So many parents I talked with said their ideal "adult time" is during the workday and school day—when kids are cared for (no extra child-care costs!) and their attention feels less divided. Meet your partner for lunch. Take a half day (or full day) of personal time and rendezvous at home, or go to the beach.

- **Work from a coffee shop together.** Can't take off work? Try working remotely for part of the day from a coffee shop together. It may not be pure romantic time, since you are focused on your laptops, but you will be sitting next to each other and proximity comes with its own set of comforts.

- **Extend day-care coverage to cover dinnertime.** For most working parents, the hours after school and before dinner are among the most stressful of the day—there's a reason it's called the witching hour. Give yourself a break once every week or two by seeing if you can get a babysitter during the dinner hour and/or bedtime— whether it's your everyday sitter who stays a little later once a week, a teenager who picks the kids up from school and helps with homework and dinner, or another parent who feeds your kids dinner one night a week as part of a swap (and you're on duty the next). A midweek adult date after work, where you don't have to deal with the witching-hour chaos, can feel like a mini-vacation.

- **Piggyback date night with business obligations.** Many parents begrudgingly make time for obligatory social events—like work functions they feel they have to go to—but don't take time for themselves. Nancy and her husband came up with a way to leverage these obligatory events into some date time. Before or after every business social obligation, they'd steal some of the evening for themselves, either by grabbing a drink ahead of time, leaving early for a walk, or grabbing dessert on the way home. It took the sting out of the annoyance of these social obligations and saved them planning time for separate date nights.

- **Keep the bond strong when apart by being kind.** Leaving a small gift or card on the kitchen table is an easy way to let your partner know he or she is on your mind. Asking what task you can take off your spouse's plate for the day will buy you goodwill, communicate care, and result in more free time when you get home at night. More romantic gestures, like leaving a love Post-it on the bathroom mirror, sending flowers to your spouse's workplace, or tucking a note into a briefcase or a purse, all require a minimum time investment but help your partner feel seen and acknowledged.

Let me leave you with one story of a couple who seems to have figured this out, or at least has *mostly* figured it out. See if you can replicate some of their approach.

Melinda, a family attorney, and Mark, a civil engineer,

have a two-and-a-half-year-old, Anna. Though both work full-time, Melissa and Mark are equally committed to their marriage and to spending time with friends—as they share the belief that "no one person can fulfill any one person's needs."

Mark and Melinda share the work of maintaining a household and child care pretty equally: Mark does the majority of meal planning and cooking; Melinda does the majority of the family scheduling and finances. They share cleanup and chores (often doing them together as a bit of shared couple time) and alternate putting their daughter to bed, each doing it every other night. Divvying up the workload has gone a long way in keeping them connected as a couple and ensuring that they both have the energy to go out.

They feel that time with friends outside the family isn't just nice, it's necessary to maintaining a healthy relationship with each other *and* being a happy parent. They sincerely believe their own and their daughter's lives are richer for having more people in their day-to-day interactions.

For social connections, once a week, Melinda and Mark go out as a couple. Often it's just the two of them; other times they'll make plans with another couple. In addition, they also give each other two or three nights a month to go out on their own, with friends—while the other parent stays home with their daughter.

FRIENDS AND FAMILY

So many parents are overwhelmed by the barrage of day-to-day logistical arrangements for their kids, they don't make plans with friends or family because it takes too much extra effort; they're planned out. When life (and work) requires so much planning, it's understandable why some parents resist

having to "schedule" any self-care activities (including quality time with people they love). But of course, without a plan,
you're less likely to have time for adult relationships. It'll just
get washed away in the swirl of everyday life.

Nurture Relationships IRL: In Real Life

Social media can be a great way to stay connected with friends
and family who live far away, and in a pinch, it can be an
essential tool during those lonely moments as a parent. There's
nothing quite as convenient as Facebook when you need a
shot of adult wisdom or companionship. Social media,
and the Internet in general, can also help you find real
people—neighborhood moms (checkout hellomamas.com,
a matchmaking service for local moms)—and offer a place to
commiserate on the wild journey that is parenthood (coffee
andcrumbs.net is a funny and tender take on parenthood).

Yet, you must resist the trap of over-relying on social
media, making it your only "adult time," often sneaking it in
when you're supposed to be paying attention to a game of
Monopoly. A study published in the *American Journal of Epi-
demiology* linked frequent Facebook use to poorer well-being.
The study tracked the Facebook activity and real-world social
lives and well-being of 5,208 adults over two years. (Well-
being included life satisfaction, self-reported mental health,
self-reported physical health, and body-mass index.) Actual
in-person relationships were, unsurprisingly, linked to better
overall well-being, supporting existing research that suggests
close social ties do our mind and body good.

Social media is okay; it has its place. But nothing beats
real, in-person contact. Get together regularly with friends
and family who live nearby. And for those who live far way,

the challenge is to create a consistent rhythm of regular visits, whether it's once a month, four times a year, or a few weeks every summer. In between "live" visits, keep the connection strong with regular phone calls, FaceTime/Skype sessions, and fun surprises care of snail mail. Set a schedule and keep to it—if you wait for time to open up, it never will!

It's Easy to Be Isolated

It's one thing to find space for quality time with the other adult(s) who live under the same roof; it's another challenge altogether to find space for quality time with friends and extended family. The hassle of coordinating schedules is a huge deterrent to getting together.

My client Shirley debated every weekend about whether or not they should pile the kids in the car to go visit her husband's family, who lived two hours away. Her in-laws loved seeing the kids, but it was a big schlep, and it was often a fight with her kids, who wanted to make plans at home with their friends. When I asked how often would be ideal for both households, she said everyone would be happy with once a month. So why not select, in advance, which weekends over the next three or four months you will go see them? I asked. That way, everyone knows the plan and can look forward to it—and feel free to make different plans for the other weekends without feeling worried about missing an opportunity.

Remove Planning from the Equation

One of the best ways to ensure you connect with others on a regular basis is to create routines and habits that zap planning from the equation. It makes connecting with others an easy, regular thing by allowing everyone to anchor their schedules around a few givens. Routine get-togethers can also make social time more efficient. For instance, if you host a weekly movie night for your neighborhood friends and their kids on Friday nights in the summer, you get faster at setting up the space, having the right snacks, and selecting the movie. Routines are a great way to solidify your tribe.

Automating get-togethers also creates glue among people—the existence of the routine communicates how much you value one another, whether those connections are daily, weekly, monthly, or annual. Reliable connecting points allow all the people involved, who likely have complicated and very busy lives, to have a few anchors they can organize their own lives around.

What social time with friends and family looks like will differ depending on proximity. If you and your family live close to another family, that's one thing. If you live far apart, you'll have to take a different approach. Here are some ways to build in regular adult time when you live near each other:

Share errand time. Building routine adult time into a few weekly chores can make mundane, obligatory tasks something you look forward to. Buddying up with a friend to go to the local farmer's market or supermarket every Saturday morning can be among your most enjoyable weekly routines. If you can get someone else to watch the kids, a one-hour trip to shop while chatting can be satisfying grown-up time, and just the shot you need to feel like an adult.

Make twenty-minute connections. It's amazing how much you can accomplish in twenty minutes with another adult. Have breakfast, grab a coffee, go for a midday walk at lunchtime, chat on your commute, meet another parent (or your partner) before picking the kids up from school or from an after-school activity, talk or Skype with a friend for twenty minutes while you do the dishes. Twenty minutes is a tiny commitment that can just do the trick.

Schedule weekly get-togethers. Build a handful of adult-time activities into the week (or every other week) that guarantee some pleasurable social time. It could be going on a power walk with a friend two mornings a week, grabbing coffee with another parent while you wait for your kids to finish soccer practice on Saturday afternoons, or staking out Friday "friends night"—a rotating potluck party to kick off the weekend.

Create monthly traditions. Monthly routines are great for groups of people (or events) that require a little more effort to make happen but are very rewarding: visits to (or from) relatives who live beyond a day-trip away; a monthly girls' or boys' night out with friends—and whoever shows up, shows up (no more spending months trying to coordinate); a monthly trivia night, poker game, or book club.

Celebrate annual occasions. There are some special events— whether tied to a holiday or a longer chunk of time away from the kids—that you may only be able to pull off once a year but are worth creating a tradition around. Consider an annual couples' or friends' weekend away that gives you a true vacation from the 24-7 supervision and responsibility of parenting. (If the kids can stay with a family member or close friend for the weekend, it can become a fun tradition for them, too!) Annual holiday events such as barbecues, dinners, and pic- nics with other families are fun for everyone—and take the hassle out of creating a whole experience yourself. You might also consider vacationing with another family—there will be another set of eyes on the kids (and built-in entertainment for your children) so the adults can actually relax a little.

Living farther away—across miles and time zones and oceans—presents its own challenges to staying connected. Nurturing those relationships can be hardest of all.

Technology is one of the easiest ways of maintaining bonds with people who live far away, but it's important not to depend on technology alone. You should also make in-person points of connection part of the routine.

If this describes some of your relationships, trying staying connected by some or all of the following:

In-person visits: It may be too burdensome (or expensive) to see each other multiple times a year, but visits are essential to nurturing family bonds. Try alternating who makes the long-haul trip each time and commit to getting together at least once a year. Then make that visit count. Go for an extended period, and make it happen around the same time each year (perhaps a holiday, perhaps summer vacation) so you can establish regular traditions. Are your kids old enough to travel on their own? Can they stay with a family member for a few weeks?

Video calls: Rely on Skype, FaceTime, Google Hangouts, WhatsApp—there is no shortage of tools that make it feel as if you and your family are in the same room. Regular old talking on the phone is good, too, but especially for young kids, being able to see a far-away family member or friend will help them stay familiar. Once on the video call, kids and grandparents can read together, or eat breakfast together—just prop up your device on the breakfast table and voilà!

Record messages: Live calls are great, but the advantage of a recorded message is that you can watch or listen to it again and again, independent of time zone.

Good old snail mail: Technology is great, but nothing replaces the thrill of receiving something in the mail. It's the person's real handwriting, their smell, their crinkled paper. Soak it up! Regular care packages—even once a month—can keep long-distance relationships feeling close.

Photos: Smartphones make taking and sharing pictures easier than ever. Apps like Facebook and Instagram (of course) make sharing pictures a breeze, but so do Line or Snapfish or Dropbox or Shutterfly. Share precious moments regularly and frame photos to keep your loved ones' faces a regular vision in your home. And talk about the people in the photos with your kids—share memories of the last time you got together and their favorite stories and beloved features, like their hilarious cackling laugh. This can keep the connections strong across distance.

HOW TO MAKE THE MOST OF THE TIME

Making the most of the time you have with other adults takes awareness and diligence. You need to switch gears and truly focus on the adult-to-adult connection for which you have made the effort to create space. You may only get small doses of time together, so follow these tips to make sure you use them to fully recharge.

Don't overdo the kid talk. Minimize talk about kids or logistics—no matter how cute, smart, and proud of your kids you are. If at first you can't think about anything but kid stuff to talk about, ask questions about life, something you read, or something you heard on the radio. Steer clear of kid and logistics talk whenever you're supposed to be spending quality one-on-one time with your spouse. Use a different time (or forum) for that stuff. (One parent I talked to told me she and her husband deal with logistics and to-do lists via email, preserving face-to-face time for connecting with each other.)

Make first moments count. Do your best to de-stress *before* getting together with other adults. Mindlessly dumping your worries and frustrations on someone within the first minute of being together—and before you even ask how they are—can steal from the value of the time you have together. Annie Pleshette Murphy, parenting expert, family therapist, and former editor in chief of *Parents* magazine, said that the first minute of positive interaction is crucial: she and her editors used to call it the "one-minute marriage saver."

Be mindful of your surroundings. While some people relax best at home, others can't turn off their to-do lists while in their everyday environment. Know yourself, and the person you're spending time with, and do your best to create the optimal conditions for connecting. It might mean something as simple as going for a walk around the neighborhood, just so you and your partner can "be here now." Or, if you and a friend have a hard time connecting while your toddler is around (even though she loves your child!), get out of the house. If being at home does work for you, have friends come to your house for dinner—and do takeout—to maximize your time together.

AUTOMATE ENTERTAINING

Stella eases the stress of entertaining (and being a guest) by deciding on a handful of signature snacks and dishes she's become known
for: guacamole and chips, a favorite eggplant dip, orzo salad, her
famous banana bread. Once that's settled, it's a no-brainer to say yes
to any party invite: she throws together a dish everyone loves that
she can make with her eyes closed.

Have quick cleanup routines. One big obstacle to a rich and
facile social life is feeling like your house is too messy to host
guests. I hear it all the time. Here are Faye and Rick's trick
for quick cleanups to always be ready for guests, because
when you have kids, messy is just part of the territory: Invest
in a handful of beautiful decorative baskets (with lids) in
rooms where messes tend to accumulate. If papers pile up on
the kitchen counter, have a single drawer, cabinet, or container
designated for the quick cleanup when guests are coming.
When you get the call, just stash the mess. It's okay. You can
also aim to have a room or area of your home that is always
ready for company. That means a room with less clutter overall
and tuck-away containers that make it easy to pull together,
without a stressful scramble to get things in order. Remember:
your value isn't a spotless, organized home!

Announce your time limits. When you are a parent, there are
practical boundaries around your time that may be obvious
to you but not to the people you are spending time with.
They don't know what else you have to do, whether that's
your spouse not knowing that you have errands to run before
the kids get home from school, or work you have to finish up
after you relax a bit at dinner. Friends (especially those who
aren't parents) can be especially tone-deaf to the time limits

you may be working under and show up late for get-togethers or ask you to travel to them for a coffee date, when that twenty minutes of travel time is going to sink your tight schedule. Share your time limits when you get together, so the other person knows what to expect.

HEALTHY RELATIONSHIPS WILL HELP YOU GO THE DISTANCE

For all the goodwill and nurturance that loving relationships can bring us, I'm no Pollyanna about how difficult and challenging they can be. Healthy, productive relationships with your friends, family, and partner require work and effort. They require having the energy and courage to speak up when things don't feel quite right and to make sure unspoken dialogues don't grow into resentments that, if left untended, can poison a relationship.

No relationship is immune to conflict, but in the ones that go for the long haul, spouses, partners, or friends develop skills to address conflict and move beyond it because they always manage to have their eyes on a longer-term goal: connection.

That's what this section is about: giving you the tools and courage to find the time to address issues, big and small.

End visits before the saturation point. Old roles die hard. Perhaps when you get together with your family, you instantly fall back into old patterns with your siblings and parents—teasing, being a pest, instigating spats about who is your parent's favorite. The purpose of maintaining connections with family and old friends is to fuel you, not deplete you, and to set a good role model for interaction and connection for your kids. Know your saturation point. If you travel to visit family, consider staying off-site (in a hotel or Airbnb) so you have a little more control over your time and environment. Or, if family comes to visit you, ask if they're open to staying close by (and offer to kick in part of the cost). The key is to know what your limits are, accept them as truth, and ensure that visits wrap up short of your saturation point.

Let the small things go—don't waste time and energy. Some small things, like subtle differences in the way a job is done (but still gets done!) may not be worth the conflict. Maybe your partner doesn't stack the dishwasher as efficiently as you do. Is it annoying? Probably. But is it a big deal? No! The dishes still get done. Maybe your mother-in-law insists on giving your kids ice cream or cookies an hour before bedtime (which, thanks to sugar, means bedtime is a little more raucous than usual). Could you make a big deal of this? Yes, you could throw a stink. Is it really worth it? Nah. These kinds of small things have the potential to create a load of resentment if you allow them to. My advice: if you can ignore it and let it go, do so.

Talk about the big things with honesty and love. There are, of course, some issues that are worth the conversation, and knowing when it's time to speak up is tricky. My belief is that when an issue is creating a wedge that makes you want to pull away from someone you love (and thus putting an important part of your support network of adults in jeopardy), then it's worth a discussion. But it must be done with the intention to repair rather than push away. The issues that seem to come up the most for the clients I work with are those that impact time, since time is such a precious commodity in the life of a parent: division of labor, which we discussed earlier in this chapter (and have more tips on in chapter 8, "**Arrange**"), and rule setting. When it comes to the children, if division of labor and rule setting are not in alignment, it costs you time and chaos, and depletes your free time to work out or to pursue a hobby. That is true for adults living under the same roof as well as extended family and friends. For example, if your sister loves to babysit but doesn't make the kids clean up before bed, you get stuck doing the cleanup at the end of what was otherwise a relaxing night out. Speak up. She's probably not aware of the time impact on you. And by having the discussion, you dissolve any wedges that could have been forming, keeping your sister (or friend or neighbor) close and in harmony—a tight circle of adult relationships that keep you going.

I will leave the hard-core relationship counseling to the therapists, but in my experience with hundreds of clients (and couples!) over the years, those who make it—who seem to be the happiest and the most content—are those who are willing to give each other a break. The same goes for long-term friendships and harmonious relationships among extended families.

Remember, every parent is figuring it out as they go, and the journey varies dramatically over the full span of the child-rearing years. How much time you have available for other adults is quite different when kids are babies, when they are school-age (perhaps the most predictable time), and when they enter the complex phase of adolescence. People in your life aren't always aware of the oscillating demands of parenthood on your time. One of the biggest surprises for most parents is how much more demanding of time and energy the teenage years are (just when you imagined your time might open up for love relationships). Whether you can give people a lot or a little time, give them something—to let them know they matter, too. And good friends, family, and spouses know and can be generous and resilient when parenthood periodically pulls you under and causes small gaps in connection.

Hanging on to resentment or hurts about being neglected in the past or present really only adds emotional clutter. Instead, know that if you didn't get it right in the first four months or four years or ten years, you can start anew tomorrow. As a couple, identify the one or two things, pre-kid, that connected you to each other, then find a way to build those things reliably into your schedule, no matter what. With friends and family near and far, commit today to a regular routine of connection that communicates in action—not just words—how important you are to each other. Resolve those unspoken dialogues through conversation and connection.

And most of all, make the time to invest in these relationships. It's worth it. They will make you a happier, healthier human being and a better parent.

14

FUN

I started working with Elena soon after she became an empty nester. With her kids finally living on their own, she'd hired me to help her transform her junk room into a craft room. For many of us, the term *craft room* connotes small projects—scrapbooks, fuzzy ribbons, projects involving hot glue guns—but in Elena's case, it meant excavating an exquisite textile collection. She'd studied textiles in college and there, buried amid twenty-five years of other stuff, were fabrics, books, special equipment, and supplies that she'd simply put on pause . . . for a quarter century. Elena's entire aesthetic (and I mean this with respect) was "frumpy mom." As long as anyone had known her, her identity was defined entirely by raising her children. No one—not me, not friends, not even her children—knew about Elena's former life as an aspiring textile artist. She'd been consumed, entirely, by the role of parent.

Looking at the impressive scope of materials, it made me wonder: what if she'd nurtured that talent and hobby while raising her children? Would it have made her role as a mom less tiring because she would have had a steady source of fuel for her soul? Would her kids have been more inspired to pursue what made their hearts sing, knowing that their mother had devoted time to cultivating this aspect of herself?

IN OUR PARENT TIME SURVEY
MOST PARENTS AREN'T GETTING ENOUGH FUN TIME

A whopping 84.51% said they spent too little time on hobbies and personal relaxation.

FUN IS FUEL FOR YOUR SOUL

Our hobbies, our passions, and what we do for pure relaxation fuel and restore us physically, emotionally, and psychologically in the most efficient way imaginable. Those restorative activities provide care and nurturance of your soul. It's what you do for you.

For the purposes of this book, I am defining *fun* as any activity that instantly relaxes, transports, or fulfills you. How you spend your free time is the unique expression of who you are as a human being. The fun stuff—your hobbies and passions—are what make you *you!* If you give all of that up completely once you become a parent, you become depleted, and that doesn't put you in a position to nurture your kids and family.

Of course, you can't necessarily devote *all* the time you once did to your hobbies and passions, fun and relaxation, but putting everything on pause isn't a great idea, either. The excuse I hear over and over is, "Julie, I'd love to X or Y or Z, like I used to, but I just don't have the time. There aren't enough hours in the week!" Everybody's felt that way at one time or another. Remember what the research says: kids want your time, yes, but they'll happily take less of it if it means their parent is fully present.

Kids want to know their parents are devoted to their well-being, but they also want their parents to be fulfilled and happy adults. And, somehow, they know when you aren't. They can sense when you're distracted, or struggling, or just going through the motions—it's like a sixth sense all kids develop in infancy.

Remember this: what's good for your own mental health is good for your children. It's good, and even important, for your kids to see you pursue fulfillment beyond their existence. It teaches them that it's healthy and normal to have interests and passions beyond the immediate influence of their family. It takes the pressure off, too: no one, not even your kid, wants to be responsible for your every happiness.

EXPERT ADVICE | **THE SCIENCE OF LAUGHTER**

- A Vanderbilt University study estimated that just ten to fifteen minutes of laughter a day can burn up to forty calories.
- A University of Maryland study found that a sense of humor can protect against heart disease.
- Humor, with its associated laughter, can reduce stress and cortisol, a stress hormone, according to *Advances in Mind-Body Medicine*.

EMBRACE THE MERITS OF FUN

As a kid, and throughout my years as a single parent, when I rattled off what was happening in my life and my work, my dad would always ask me, "What are you doing for fun?" I found the question annoying and irrelevant. Fun?! I'm conquering mountains here. I'm building a business. I'm raising a kid. I'm accomplishing great things! Fun seemed so trivial.

It took me decades to fully appreciate the value of his question.

The first chink in my armor occurred around five years after I launched my professional organizing business, Task Masters. At networking events, as the chitchat unfolded, people would inevitably ask what I did for fun. "Oh!," I'd explain with genuine enthusiasm, "running my own business and being a parent are two of the most fun and creative ventures I've ever embarked on." My fellow networker would politely correct me: "No, I mean like hobbies . . . what do you do for fun?" Gulp. I didn't have an answer. As silly as it sounds, I realized that in the best interests of my business (and networking opportunities), I better develop a hobby.

I spent a little time pondering possibilities. I'd always been interested in learning Portuguese, but picking up a new language seemed too hard and time-consuming. I'd often fantasized about taking cooking lessons, but classes were expensive and time intensive. I needed something with a short learning curve.

Then it hit me: dance! I used to be a dancer, and nothing brought me more joy than being on the dance floor. I'd been hearing about swing dancing at the Continental Club on Sunday nights in Manhattan, led by the legendary Frankie Manning, a short subway ride from my Brooklyn apartment. I'd always wanted to go but just never found the time.

So, newly motivated by a desire to up my networking game, I shoved Sunday night swing dancing into my already overpacked schedule. It was a blast. Big bands, Jerry Lee Lewis, Dianne Reeves, and Chuck Berry were blaring on the speakers.

Old hoofers, eighty-something years young, flipping me upside down. I felt newly energized, newly productive.

To my amazement, adding something new and joyful to a crammed schedule had the effect of stretching the hours and days. I had more time than I'd had in years (or at least it felt that way). During the workday, I'd have my head down for hours and look up thinking it must be close to five, to find out it was only three. In the evening, during dinner with my daughter—which used to feel too short—the time felt rich and "enough," because I was fully present. Deciding to spend my Sunday nights swing dancing to Benny Goodman was the best thing I ever did for myself, my parenting, and my business.

Not surprisingly, most parents I work with now have the same reaction I had to my dad's persistent question, "What are you doing for fun?" They stare at me blankly. Am I nuts? Do I really not get the time crunch they're experiencing? There will be time for fun when the kids are older, they tell me. There's just no time for that now, they tell me. Any time I can save them should be devoted to work or sleep, they assure me. Fun doesn't even enter their orbits.

But it must. I've shared my personal experience with what fun can do. But you don't have to take my word for it. Play is also an element of human nature. According to the National Institute for Play, a nonprofit, play for adults does three essential things: it helps us make connections and build community (remember my Sunday-night swing dance pals), it helps keep the mind sharp (you've heard how beneficial puzzle games like Sudoku and Scrabble can be in maintaining memory and thinking skills), and it can help us stay close to the loved ones in our lives. "When there's major play deprivation in an otherwise competent adult, they're not much fun to be around," says Dr. Stuart Brown, a psychiatrist and founder of the

National Institute for Play. Check out his TED Talk. "You begin to see that the perseverance and joy in work is lessened and that life is much more laborious," he says.

In my experience, there are three common mind-sets you'll need to let go of to make more time for fun.

1. **If I'm not taking care of someone or being productive, I don't have value.** This is a biggie. Many people, and women in particular, believe in their veins that they are being irresponsible and have no value unless they are working or taking care of someone. That belief system is ingrained in our culture and hard to transcend, particularly for women. I've had the chance to coach several senior editors at women's magazines. Those women (by and large) put in long, punishing days—and it's no surprise that in the publishing business, where profit margins are razor thin, there is enormous pressure to do more with less. I've had clients whose colleagues had to strong-arm them to leave their desks by three p.m. on a summer Friday and ban them from checking email! If you are in the grips of this mind-set, it'll be hard to let it go until you experience fun for yourself—as I experienced swing dancing. You won't believe it. If doing something for yourself (just for fun) is too big a leap, do it for your family and your job. After all, allowing yourself the chance to be an interesting, well-rounded, and whole human being puts you in the best position to come up with creative solutions and care for others.

2. **Taking time for fun is selfish and/or not fair to my family.** Nearly every client says this: "Oh, Julie, I would feel so guilty asking my wife for time to do my hobby," or "My husband will laugh me out of the room if I say I want

Sunday afternoons for going off on my own to a museum."
I get it. But you have to find a way to make the case to your
family, because it's good for everyone. Consider making
fun part of the values your family lives by. Trade time for
fun with your spouse—you'll cover bath time and bedtime
on Tuesday nights, if your partner takes Wednesdays (so
you can attend gospel choir practice). Or, if you can swing
it, hire a sitter to come once a week for the sole purpose of
giving you time to pursue your passion.

3. **Work first, play second.** America—and particularly
American adulthood—seems defined by this ethic. For a
while, when kids are really small, all they do is play. Then,
at some point, parents intervene under the auspices of
helping a kid "grow up" and say, "Okay buddy, you can
play, but first you have to do your chores." Or, "No playing until you finish your homework." The principle certainly has its merits. But as that message seeps deeper and
deeper into your unconsciousness, it can drive you to be
all work and no play. And if you apply that principle to
your life as a parent, you will have zero chance of ever
getting to play because your work is endless: as you check
things off your to-do list, more tasks are added all the
time. Ironically, as an ultra-conscientious parent, you'd
do well to flip the work-first-play-second mentality every
so often. If you start with play, you'll have more energy
for work! It's my "when you have fun, time expands"
theorem.

My dad was on to something.

I am a fan of Brené Brown, the author, researcher, and social
worker. She writes in her best-selling book *The Gifts of Imper-
fection*, "A critically important component of wholehearted

living is play. . . . Play is as essential to our health and functioning as rest (but) spending time doing purposeless activities is rare. In fact for many of us, it sounds like an anxiety attack waiting to happen."

It doesn't have to be that way. I promise. Let's get to it.

BACK ON THE FUN TRAIN IN THREE STEPS

If you've been off the fun train awhile, it can take a little while to figure out what you actually enjoy. It's not uncommon for parents to be so consumed with planning for their kids that they lose steam when it comes to planning for themselves. One client, Cynthia, begged me for mercy when I told her she needed to plan more time for fun in her life: "I need a break from all the planning!" I get it. The problem with *not* planning, however, is that we end up defaulting to lazy forms of relaxation—like binge-watching Netflix or folding laundry—that are not actually restorative. Here are guidelines to help you move beyond what's most convenient and rediscover what actually brings you joy:

1. Break the Train of Everyday Thought

Herbert Benson, director of the Division of Behavioral Medicine at Beth Israel Hospital, a training hospital of Harvard Medical School in Boston, advises using a relaxation technique that will break the train of everyday thought and decrease the activity of the sympathetic nervous system (the system responsible for our fight-or-flight response). "Just sitting quietly or, say, watching television, is not enough to produce the physiological changes," he said. While those things may be enjoyable, they don't bring about the physical response that make it count as an authentic relaxation technique. Here are some suggestions:

Avoid mindless screen activity. When you are in need of a little fun break, resist the urge to drift to channel surfing or Web browsing, logging on to Facebook and Twitter, checking email, or texting—these activities don't truly relax or restore you, so they don't really count as rewarding forms of fun.

Step away from your to-do list. When parents find themselves with spare time, they often mindlessly gravitate to their never-ending lists. Here's a chance to compile photo albums, or organize the attic, or clean out the fridge, or fold the mountain of laundry in the guest room. Unfortunately, any endeavor that feels more like an obligation than a joy is not fun or relaxing. Relieving? Yes, maybe. But not relaxing. (Plus, if your idea of "fun" is getting more to-dos done, something is off-kilter.) Life is about experiences and energy, not all the tasks on your to-do list. To start, when you have a free moment, neglect one small task—don't do the dishes in the sink, don't rearrange the pillows on your couch, don't carry the laundry basket upstairs—and do something fun and just for you instead. Your family will survive; heck, they may even fill in for you.

Create a relaxing space. You know the sayings, "you are what you eat" and "dress for success"? The same logic applies here. Create a physical space in your life for the thing you love to do, and you're more likely to actually do it. I worked with a young mom who, before having children, loved going to her local meditation center—the space, with its natural light, clean scent, and positive energy, was restorative. As the parent of two young kids, a sixty-minute meditation class (plus travel and shower time) was out of the question. So she created a meditation corner in her bedroom, away from the hubbub of her busy home, near a window that over-looked a giant oak tree. It transported her away from the hustle of everyday life and helped her focus on the moment. If your thing is drawing or knitting or you-name-it, desig-nate a corner or a basket or a cabinet as a sacred space just for you.

The goal here is productive fun. An activity that brings about a relaxation response—which is actually a mentally active process (unlike vegetating on the couch and channel surfing)—leaves the body relaxed and the mind calm and focused.

2. Find Fun That Will Fit into Your Schedule

What activities instantly transport you to a place of pure joy and relaxation? It could be reading, gardening, painting, danc-ing, listening to music, or pampering yourself. Brainstorm activities that eat up small bites of time—fifteen to thirty min-utes a day, or one to three hours a week—but will reasonably fit into the rhythm of your life. (A snorkeling vacation to Tahiti—while fun—doesn't make the cut.) The goal is some-thing you can commit to doing regularly. Here are a few ideas to get you started:

Go back to what you used to love. Recall activities you loved in childhood and find a way to bring them back into your life. Did you love to sing? Take up the guitar or join a choir. Love to sketch or sculpt? Grab a sketchbook or some clay. There's no need to wait until your kids have flown the nest to bring a little of what you always loved into your life.

Try something totally new. Experiment! There's a great sense of adventure and wonder in trying something new. It could be something purely relaxing and quiet, like meditation, or a new sport, or an activity you were always curious about but have yet to try. Create a short menu of things to start with.

The logistics of researching and starting something new can be a barrier, so I've suggested several things below, organized into three broad categories: chill out, hobbies, and self-development.

Chill Out

Read. Escaping into a good novel can make you feel like you're on vacation. Rachel Smalter Hall has a great book, *How to Read After You Have Babies*, with tips that I have adapted below—designed for reading during the parenting years.

- Don't get discouraged. It will take longer to finish a book.
- Read (or listen to audiobooks) while your baby's feeding.
- Listen to books while your baby is bouncing and playing.
- Listen to books while going for walks and drives.
- Read after your baby goes to bed.
- Take turns having free time with your partner and use your free time to read.
- Learn how to "DNF." If you're not super-digging whatever book you're reading, I have three words for you: *do not finish.*

Listen to music. Music sets a mood and has the power to transport you instantly. Refamiliarize yourself with music from your youth. Choose music to drive home to, to cook dinner to, to clean the house to, and so on. Sick of your collection? Create a Pandora station based off artists or songs that you like—their algorithm will choose similar songs and create a unique station, just for you. Spotify is also a great way to discover new artists with almost no time invested on your part.

Tune in to your senses. Slow down and pay attention to what's around you. A simple walk around your neighborhood can become an escape if you pay closer attention to the sights, sounds, and smells around you. Let your own environment be an escape.

Try finger painting! It's a throwback to childhood, but the tactile feel of the paint on your fingers as you create your next masterpiece is wonderfully calming. Want less mess? Try watercolor crayons or adult coloring books. Revel in the comfort of bygone days as you release the stress of today.

Journal. Taking five to fifteen minutes to record your thoughts, experiences, and what you feel grateful for can be extremely relaxing for many people (just not those with writer's block!). A dream journal (where you record your dreams) can help you feel more in tune and spark creativity.

Get pampered. For a busy mom, nothing seems to soothe the soul more than being taken care of while your mind wanders: a massage, manicure, pedicure, or haircut. For a less expensive self-pamper, add Epsom salts to a hot bath, light a candle, and pour a glass of your favorite adult beverage.

Listen to podcasts. Audio storytelling is experiencing a renaissance. It's possible to consume almost any type of information in podcast form these days. Among podcasts, there are news programs, murder mysteries, serialized fiction, and podcasts about start-ups and knitting. Explore!

Do puzzles. Can you designate a table or corner of your home for puzzles and games? Stick to good, old-fashioned versions of games in lieu of the digital versions (solitaire with real cards, Scrabble with real tiles) for the best effect.

Hobbies

Play an instrument. Thanks to YouTube, you can teach yourself to play an instrument at home. Focusing on the guitar or harmonica, for even ten minutes in the evening, is tremendously relaxing—far more so than an hour of television. You're never too old to learn how to play an instrument.

Take up writing. Like to write but never thought of yourself as a writer? Start out by writing short compositions: haikus, silly poems, a short story, an autobiographical sketch. Writing is like a muscle: the more you exercise it, the stronger it becomes. Once you've got something down on paper that you like, share it with family and friends.

Do model building. There's something soothing, absorbing, and tangibly satisfying about building a model. Kits are available at your local hobby shop, or check out www.scalemodel.net (for all kinds of model building) and www.nmra.org (for model railroad building) to get more information and tips on how to get started.

Knit and sew. They're not only useful skills to have but cost-efficient ones, too! You can add new sweaters to your wardrobe and make some of your own clothes (you can then apply the money you save toward other activities you never dreamed of doing). Check out www.learntoknit.com and www.sewing.org for tips, resources, patterns, and leads on classes nearest you.

Flower arranging. Developing the art for mixing colors, shapes, heights, and styles in a vase is peaceful and will bring more beauty (joy) into your home. Check with a nursery or local flower shop in your area to see if it offers classes.

Gardening. Getting your hands dirty and solving the problems of gardening (weeds, animals, bugs, a watering plan) can be a soothing escape, and the results are visible every day! Try growing vegetables, herbs, or flowers. Focusing your mind on one tiny patch of land—your backyard—can be relaxing and rewarding.

Crafting. Activities such as jewelry making, pottery painting, and scrapbooking can bring out your inner artist. Many community colleges, as well as local artists and craftspeople, offer classes to help get you started. You can also check out www.craftdaily.com and www.ourdailycraft.com for DIY ideas.

Self-development

For some, self-improvement may feel like work, but for many, learning, skill-building, and self-development generate energy and bring a spark to the humdrum of daily life. Here are some of the things my clients often want to learn—and superefficient ways to learn them:

- **Learn a fact a day.** Spend less than five minutes a day learning a small, interesting tidbit, then share what you learned with your children:
  - Read *An Incomplete Education: 3,684 Things You Should Have Learned but Probably Didn't*
  - Visit the website Today I Found Out
  - Subscribe to a daily art feed like *Contemporary Art Daily*
  - Subscribe to the feeds at *Did You Know?* and *Tell Me Why?*
  - Listen to podcasts like *Stuff You Should Know* or *How to Be Amazing with Michael Ian Black*

Improve your public speaking skills. Toastmasters and Dale Carnegie Training are two of the biggest international organizations aimed at helping anybody who wants to up their public speaking skills. Check out their websites for a location near you at www.toastmasters.org and www.dalecarnegie training.com.

Master the art of joke telling. Ever wish you could be like that person at the party who can get everyone cracking up? People who seem to always have a joke to tell actually work at remembering them. It can be fun, and socially handy, to develop a repertoire of good jokes to have at the ready. Write down any joke you hear and love on index cards and practice telling it until it becomes natural.

Master the jazz greats. Or blues. Or country. If you enjoy music, and want to become an aficionado, dedicate a year to learning all the greats in a particular genre, starting with a Wikipedia lookup of the significant players, downloading albums, watching videos (try academy.jazz.org, for example), and learning, maybe one artist a month for a year.

Learn a new language with an app on your phone. Spend just ten minutes a day with Duolingo or its paid cousin, Babbel. You can also learn online by checking out www.rosettastone .com, which provides interactive learning software in twenty-eight different languages.

3. Steal Back Time

Once you've selected the fun activities you want to build into your routine, you can't rely on doing them in your spare time. As you know, spare time is the unicorn of parents everywhere—it rarely exists! You need to block fifteen to thirty minutes a day or one to three hours a week to dive in. (The idea is to make it a routine—a regular source of fun, to generate regular fuel.)

I know what you're about to say next: "Julie, I don't have time. I don't have fifteen minutes a day!" Nonsense. Just think about how many twenty-minute blocks of time you waste every day, because you didn't have a plan or didn't think you could accomplish anything in such a short amount of time. A challenge: for an entire day, note every time you had an unscheduled fifteen minutes (or more) and didn't have a plan. Also note how you spent the time—did you mindlessly check email, rewrite your to-do list, check Facebook? We can steal back that time.

Here are some great times to steal back for fun:

Get up early or do something late at night. Get up a little early, before the house wakes up. Or, instead of turning on the

TV after your kids go to bed, take out your guitar, play some music, and allow yourself to relax. It's a few minutes you can look forward to every single day.

Take advantage of waiting time. As parents, we spend a lot of time waiting . . . in the car at school pickup, in doctors' waiting-room offices, at sports practices. Instead of just waiting, pull out a sketchpad, listen to a podcast, write a poem, or read a book. Time spent waiting doesn't have to be time lost.

Piggyback on your child's schedule. Take advantage of when your kids are doing their homework or when they're engaged in a game with friends or siblings. That can be "fun" time for you. While kids pursue their hobbies, you do the same.

Batch chores and errands on one day. Janice made the mistake of using every moment her kids weren't with her to knock out errands and housework. Instead, corral chores and errands to one or two days a week (if possible) to free up one or two reliable blocks of time you can devote to your hobbies or pure fun every week.

Hire some help for the witching hour! After school and right before dinner are tough times for every kid. It must be something in the atmosphere. Catherine, a single mom of a five-year-old, loved yoga. There was a class taught by a teacher she adored right after work, but she'd stopped going because of her daily routine with her child. Once a week, she hired a student to care for her son after school and prepare dinner so she could attend her favorite class. It made that one night each week less stressful and more enjoyable. And she still was home in time to have dinner together and tuck him in!

Don't be afraid to trade off with your spouse or a friend. My client Mel wanted time to do creative writing, so he figured out a way to trade time with his wife. She went to lunch for a couple of hours with her girlfriends each Saturday, and on Sunday she managed the kids while Mel went to the library to work on his novel. They spent the rest of the weekend together as a family.

REAL PARENT VOICES

MAKING USE OF SUDDEN OPPORTUNITIES FOR FUN

With three kids, aged nine, eleven, and thirteen, who had busier and busier lives, Lucy often found herself with an unexpected pocket of free time that she was unprepared for. Without a plan, she'd squander that gift of time and feel like it went to waste. Over time, she realized the best defense was to always be ready. She came up with a short menu of three to five fun things she truly loved but rarely had time for (manicure, walk in the park, museum visit) and wrote them down on a Sudden Opportunity list. She kept that list in the "Notes" app on her phone, but you can keep yours on an index card in your wallet. From that point forward, when she was suddenly gifted with a window of free time—her kids are at a birthday party, soccer practice runs late—she was ready to seize the moment and know what to do with it.

FUN TIME IS SACRED TIME

My client Ella is a mother of two—a fourteen-year-old girl and an eleven-year-old boy. As a kid, Ella watched her mom completely subsume her individual identity and sacrifice her own interests in order to care for her kids and husband. Ella's mom never took time for herself in order to pursue her own interests. When Ella's parents' marriage ended in divorce, Ella watched her mom completely fall apart because she had lost any sense of her own identity beyond "mother" and "wife."

It was a mistake Ella was determined not to repeat. Ella and her husband have organized their family life to be sure that each family member has time for their own hobbies. That includes Mom, Dad, and the kids. Her daughter is into dance and volunteering with deaf children; her son is into robotics and skateboarding; her husband likes to garden; and Ella is in her element when painting or playing the harmonica. To keep it manageable schedule-wise, each child is limited to one or two hobbies at a time, and they try as best they can to stack time, so everybody is pursuing their passions at the same time. It takes work to puzzle all those activities into one schedule, but making fun a family value communicates many life lessons that Ella and her husband hope will stay with their kids forever: that fun is not "pointless"—it's a part of being a whole human being, and that even with responsibilities as serious as school and parenting, one should always make space for the full expression of one's soul.

Maintaining the time for fun isn't always easy or a given; it's a fluid process. Oftentimes, you may find yourself scrapping and clawing to salvage it from the gravitational pull of your daily life: the endless to-do list; the voice imploring you to do one more task; to bring home work on the weekend; to postpone a vacation; to skip dinner with a friend after work.

My advice? Make time for fun and protect that time. The rewards you gain—in energy, happiness, patience, and quality time with your kids—will motivate you to keep it. You'll start considering that time as sacred, knowing that while it isn't much (in terms of percentage of hours each week), the rewards are enormous and worthy of your fierce protection. Like my dad taught me—making time for fun is one of the greatest gifts you can give your family and your job.

PART V

LIFE HAPPENS

15

WHEN LIFE THROWS YOU CURVEBALLS: MOVING, DIVORCE, ILLNESS, JOB LOSS

We've been talking for the previous fourteen chapters about how parents are constantly juggling eight responsibilities: P.A.R.T.—**Provide**, **Arrange**, **Relate**, **Teach**—and S.E.L.F.—**Sleep**, **Exercise**, **Love**, and **Fun**.

On a good day, managing this juggling act is a delicate balance. What happens when you are thrown a major curveball?

Aside from managing the everyday ups and downs, there are unpredictable and disruptive life events—including moving, divorce, illness, and job loss—that can derail schedules and routines, throwing off any semblance of balance you may have had. Often, during these times of crisis, the first things to "go" are the very things this whole book has been devoted to helping you create time and space for: quality time with your children and for yourself.

The curveballs are huge, temporary projects that eclipse your time, energy, and brainpower with a million and one additional things that have to be decided, organized, and executed. What's worse, each situation takes an emotional toll on you and every member of your family. As a parent, you have the added responsibility of managing your own additional emotional load and helping your kids cope with theirs.

When confronting any difficult situation, there is no better resource than sesamestreetincommunities.org, headed by the very bighearted and extraordinarily experienced Jeanette Betancourt, whom I had the opportunity to interview for this book. The website is another arm of Sesame Workshop, whose mission is to help children grow stronger, kinder, and wiser. The site is chock-full of practical, insightful, and free tools and resources to guide you and your kids through a huge range of tough topics.

This chapter shares practical strategies to manage the onslaught of to-dos, while still carving out essential time to tune in and take care. The goal is to manage these situations with as much grace as possible and help you create and contain time to keep the rest of life on track. We'll focus on four of the most common curveballs, but you can apply the principles to almost all tricky situations.

ADDITIONAL DEMANDS ON YOUR TIME

No matter what curveball you are dealing with, there are generally three categories of tasks and activities that demand your time and attention.

The first is the time required to conquer extra work. Every curveball brings with it a tidal wave of additional tasks, activities, concerns, and decisions to be made, usually without much warning. If you've never had to weather the situation before, it can be even more challenging because you are in a constant state of surprise and doing things for the first time.

The second is keeping the existing trains running on time

by not letting the most basic household logistics go to the dogs. It means completing the regular chores, like cleaning up and mowing the lawn, getting the kids to school on time, making dinner, doing laundry. It's hard enough to do these things when there isn't a crisis looming, but it's arguably even more important to get them right in curveball times because these routines can help everyone in the household maintain some sense of normalcy and control.

The third—and often the hardest—additional responsibility for parents is helping their children cope with the disruption. It's hard because parents are usually dealing with their own emotional and physical stressors. Amid all of that disruption and uncertainty, it can be difficult to find a way to ensure that kids don't feel forgotten or invisible. Parents must find a way to communicate the change to their kids in a way they can understand; create the space for them to share their thoughts, feelings, and concerns; and encourage them to continue with their normal routines, making at least a little time to have fun and blow off steam. It can feel like an impossible mission!

With all of the added responsibilities on your plate, navigating the curveballs will require you to master two rules that don't always come easily: 1) you'll need to ask for help, accept it, and divvy up tasks with grace; and 2) you must triple down on self-care. These two go hand in hand. Master them, and you'll be able to withstand all the heavy lifting without missing a beat for your kids.

Rule # 1: Divvy Up the Labor

No matter how independent and self-reliant you prefer to be, dealing with extraordinary circumstances is an enforcing mechanism for all parents to learn to reach out for and accept help. One client—the mom of a child with special needs—said the lesson she learned when her son was first diagnosed was that it doesn't just take a village, "it takes a universe."

In curveball moments, there are really three things you should preserve your time and energy for: learning and discovering all the new things to deal with; making strategic decisions that affect your family; and providing love and comfort to your kids, your partner, and yourself. With everything else, be open to getting help. Here's how:

Let people step up. Friends, neighbors, extended family, school contacts, and even your workplace may offer to help—let them. Make the delegating easy on yourself by preparing a list of tasks that you could potentially move off your plate, that helpers can pick and choose from. Some tasks on the list might require specialized expertise, so you may need to track down a professional moving company or insurance claims specialist, but most will cover everyday routines—like meal prep, carpooling, laundry, changing the sheets, or doing yard work—that most people can take on. Caregiver.org has some really smart tips about how to do this the right way. The most important things to keep in mind are: vary who you ask for help (don't ask the same person over and over!); be as organized and concrete as possible about the help you need; and don't be shy about giving explicit instructions (e.g., if you send them to the store, name the item, brand, and text a picture)—it actually makes it easier for your helpers to help.

Keep your sense of humor. Your helpers may be doing things they've never done before. As a result, it may take them longer or they may do things differently than you would do them yourself (e.g., buying the wrong brand of toilet paper or overcooking the pasta). In Ned's case, he managed to permanently seal the pressure cooker lid during a brave foray into the kitchen in which he tried to make his wife a healthy chickpea stew. The whole family got involved trying to figure out solutions—no dice—and had a big laugh at the mystery of the sealed pot. Two weeks later, they gave up and dumped the whole cooker, lid and all, into the trash. It's okay if your helper messes up. Thank them—and laugh it off.

Get extra kid care. Delegating child care is essential if you need to spend extra time away from the house or know that something inappropriate for kids' eyes and ears may be happening. A babysitter, friends, or extended family that can commit to being there last minute—and maybe even take the kids overnight—can help you to provide a stable environment for your children. It's good for kids to have an extra layer of love and support outside their immediate family during tough times. They may even find it easier to talk about what's going on, or just escape the stress by being with others.

Rule # 2: Take Impeccable Care of Yourself

It's hard to be a rock when you feel out of sorts. In order to be in a position to soothe your kids, you first need to soothe yourself. Children rely on adult reactions to help them figure out how to understand and interpret what's happening around them. The way you handle your attitude and emotions will set the tone for the way your child copes.

Here's how:

Build in daily pauses. Resist the urge to become all about your to-do list—that will make it hard to slow down and tune in to your own emotions and gauge how your kids are doing. Instead, take a break at least once a day (if not more) to detach from your to-do list and just breathe. Be confident that it will all get done. As the British say, "Keep calm and carry on."

Build happy moments into every day. Sometimes, it really is the little things. Cook your favorite meal for dinner, listen to your favorite album as you tick through your household routines, invite a friend or neighbor to come over for a Popsicle break, blow bubbles with your toddler, catch bugs in your backyard. Making time for life's joyful moments is a breath of fresh air.

Stay in fighting shape. You won't be good for anyone—or at handling the crisis at hand—if you run yourself so ragged that you get sick yourself. Instead of overindulging in food, alcohol, or other unhealthy escapes, commit to eating well, getting enough sleep, and exercising regularly.

 BOOST YOUR IMMUNE SYSTEM!
OVER-THE-COUNTER REMEDIES

Vitamins/Supplements: vitamin C, vitamin B$_6$, vitamin E, zinc, elderberry flower, echinacea, oscillococcinum, reishi mushroom, lion's mane mushroom, colostrum, colloidal silver, probiotics, ginseng, myrrh, oregano, and astragalus root.

Foods: broth, garlic, ginger, turmeric, lemon, manuka honey, yogurt, shiitake mushroom, fruits, vegetables, fermented foods (apple cider vinegar, kombucha, kimchi, etc.), healthy fats.

Have a neutral confidant. It often helps to talk with someone who has no attachment to the particular curveball you've been thrown—in other words, someone who doesn't know your soon-to-be-ex-spouse, or your employer, or the person who's sick. A neutral confidant can offer an unbiased ear. It's a person with whom you can talk freely—and without worry—because they don't have any skin in the game. These friends can also be an escape—you can talk about topics that have nothing to do with the tricky situation at hand.

Tap into your mojo. Curveballs can deal a leveling blow to your ego (especially divorce and job loss). Don't dwell on what went wrong. Instead, focus on your strengths and what you have done right. Embrace the strong relationships you have been able to cultivate and rely on them to fortify your confidence as you move through the transition. Review your résumé and think about jobs where you thrived. Spend time with beloved family and old friends who help you connect to the very best version of yourself.

With those two rules in mind, let's dive into how you can plan to manage each of the four curveballs using the framework introduced earlier in this chapter: 1) organizing extra work; 2) maintaining existing routines; and 3) helping kids cope.

MOVING

Moving can be exciting and a chance to start anew, but leaving a home where you have comfortable and familiar routines, objects, friends, and surroundings can trigger anxiety in adults and kids. Whether you are moving to a home in the same neighborhood, to another town, across state lines, or overseas, the process of moving is a huge project that is mentally, emotionally, and physically strenuous.

1. Organize the Additional Workload

Moving is a massive logistical task, with many moving parts—from the grand (choosing your next home), to the most mundane (do we have enough boxes for moving day?). Many of the activities are time demanding and time sensitive, so it is essential to figure out where you can get as much help as possible. Here are a few ways to find and organize labor and help you decide what's best for you to do and what's best outsourced:

Buy/sell your home. Both sides of this equation require a huge amount of time. Get a realtor with whom you don't mind spending time and who seems to authentically "get" you, your priorities, and your needs. On the sell side, staging your home is often a good idea, though it is especially difficult when you have kids. It's darn hard to keep your house "showroom" perfect! Sara, a mom with twin four-year-olds, insisted her broker do three open houses in a week (rather than across three weeks) because that was the longest period of time she could keep the impending chaos at bay. During that week, she and her children went to stay with her mom.

Declutter. Many parents love the idea of moving as an opportunity to finally "clear the clutter." And they're right, moving is the perfect excuse to hit Reset in your new home. My warning to you is this—don't declutter without involving your kids (if they are old enough to speak). They may have surprising attachments to things you aren't aware of. And you don't want them talking decades from now about how you threw out their favorite picture. As soon as you know you are going to move, use a color-coded system (Post-it notes work well) to tag KEEP, TOSS, DONATE, and STORAGE. Give every family member their own stack of Post-it notes and tag away.

Hire movers. Get estimates from three movers before deciding which one to hire, so that you can compare and contrast to be sure no one is vastly over- or underbidding. Ask for a separate estimate for the packing and unpacking—two functions that few people realize are available and are actually wise investments. Movers can and should do most of the packing, especially anything that is fragile—their insurance won't cover anything that is PBO (packed by owner). When the movers show up, keep things organized by assigning someone the role of overseeing the packing. Ask them to label boxes so you actually know what's inside (e.g., twenty-eight boxes labeled KITCHEN doesn't help you find the toaster in a hurry). This is a great job for a professional organizer if you can afford one.

Research the new neighborhood. Research and select new schools, doctors, services, and so on. Ask a resourceful friend or relative for help doing the initial legwork. Give them a list of criteria that you want to compare (distance from home, years in business, fees, etc.) and let them share a summary of their findings. Then, you do the choosing.

Transfer paperwork and records. For purely administrative, tedious tasks such as transferring medical records, transcripts, utilities, addresses, and so on, make a master checklist. Then ask a friend or relative for help or hire a TaskRabbit to spend time on the phone, making requests and confirming transfers. Save your energy for the bigger decisions.

Plan out the new space. If you are not naturally good at space planning, it helps to bring in a talented eye. Do you have a friend or family member with a good eye for space and/or design (they are two different things)? An organized friend (or a professional organizer) can help you map out what goes where from a storage point of view. Someone with a flair for decorating can help you select paint colors, furniture placement, and art to hang on the walls.

Unpack. Create a comforting bridge between your old and new space by inviting extended family, friends, and your kids' BFFs from the old neighborhood to help unpack the new house. Though it may sound like an extra to-do, more hands will definitely make for a merrier move. And you'll benefit from having extra sets of eyes to watch and entertain the kids.

2. Maintain a Steady State

Leave packing to the (gasp!) last minute. At some point in your pre-parenthood life, you may have been an early packer. It was easy enough then because living out of boxes was no big deal. But for the kids' sake, the longer your household feels normal, the better for everyone's sanity. I recommend leaving packing until two days before the moving truck arrives.

Make clever use of last-on/first-off boxes. To have a few organized living spaces to immediately relax in the very first night, designate certain key boxes to be loaded *last* onto the moving truck and, therefore, unloaded *first*. These are boxes you strategically choose to unpack first, to help ground you until the rest of the boxes are unpacked. Make sure to mark these special boxes so you can immediately identify and access them the first night:

- **Kids' bedrooms:** Yes, your kids' entire bedrooms should be the very last to get packed and the very first to get unpacked. This allows them to enjoy their space (and be out of your hair), even as the rest of the house is getting boxed up, and they can settle into the new space as you continue to make your new house a home.

- **Kitchen essentials box:** With all the paper and bubble wrap, kitchens can take a long time to unpack. Set yourselves up to be able to make a basic meal within the first twenty-four hours by packing a single box or two with a saucepan, coffeemaker, and one plate, bowl, mug, and set of eating utensils for each member of the family. If you have pets, add their food bowls and food, too. Don't forget a corkscrew and two wineglasses for a celebratory toast on your first night!

- **Bedroom essentials box:** At the end of an exhausting moving day, you will undoubtedly want to sleep in a freshly made bed. Pack one set of sheets, pillowcases, pillows, and blankets for each bed. Toss in your bedside essentials, too: alarm clock, reading glasses, book, and one change of clothes so you can get a good night's sleep. If you don't have curtains up yet, bring a tension rod and a sheet for privacy.

- **Bathroom essentials box:** After you work up a sweat loading and unloading boxes, you'll be happy to shower and relax the first night. Pack one towel for each family member along with soap, shampoo, bath rugs, shower curtain, toothpaste, and toothbrushes.

- **Cleaning/basic toolbox:** No matter how much prep, a move creates messes and there are quick repairs you'll need to make. Pack a special box ready for the last-minute cleaning and fixing jobs that emerge on moving day. It might include: a vacuum cleaner, a broom, a mop, a dustpan, cleaning supplies, paper towels, sponges, cleansers, trash bags, string for flattening and tying up empty moving boxes, lightbulbs. Throw in a few basic tools, too: utility knife, hammer, screwdriver, nails, masking tape, tape measure, and flashlight.

Unpack every box within two weeks. Any box that is not unpacked within the first two weeks stays in a box forever—or at least until your next move, in ten years. Give yourself a deadline of two weeks to unpack every box in your new home. To maintain calm and order until you fully decorate, designate a staging area for all the decorative items: a room where you place all your decor, pillows, picture frames, and so on, that don't yet have a home. With all your miscellaneous stuff in one place, you can establish "move-free" living zones to relax in: the family room, bathrooms, and other areas without the visual clutter of items or boxes stacked in corners throughout the house.

REAL PARENT VOICES

CLONING ACTIVITIES WHEN MOVING FAR AWAY

Jennifer and her family moved overseas, to Hong Kong, when her husband was offered a once-in-a-lifetime job opportunity. In order to maintain a steady state for her three children (ages two, seven, and ten), they tried to replicate as much as they could about their old life in their new one. They connected to the ex-pat community, replicated the kids' after-school activities, prescheduled a grandparents' visit for six weeks after their move date (so they had ample time to settle in but also had something to look forward to), and planned a summer trip back to the United States, complete with summer camp for the kids.

3. Help Your Kids Cope

While you are in the heat of planning, your children will likely have completely different concerns. They might be worried about making new friends and settling into a new school. Or, if your family is moving to a smaller space, they might wonder what it will be like to share a room or whether they will be able to keep all of their favorite clothes and toys. Kids are resilient and will take cues from you on how to feel about living in a different place. Your goal should be to reassure, reduce disruption, rebuild, and make getting settled as fast and easy as possible. Here's how:

Remember the phrase "Home is what we have between us." This is something my daughter said to me when she moved out after she graduated from high school. I found it to be extremely liberating and true. You and your kids likely have an emotional attachment to the house they grew up in—so it can be scary to go to a new place. Remind them that a house is not a home—home is where your family is.

Help kids plan their new space. You may have seen the new home and have an idea where you are going and what your new life will look like. Help your kids do the same. Will they have the chance to pick the colors in their room? Can they get a new bedspread or curtains? When my daughter was in junior high school, she heard somewhere that every room is defined by seven objects that you become accustomed to seeing. Which ones they are will often surprise you, but if any one of those objects is taken away, the room feels different. Figure out what those seven items are for your kids' rooms and try to bring those along to the new space.

Experience the new neighborhood *before* you move. If your new home is reasonably close to your old home, schedule a day or two to visit before the move. Check out the local park or playgrounds, visit the community pool or ice cream shop. If you are moving out of state or overseas, take advantage of Google Maps, Google Earth, and Google Street View and take your kids on "virtual walks" through the neighborhood. After you've moved, plan family adventures to get to know your new hometown. Help your kids find points of comfort by identifying similarities between your new and old neighborhoods and by helping them appreciate the things that make them special because they are different.

DIVORCE

Divorce is not a decision taken lightly and usually comes after a couple has been unable to resolve big problems. When I decided to get divorced, it was a painful choice. Yet, after years of an unsatisfying marriage, I felt a certain relief, excitement, and hope for the future—for myself and for my daughter.

I called my dear old friend, Ric, who'd known all I'd been through, after I made the decision. I thought he would be proud of my choice to move forward, so his response took me a bit by surprise when he said, "Jules, please take impeccable care of yourself; a divorce is like ripping skin—more sad and painful than you can anticipate—for you and your whole family." He was right.

Divorce is a process of disassembling intertwined lives connected with fibers you don't even realize exist. Divorce involves restructuring a family's entire ecosystem. There are inevitable changes to the rhythms and routines of everyone's lives.

Unlike moving, job loss, or many illnesses, divorce is not just a moment in time but a series of stages that can be incredibly painful.

1. Organize the Additional Workload

Whether you welcome the divorce or not, it's a heck of a process. It takes a long time (two years, on average, and sometimes longer), and navigating the logistical and emotional potholes for yourself, your spouse, your kids, your extended family, and your friends is a marathon. You'll need help to stay as steady as you can for your children.

Hire a lawyer and/or a mediator. Whether you decide to use a lawyer or a mediator, you need to find professionals who can help you and whose approach matches your values. Ask friends who've been through a divorce how they chose, who they chose, how happy they were, and what lessons they learned. Piggybacking on their research and experience may keep you from making similar (costly) mistakes.

Assess and divide your assets. Most people's assets, bank accounts, budgets, and spending are somewhat disorganized, which makes divvying them up and figuring out alimony and child support a daunting job. When things are accessible and clear, at least the logistics will be easier. But don't try to go it alone. You'll need to gather and organize financial documents and inventory assets, debts, property, and belongings. Wills, retirement plans, insurance, and tax filings also need to be looked at and evaluated for modifications. An experienced and levelheaded professional organizer, an adult family member, or a trusted friend can help you pull the paperwork together to pass along to an accountant or bookkeeper to create spreadsheets and fill out forms.

Develop a co-parenting strategy. Deciding custody, living and visitation arrangements, and holiday schedules can be (and usually is) an emotionally charged and draining process. If you and your ex struggle to communicate effectively, look into hiring a parenting coordinator (PC). Parenting coordinators are professionals who help separated and divorced parents create a parenting plan that minimizes conflict and helps build on parental cooperating and communication.

Get family counseling. Connect with your child's school and let the teachers and counselors know what is happening. Find out if there is any special support they can offer your child. Also, ask if there is a family therapist they recommend to help your child navigate the transition. Therapists and counselors can help create a safe space for your children as they go through the transition.

2. Maintain a Steady State

A divorce is, by definition, disruptive to the family ecosystem. Here's how you can offer stability and consistency amid the storm:

Avoid the blame game. It may soothe you in the moment, but it creates a time boomerang, adding stress and more angst to deal with. Remember, your ex is part of your child's identity and your child sees themselves in both of you. Anything negative you say about your ex runs the risk of your child internalizing it and thinking, "Oh, that is me. I am a liar, I am a cheat."

Furthermore, a 2010 study published in the journal *Family Court Review* found that in divorced families, the opposite-sex parent (your daughter's father or son's mother) has the greatest influence on children's academic outcomes. It's worth doing what you can to maintain a constructive relationship with your ex as co-parents.

Insulate your kids from the details. Don't let your dining-room table become divorce paper central. And if your kids are within earshot, avoid venting to a friend or confidant. What your kids really care about is what's going to happen to them, and what it means for their sense of stability, family, and values.

Highlight what is consistent. In an ideal world, ex-spouses will be cooperative and maintain the exact same practices in both homes. But that's not always realistic. You and your ex may not agree on things like bedtime, discipline, and nutrition. So, if things are going to be different at each household, point out to your kids any little thing that will remain the same. For instance, even though bedtime is different, or they have to share a room with their sibling in one place and not the other, in both houses your children will get a bedtime story before going to sleep and will wake up in the morning, brush their teeth, get dressed, and have breakfast.

If possible, live near your ex. The best possible outcome for your children is to live as close to your ex as possible. It makes it easy for them to invite the same kids over after school, frequent the same parks or candy shops, and take the same route to school. Make geography one less change your kids have to navigate.

Restructure your life during non-kid days. On the days you don't have your kids with you, you may feel lost. If you have entire weekends sans children, choose one block of time (Saturday nights are a great starting point—the loneliest night of the week) to build in a new ritual for yourself. Try something that restores you: go to the market with a friend, find a cultural event to attend, enroll in a weekly art class, go to a yoga class. If many of your weeknights are now kid-free, don't pour all of your free time into working late since there's no one to go home to. Once you have a single block of time worked out to look forward to in your free time, it anchors you—you panic less, and you can start building other new routines from there. Before long, you'll have structure when your kids are with you and when you're on your own.

3. Help Your Kids Cope

Divorce is a painful and, at minimum, disruptive event for any family. Keep this in mind: when it comes to your children, focus on how you navigate the change, not the change itself.

Settle into a positive co-parenting style. By far the healthiest thing you can do for your children is define and agree on a co-parenting style. The good news is there is more than one way to create a healthy co-parenting arrangement that helps kids thrive. Author Edward Kruk, associate professor of social work at the University of British Columbia and president of the International Council on Shared Parenting, identifies four different styles of co-parenting that couples fall into, consciously or not (the first two are positive, the last two not so much). How would you characterize your relationship?

- **Cooperative co-parents** are involved with each other's lives, share and discuss information about the day-to-day stuff, and maintain a very low level of conflict. About 25 percent of divorced parents fall into this category, and their children benefit. Kids from cooperative parents tend to heal and do well.

- **Parallel co-parents** have a low level of involvement and don't collaborate on much but maintain a low level of conflict with each other. Each parent runs their own household, and their kids adjust to going back and forth. About 40 percent of divorced parents fall into this category, and—drum roll—kids do just as well in this environment as those with cooperative co-parents.

- **Conflicted co-parents** are characterized by a high level of involvement and a high level of conflict. Every interaction between these ex-spouses is heated. Only about 10 to 15 percent of divorced parents fall into this category—and children pay dearly for it in feeling torn between sides, thrust into the role of caretaker to their own parents, and unable to focus on their own upbringing.

- **Alienated co-parents** typically have a low level of engagement but a high level of conflict. About 10 to 20 percent of divorced parents fall into this category and rarely talk, but when they do, things get ugly. This, too, creates issues for kids who end up without cohesive guidance and a lack of security from turmoil and worry.

Professor Kruk advocates developing a co-parenting plan that focuses on the needs of the children, to maintain routine relationships with each parent and to shield them from ongoing parental conflict. He recommends a co-parenting plan that builds on five dimensions of co-parenting—two aspects of decision-making and three that actually relate to time: *overnight stays* (sleepover schedule for each parent's home), *routine time* (time parent and children spend together doing daily caretaking), and *recreation time* (time spent together in special activities). If the lion's share of recreation time goes to one parent and routine caretaking goes to the other, there will be difficulties. A more balanced arrangement in which each parent shares some of each type of time is ideal.

Create a calendar. Kids find comfort in concrete schedules. Print out a few weeks' worth of calendar pages at a time and talk through the plan for the coming weeks. You can color code days (visual cues help memory) by assigning different colors to Mom days and Dad days and write in fun stuff they can look forward to. If you have young children who don't have their own paper or digital calendar, let them hang on to a copy of the calendar (or make it a craft and let them draw their own).

Give kids a chance to transition between homes. Ping-ponging between houses can be difficult—children need to adjust to different atmospheres, rules, and routines. Each transition is a painful reminder that their lives feel divided and they feel split. It's not unusual for kids to be cranky at the beginning of each transition. Once your child is ready to engage, keep your focus and questions on them and don't dig for information about your ex. Sesame Street in Communities suggests a few great questions for when you do reunite: *What was one good thing that happened today/this weekend/ this week? What was the best thing that happened this week? What made you laugh this weekend? Who would you like to spend more time with at school, after school? What part of the* *day do you look forward to? What makes you a good friend to classmates? What's something you'd like your teacher to know about you?*

Be sensitive to tricky times. Holidays, birthdays, graduations, and celebrations are especially difficult for parents and children of divorce, no matter how recently or long ago you and your ex split. It helps to create new traditions that expand kids' experiences, not to compete with your ex's household but to give holidays a distinct flavor in each place.

Balance between time with parents and time with friends. Kids who split time between two households can get into a time bind—they're doubling their "family time" because they have to spend time with Mom and Dad separately. Make it okay for your kids to spend time with their friends. That communicates you are there to support *them* as whole people. A social life, apart from family time, is important. It's fun and may help them maintain a sense of stability and comfort amid the upheaval of a divorce.

ILLNESS

Illness is a curveball whose disruptive potential can range across a wide scale. Regardless of who is sick (parent or child), illness throws off the family ecosystem. Whether it's an ear infection, the flu, or something much more serious, when someone in the household gets sick (or injured), there's more to do and fewer people to do it. Not only is the sick person out for the count, but so are the people taking care of them, who may feel stretched thin as they take on extra duties while keeping up with their regular responsibilities.

Ellen is a full-time working mom of a fourteen-year-old, a twelve-year-old, and an eighteen-month-old. Her fourteen-year-old son, Noah, suffered a stroke during birth that left him with cerebral palsy. It took time for her to accept that she had a child with special needs and then learn how to adapt to the increased demands on her time and figure out tactics that were sanity saving.

She learned three key strategies fairly quickly. First, she realized that she had to accept being a person who needed help and a person who accepted help. It was a hard lesson—prior to her son's birth, she'd been fiercely independent. But between juggling therapy appointments and specialist appointments and managing her own worry, there was too much going on to take it all on alone. When her babysitter offered to come by and do her laundry, she said yes, and then she took an hour to run errands and have an hour of alone time. When friends offered to research therapists, she said yes—she didn't have a monopoly on the Internet and the more brains focused on her son's condition, the better.

Second, she came to accept that it doesn't just take a village, it takes a universe. She worked diligently to develop a team of experts to ensure that her son had a top-notch team. If someone wasn't up to snuff, she asked for someone better and made a connection.

Third, she learned the value of crowdsourcing. She wasn't the first person to have a child with special needs, and she wouldn't be the last—so many parents had experienced what she was going through, and she learned to tap into that. Two online communities worked best for Ellen—a Facebook group and the message board of a program her son belonged to. When she needs insight on anything from "When do I need another referral?" to "What socks do you love?" she crowdsources and gets instant and generous answers from her community.

1. Organize the Additional Workload

Any family facing a more serious illness knows that the logistical and emotional load is amplified and even harder to adjust to. But even everyday derailments (like colds, ear infections, and playground injuries) bring a lot of extra work to manage. The duration and severity of the illness impacts the family's functionality—a flu contained to one family member may cause a few sleepless nights and a day or two of missed work, but if the flu rips through the house like wildfire, the workload (and lost work, and sleepless nights) can go on for weeks.

Since the average child catches between six and eight colds per year, and the average adult catches between two and four colds, chances are you and your family will need to learn how to manage these more routine curveballs with some regularity.

While I hope you don't ever have to deal with a more serious diagnosis, below are some tips from parents who have. Their insights will help you navigate whatever situation you find yourself in.

Making doctor appointments. When Ellen was told her child had to wait four months to see a certain specialist, she got resourceful. She found out who the specialist's in-house social worker was, made an appointment, and gave an in-person pitch for her kid's case to be handled sooner. There are simpler ways, too. Ask the office secretary about cancellations. Inquire about a wait list. Ask, does the doctor ever stay late?

Even send the doctor an email, sharing your child's story. Whether the sick family member is an adult or child, you are the patient's advocate—don't be afraid to ask.

Going on doctor visits. Arranging transportation to and from the doctor and attending doctor appointments are best done by close family members, who can be advocates for the sick person. If someone has a lot of regular appointments (physical therapy, tests, treatments), ask friends or neighbors who are not working to help with driving and to keep you company and be an extra set of ears. To make the most of doctors' appointments, write down questions *before* the visit (include in your list the questions and concerns from your children). You can also tape-record the visit to make sure you don't miss anything. Remember: it's impossible to do this on your own.

Researching remedies and treatment options. Whether you are seeking a natural remedy for a stubborn sore throat or confronting a graver illness, you will feel compelled to learn more and see what options may exist. Think about any friends or family members who have exceptional research skills or anyone who has faced a similar illness. Ask them to do the digging on treatment alternatives and find out who the leading specialists/treatment centers are in the city or county. Even if you still do some research on your own, getting a jump start from others makes you feel more confident that you are leaving no stone unturned and moving in the right direction.

Submitting insurance paperwork. Dealing with insurance companies is tedious and aggravating work. They will fight you on what is and is not covered by your plan and are basically designed to make getting reimbursed so complicated, you'd rather just give up. Ellen told me it was essential to be the squeaky wheel and immediately ask to speak to a supervisor. The first person who answers your call isn't high enough in the food chain to handle complicated matters. Just cut to the chase. Assign this chore to a family member who is great at administrative details and has an eye for numbers—and show a lot of appreciation. You can also ask if your doctor's office is willing to help with paperwork—some will fill out forms with the diagnosis and treatment codes, and even mail them in for you. Ellen saved time on all of the paperwork by filling out one form with the basic info—name, birthdate, and insurance number—then made a bunch of copies to have on hand. The next time she needed to apply for insurance coverage, she grabbed the prefilled form, attached the bill, and submitted it.

Extra cooking, cleaning, errands. If you are taking care of someone with a contagious sickness, delegate meal prep and lunch packing to a healthy, less exposed member of the family (or you might inadvertently infect everyone else!). Shopping for supplies, preparing special foods, and organizing medication are the perfect tasks to divvy up among friends, neighbors, and volunteers. "Today a friend and fellow mom on my son's football team set up a meal train," said Lola, who'd been through a mastectomy. "We were reluctant to accept the offer, but she made me realize that if there was ever a time to accept the help, it was now. We had a home-cooked meal for each day of my recovery. I told my boys, 'Don't get used to all this home cooking—as soon as I get better, its back to takeout.'"

2. Maintain a Steady State

Get dressed every day. Whether you are the sick person or the caretaker, it's so easy to lose track of time and self-care in the smallest ways. The first rule of every day should be to wash, dress, brush your hair, and feel good. Simple self-care routines will help you to mark the days and keep them from blurring into nights. It may be difficult and feel like you are just going through the motions, but in the end, it will help to keep your feet grounded in a sense of normalcy.

Stay connected. Being sick can be lonely. Having people around—whether they call, write a letter, or sit in silence—can help the ill person feel more normal. Encourage your child to reach out and share a funny story or tell them about school or a sports game. Enlist other folks—friends, neighbors, extended family, babysitters—to be your regular rotation of TLC givers.

Confine germs. Confining the sick person (and their germs) to one room can lead to loneliness and add strain on the caretakers, who are constantly running back and forth to spend time with everyone. It can be fine to hang out in the same room, as long as everyone agrees to practice a few tried-and-true germ-stopping maneuvers: sit six feet apart, keep disinfecting wipes on hand for quick swipes (on the iPad, light switch, doorknob, faucet), and give the sick person their own books, toys, and blankets (off-limits to healthy family members). Also, teach the sick person to cough or sneeze into their elbow and make sure everyone washes their hands regularly with soap and warm water for at least twenty seconds, about as long as it takes to sing two renditions of "Happy Birthday."

Keep family routines going. It's helpful for kids to keep up their school schedule—a sense of routine helps them cope. Remind your children that their job—as a kid—is not to worry or help with adult chores but to go to school, do their homework, see their friends, play sports, and have fun.

Give your healthy children extra TLC. If you are taking care of a sick family member, it's understandable why you might focus all of your energy and attention on them. Make sure to take the time to give your other children attention, too. If they are old enough to write, give them a special notebook to record ideas of things they want to share with you: stories from their day, questions they have, worries on their mind. Then dedicate a special time each day when they get your 100 percent focus. A little TLC will go a long way.

3. Help Your Kids Cope

Being sick, seeing a parent sick, or visiting someone who is sick is a hard experience for adults, let alone for children. But the way you approach the situation can make it less scary. Here are a few ways you can help your child feel connected:

Convey that sick people are just people. Sometimes kids can be fearful of illness. They may be genuinely concerned about the sick person's well-being or worried that they might get sick themselves. Ensure your kids that the sick person is the same person they were before! Kids can help a sick person feel more normal (and like less of an outcast) by doing an activity that helps lighten the mood. Bring cards, games, a craft, or your child's favorite movie. Remind your child that it always feels good to know that someone is thinking about you.

Let your child help. You may find that your child wants to help but isn't sure what to do. Offer up simple tasks, like making sure the sick person's water glass is full, feeding the dog, or washing dishes, and let them know you value their contribution. Ask your child to draw a picture, make a get-well card, or pick a bouquet of flowers from the backyard.

Prepare your child for what's to come. If a member of the family is dealing with a more serious illness, tell your children about the potential side effects of treatment in advance. Because different people respond differently to illnesses and treatments, let them know if you are not sure what the side effects will be, but that you or another important person in their life will be there to help prepare them for any changes.

JOB LOSS

When you are out of work, the structure of your day-to-day life changes as much as you do. Whether you lost or quit your job, the transition period that follows can challenge your confidence, identity, livelihood, and sense of stability. Worries about being able to pay the bills and adjust your spending while maintaining your family's lifestyle commingle with trying to keep your head clear and find your next job opportunity. It may seem like you have more spare time than you know what to do with. What's worse, being home might even feel awkward and like you are disrupting your family.

Emily was a marketing executive at a pharmaceutical company that went through a series of downsizings over a five-year period. When her job was eliminated, she was one of the last people standing. The five years of living in fear that she "was next" had taken its toll. The culture in her office had turned cutthroat—everyone out for themselves, everyone watching their backs. "I was done, emotionally spent," she told me. "I had no confidence in my professional self."

She worried about how her job loss would affect her family's finances—and she feared she'd never find a job that was as well paying again. The fifteen to twenty hours of weekly consulting work she picked up was fine, but a little uneven and less secure. But the fear of not knowing where her next gig might come from was nothing compared to the emotional turmoil she'd endured for the previous five years.

With the extra time on her schedule, Emily started to take better care of herself—she went to the gym and saw friends—and also became a much more involved parent. Her daughter, Bella, was ten at the time Emily lost her job and on the cusp of adolescence. In true preteen fashion, when Emily first lost her job, Bella said, "I didn't mind not having you around." That stung. It took a little while, but eventually everyone adjusted to Emily being more available. They had dinner together every night and went to church each week, and Emily started volunteering weekly at Bella's school. Soon enough, Emily was finding an enormous reservoir of self-worth in her role as a mom—she felt valued and cared for in a way she hadn't felt in a long time. It gave her energy and a renewed sense of confidence. A job loss ended up being a good thing—for Emily, who discovered she was more valuable than her job title, and for her family, who benefited from a present and relaxed mom. The goal of this section is to help you and your family maintain stability and stay connected as you find your stride.

1. Organize the Additional Workload

Explore new job opportunities. We all have many careers inside of us—and each job transition presents a chance to reconsider your next move. Do you look for something exactly like what you were doing, or are you exploring new opportunities within or beyond your current field or industry? Make one list focused on opportunities within your field (opportunities with similar companies) and another list with other jobs outside your field. Then talk to people who know you well and ask them to help you think through the possibilities and your potential. Where do you match up? A fresh, objective perspective may uncover possibilities you might have missed. You might also consider getting help from a career counselor or taking a free online self-assessment test.

Network. Networking, for most people, is hard enough when they are employed—it's difficult to find the time, and it often feels awkward to schmooze. Networking as an unemployed person can be especially intimidating because you are afraid of asking for help. Don't be. People love to help. Just make it easy for them to be helpful. The key is to be methodical. Start by brainstorming a list of twenty possible people who could help you by just being a sounding board. Aim for seven coffees or meetings per week, and out of each meeting, try to leave with referrals for three more meetings. Focus on getting advice: "I'm looking for X, and here's how I think you can help me." Build a list of all the people you connect with, note who was helpful (and who wasn't), send thank-you notes (handwritten, if possible!), and keep people posted on your progress. Once you get started, you'll enjoy the process.

Apply, prepare, and interview for jobs. While it'd be nice to delegate job interviews, that's kind of like delegating going to a dentist appointment. But you can get help with the prep. Use your LinkedIn account to see how you may be connected to your potential employer. If you see a connection, reach out to your mutual contact and ask them to share what they know about the person and the company, and provide any tips on what might make you successful with them. Practice answering interview questions with a friend. If writing thank-you notes is so hard that you put it off—use your pal Google to identify a few templates that you can personalize and get out the door.

2. Maintain a Steady State

Just because the way you spend your days has changed temporarily doesn't mean that you have to reinvent your entire daily routine. Do what you can to limit the upheaval to your own and your family's schedule.

Make your job finding a job. When you are out of work, it's best to use the same nine-to-five schedule to look for your next opportunity: your job search becomes your full-time job. I've coached plenty of clients through these transitions and usually we divide the day into three distinct parts: 1) morning is used for research and to send out cover letters and résumés; 2) midday is best for networking lunches and coffees; and 3) afternoons are best for meetings, follow-up notes, and making new contacts. The more routine your schedule, the easier it is to maintain a steady state (and find a new gig!).

Have a daily family huddle. Though you may be tempted to withdraw because of your own anxieties or financial stress, that's one of the worst things you can do! You are likely to be home earlier for dinner than when you were working, so take advantage of that time to have the whole family update each other on their day. Have everyone name something great that happened, something they learned, and something they could use some ideas about. Your unemployment is temporary—so take advantage.

Have cheap fun. Just because money is tight(er) for the time being doesn't mean you can't have fun. If you usually do Sunday brunch out, learn to make your restaurant favorites at home together. Instead of going out to an amusement park, do a scavenger hunt at a nearby playground. Make your own popcorn at home to tote along to the movies. You'll have a little more time to conjure up creative ways to hang out. It's a way to show your kids that they bring you more joy than any job and that you can't put a price on fun or appreciating connections and family.

3. Help Your Kids Cope

Kids crave a sense of consistency and security. They are also incredibly intuitive and sensitive. Let them know that some things will change and allow them the chance to help out, so they have some sense of control over the situation.

Add a bonus activity or two. With the increased flexibility of your schedule, ask your family what additional activity or task you can do now, but normally can't—aim for something that's fun and helpful. Maybe it's taking the kids to school in the morning, volunteering in your kid's classroom or on a field trip, taking them on an outing after school on Fridays. Don't get so involved that it throws off your structured job hunt, but providing them with a little extra "you" time can fortify kids. Instead of worrying, they will be excited to spend more time with you.

Teach your kids how to save money. Rather than approach it from a place of stress, make saving money a game that involves the whole family. Saving money will help ease pressure on you, give your children a measure of control, and allow you all to share in the satisfaction of spending wisely. Here are a few ideas from the Sesame Street in Communities website on managing economic hardship:

- Write down frequently purchased items and see who can clip or find the best coupons.
- Make a list of little things they can change to help save money, like drinking water instead of juice or sports drinks.
- Ask your children to collect clothes or toys that they rarely use, and other household items, for a garage sale. Let them keep the money from the items they sell.
- Visit the library rather than the bookstore. Borrowing is cheaper than buying.
- Put spare change in a jar labeled FAMILY BANK. Once the bottle is full, use the money for something fun or to buy something your family really needs.
- Scour the newspaper, Internet, or library bulletin board for upcoming free events. Take advantage of what your community offers!

- Model resilience. If one area of your life isn't going well, that doesn't mean you can't enjoy life in other ways. By staying positive, you'll show your family that facing challenges and solving problems are a part of life and that setbacks won't hold you back.

Because this is a book about finding time to parent, I'll wrap up this chapter with a few additional tips about how you can help kids cope in uncertain times. Resources including pbs.org and the Sesame Workshop have incredible tools for parents— visit their sites for even more.

Talk and listen to kids. Not just when you initially break the news about a change, but throughout the entire journey. It's essential to set aside a specific time to let kids know about what is going on and give them time to process, ask questions, and understand that no matter what is happening, you will always be there to support them.

Maintain a calm and positive tone. I'll use the old flight attendant analogy here. If a plane hits a spot of turbulence—and the flight attendant looks afraid—you may be, too. If they're calm, you figure the plane won't go down in flames. You're the flight attendant for your children.

Make sure kids know it's not their fault. A child's natural instinct might be to blame themselves when bad or unexpected things happen. If a sibling is sick, they might think they caused it when they said, "I hope you get sick!" in a fight; if you lost your job, they might think they caused it when they said, "I hate your job!" Get that nonsense out of their heads.

Avoid overwhelming your children with more information than they need. Curveballs are adult matters. Don't overburden your kids with too many details, but ensure they know enough that they don't feel surprised by anything in the process. When you talk to them, share the facts that will affect them, and then ask them what they understand. Their answers will let you know where misconceptions lie. They may actually surprise you with understanding far more than you imagined.

We've only tackled four of the many curveballs life throws at parents. Whatever unexpected situations life has in store for you, remember they are made more manageable by getting some help and taking care of yourself first.

AFTERWORD
ENJOY THE RIDE

Parenting is the toughest job in the world, the most important job in the world, the most perplexing job in the world, and undoubtedly the most rewarding job there is. Moms and dads are blessed with the extraordinary privilege of raising human beings and preparing them to make their unique contribution in the world. As I said at the beginning of this book, the universal goal of parents I meet everywhere I go is to truly be there for their kids: to raise happy, healthy, and productive members of society and to be present for the experience.

For years, parents have been doing this job without a clear job description, an impossible task with any normal job, let alone one of the most important in the world. Every generation tries to do better than the one before it, but without a clear job description, it's hard to know how they're doing, and that doubt and ambiguity can steal away some of the pleasure of parenting, making it harder to relax and be present.

I hope I've eased some of that distractibility by offering a job description. With the P.A.R.T./S.E.L.F. blueprint in hand, you can see the edges of the job and that will help you to find a balance among all the things you need to do to *raise* a human being and *be* a human being. You can be present and worry less about what you might be missing and be more focused on where you are in the journey.

You can take credit—and feel joyful—about all the things you are doing well.

You can see the concrete ways in which you might be falling short and work to improve in those areas.

By now, you've probably learned a few unexpected lessons, too: how essential self-care is, for one, to being there for your children—if parents don't nurture themselves, it's awfully hard to cultivate the energy, capacity, and joy required to nurture their children. Hopefully, you've taken to heart the message of quality over quantity when it comes to the focused time and attention you devote to your children. Your kids receive tremendous benefits from time and attention, delivered consistently and reliably, even in relatively short bursts.

I also want you to remember that being a great parent doesn't mean never making mistakes; it means learning from them. You *won't be perfect*—that's a given. But instead of berating yourself for your shortcomings or worrying endlessly that a decision you made when your child was in kindergarten will be his downfall from now until eternity, know that you can do better next time. Don't be afraid, as Claire Lerner, social worker and parenting educator of ZERO TO THREE, suggests, to take a redo and say to your child, "I'm sorry, I made a mistake. Let's try this again."

You and your kids are resilient—remember that.

It takes a village. That, too, should be something you learned from reading this book. I've written a lot about how important it is for you, as a parent, to expand your circle, nurture a community, and delegate when required. The larger your village of loving caretakers, the better you and your children will be. Mr. Brown and his incredible legacy taught me that.

By looking to science, psychology, economics, and sociology, we've learned so much about this adventure called parenthood, as moms, dads, and caretakers everywhere have done their best to replicate the positive aspects of their own childhood and do better where their own parents fell short. But, in the end, I think what we've discovered is perhaps what we've known all along: that no matter what parents and caregivers bungle, the most important nutrient of all—the thing with the power to salve all wrongs and bring out the potential in every human being—is feeling loved and listened to. Being fully present for your kids is as vital a nutrient as food, shelter, and sunshine. When you organize your life to make time for what matters, parenting—with all its messy challenges— becomes more joyful and your connection with your child will thrive.

ACKNOWLEDGMENTS

It takes a village to raise a child, and so it was with this book, whose evolution was nurtured, encouraged, and influenced by so many people along the way. I am profoundly grateful to each and every one of them for their contributions, and feel enriched to have been part of something that so many people enthusiastically supported.

First and foremost, I thank Maggie Richards, head of publicity and marketing at Henry Holt, who welcomed my call to meet about doing another book together, and who plucked this topic from the long list of ideas I presented and said, "*This* is the book the world needs, and that you need to write." Thank you for being game to bring the band back together. It's been amazing to be back home at Holt.

Thanks to my devoted editor Serena Jones, who has loved this book from beginning to end, serving up enormous patience, respect, and practical support every step of the way. To assistant editor Madeline Jones, for her attention to detail and her advocacy to ensure the book production schedule was met. To Hannah Campbell, the production editor who made sure I dotted my i's and crossed my t's. To superstar Nicolette Seeback for brilliantly capturing the soul of the book with the most warm, elegant, and joyful cover art. To Jason Liebman for sharing his wealth of IT expertise and providing support to get the digital realm right. I am so deeply grateful to Mary Murphy, who shared her extraordinary gift of distilling a massive amount of material into a succinct and compelling message. And to every member of the magnificent marketing and publicity team, Pat Eisemann, Marian Brown, and Jessica Wiener, for so brilliantly dividing and conquering the complex new media landscape and getting the book out there for all to see.

One could not ask for a wiser, more nurturing agency than WME. Suzanne Gluck, you were brilliant to assign this book to Margaret Riley King, a true author's agent. Margaret, thank you for going above and beyond to read every word, nurture the content, encourage me, and go to bat for the time and attention the book needed at every juncture. Strand Conover, I count my lucky stars every day for your loyalty, bright mind, brilliant guidance, and steadfast partnership over all these many years.

Any author will tell you that birthing a book is like labor, and for this one, the process was especially protracted because of the vast scope of research and the tenderness of the subject. My deepest gratitude goes to Cloe Axelson, the true midwife of this book, and also the Rogers to my Hammerstein, the Moss to my Hart, the Cole to my Porter. Your commitment to this project, along with your unique ability to find clarity amongst my clutter of thoughts, to drive the process forward, and to make my words sing brought this book into being. And Tatiana McPartland, my multitalented, bighearted, Swiss Army–knife assistant: holy moly, how blessed I am that you arrived when you did, rolled up your sleeves, and made yourself instantly invaluable as assistant doula. Thank you for sharing all your extraordinary gifts while keeping me sane and steadfast to go the distance. Gratitude to Dawn Raffel and Emily Rapp for help at key moments along the way. And to my amazing research assistants, Maresa D'Amore and Anna Rooney, who took on the brave act of culling through seemingly infinite studies, books, and websites, and expertly selected the richest sources with the most innovative ideas.

Every page of this book came to life because of the extraordinary

time, input, love, and support of Steve and Sue Morgenstern, Amanda and Aaron Rios, and Ric Murphy. Thank you for being in it with me for the whole important ride. Your handprints and heartprints are all over this book.

Eva Bloomfield, Josephine Mogelof, and Amanda Libman provided special assistance on this project at so many critical junctures, giving incisive feedback on concepts that shaped content, designing our parent survey and self-assessment, connecting me to thought leaders and experts who made the book better, and helping disseminate this book in so many extraordinary ways.

My ability to synthesize seventy years of research on the science of human development was made possible by a generous group of experts who shared their time, knowledge, and insights. You were incredibly valuable allies on my hunt for the answers parents most want to know. Thanks to the very special Jeanette Betancourt, Claire Lerner, and Dr. Melissa Milkie, who not only did multiple interviews, but also read through manuscript pages to make sure the material was thorough and true. For extraordinary interviews, I thank Martin K. Brown, Dr. Laurence Steinberg, Dr. Bernard Dreyer, Dr. Michael Yogman, Dr. Amanda Rios, Dr. Matthew Biel, Emily Bloomfield, Annie Pleshette Murphy, Karen Spencer, Nina Perez and Donna Hoffman Cullinan, Tara Oakman and Courtney Hayne, Brigid Schulte, and Susy Kremer. And to Linda Jacobs, PhD, who has been my greatest teacher in understanding the powers of attention, attachment, and nurturance.

Many parents participated in focus groups and interviews to ensure that what made it into the book was universal and relatable. Very special thanks to Cary and Tiffany Friedman, Candace Lun Plotkin, Maria Valdivieso de Uster, Ellen Seidman, Brett Lyons, Diana Limongi, Megan Carolan, Catherine Depret, Elizabeth Moshier, Jacquelyn Sumer, Simon Isaacs, Paige Trevor, Don and Laurie Graumann, Jenn Berube, Kerry Martin, Kelly Clyne, Susanna Baird, Tricia Pini, James White, Michelle Grundy, Lorena Sergent, Heidi Rome, Deborah Amster, Celia Pergola, Rebecca Carroll, Erica Cohen, and Heidi Frederic, for sharing your perspectives.

I am indebted to a very dear and trusted circle of readers who provided invaluable feedback on many drafts along the way. Thank you to Adira Amram, Jonathan Horn, Jennifer Buchman, Andrés Hoyos-Gomez and Viktorija Gecyte, Jeanette Betancourt, Claire Lerner, Dr. Melissa Milkie, and Faye Cone. Your handprints and heartprints are all over this book.

And thanks to my longtime champion and dear friend Joni Evans, who is in a league of her own, who slogged through every single blessed word of the final manuscript, and knew just what the book needed to bring it into sharp relief.

I am eternally grateful to my team at Julie Morgenstern Enterprises for keeping the business afloat and healthy while I got lost in the stacks and went deep into the writing cave. Thank you to Jessi Colon for ensuring clients got white-glove service and for basically running the business; to Tatiana McPartland, who made sure every item on my schedule and task list was executed to perfection; to Kelly McLaughlin, who used her marketing talents and get-it-done drive to keep us visible and polished; and to Maresa D'Amore for filling the gaps each time they appeared. To Bud Libman: you have been my guardian angel and an extraordinary friend. Thank you for providing a steady and flexible rudder so that we never lost sight of our goals. And to two rocks of the business, Bob Muller, our rabbi/accountant/funnyman, and Urban Mulvehill, our wise and compassionate lawyer: thank you for providing unwavering friendship, support, and world-class guidance through every evolution of the business.

Of course, this book didn't begin with the writing process—it ruminated for many years, influenced by many special people on my own life's journey.

I was truly schooled in parenting by my own village of friends and family, who brought out the best in me and made sure I never felt alone as a single mom. A special thank you to: Liz Ezra and Bill Derman, Cati Sorra, Susan and Richie Sporer, Ellen and Drew Driesen, Marilyn and Joel Duckoff, Amy and Jack Cohen, Judy Wineman, Gordon Mehler, Bob Rubenstein, Zoe Anderheggen and Courtney Gwynn, Camille Pucci and Peter Ehrenberg, Kathryn Grody and Mandy Patinkin, Robin Goldfin, Nelson and Nellie

Colon, Gerry and Lillian Colon, and my own parents, David and Sonia Morgenstern.

The concepts in this book were fed for nearly thirty years by the thousands of clients around the world who deeply trusted me to bring order to their lives from the inside out. Their honesty gave me insight into the common drive we all have to be loved and listened to, and to connect the dots between that drive and our ability to be organized as grownups.

My commitment to writing this book fully catalyzed thanks to the courage of Oprah Winfrey, who has dedicated her life to illuminating the importance of being seen and feeling worthy. One episode of her show in particular hit me between the eyes with two life-changing aha moments: first, that children who are starving for attention are the most vulnerable, and second, that statistics show how common it is for children to feel starved for attention. Oprah, you know which show that was, and I thank you. Thus began my quest to answer the question on every parent's mind: how much time and attention do children need to feel secure and loved?

And to Libby Moore, you were the first person I uttered this idea to, and your validation and encouragement was fuel that propelled me to pursue and develop this idea over the years.

Throughout the long, arduous road of writing of this book, I will always be grateful to my partner, Mark, who provided me a steady and welcoming place to come home to, keeping me balanced, present, and nourished so I could recharge and go the distance.

This book would never have come to be were it not for the birth of my own daughter, Jessi, whose goodness and light motivated me (and still does) to find the path to be the best version of myself, to bring out the best version of her. Jessi, you are the greatest blessing in my life. I am humbled by my luck in being your mom and proud of the positive force you are in the world, spreading your compassion, talents, and love with everyone you meet.

ABOUT THE AUTHOR

Julie Morgenstern is the author of five books including the *New York Times* bestsellers *Organizing from the Inside Out* and *Time Management from the Inside Out*. She is an internationally renowned organization consultant and has been featured on *The Oprah Winfrey Show*, NPR's *Fresh Air*, and *Today*. She is quoted regularly in *The New York Times* and *USA Today* and has been a columnist for *Redbook* and *O* magazine. Julie lives in New York City, where she raised her daughter as a single mom.